CIRCLES OF DELIGHT
Classic Carousels of San Francisco

Quite by chance, San Francisco has become one of the carousel capitols of the world. It today hosts carousels from all three of the most important historic American carousel makers—the only city anywhere with that distinction! What's more, each carousel has been restored close to its original condition. *Circles of Delight* celebrates the beauty and diversity of these traditional, hand-carved wood carousels of the Golden Gate City.

Aaron Shepard is an independent writer and photographer. He has been entranced by carousels since childhood—but his love and interest were rekindled when his wife, Anne L. Watson, wrote a novel about a young carousel restorer. When a business trip brought them to San Francisco in April 2004, Aaron spent three days photographing the city's carousels, giving him the photos for this book. He currently lives in Bellingham, Washington, and can be found online at **www.islanderimages.com**.

CIRCLES OF DELIGHT

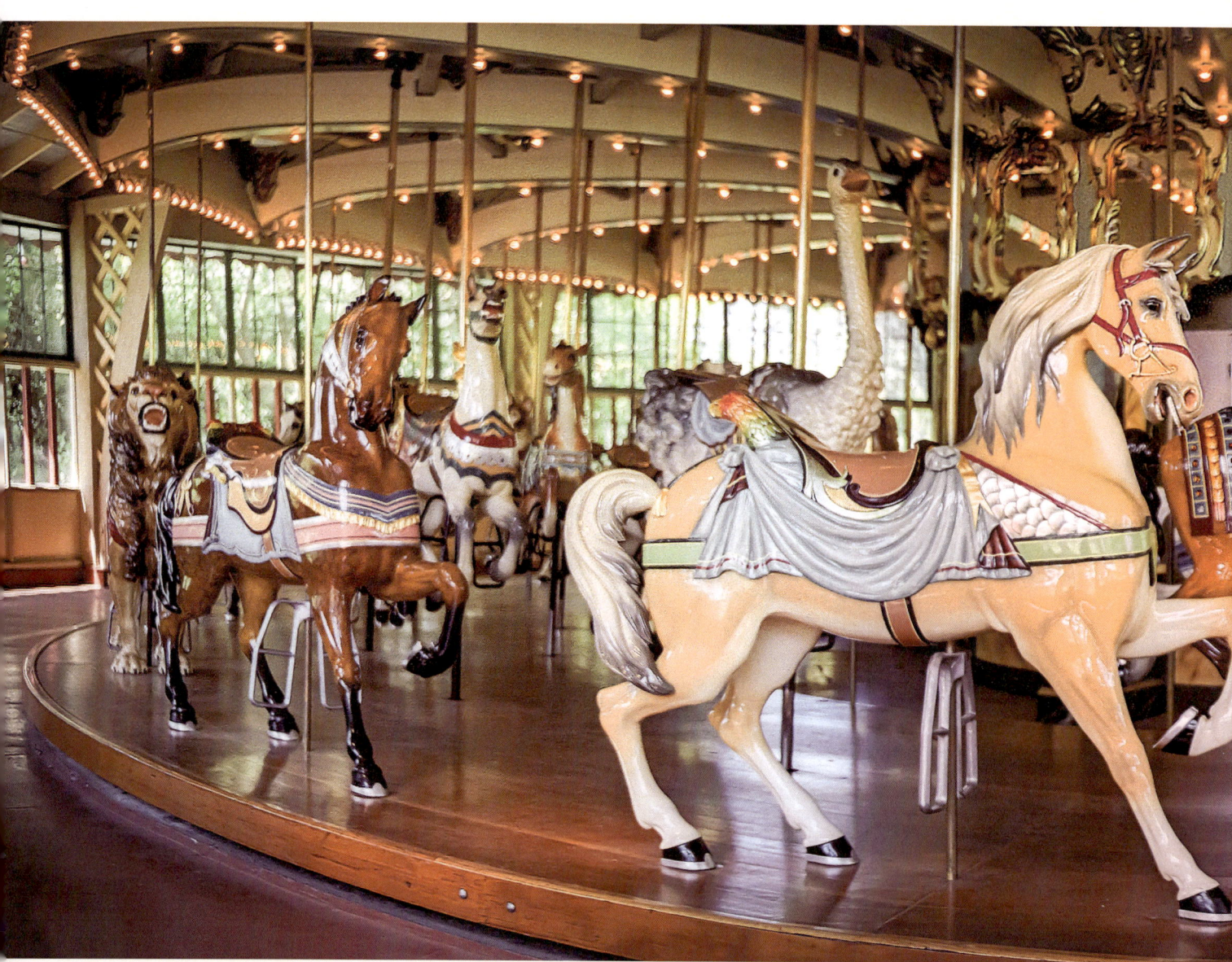

Photography and Text by Aaron Shepard

Classic Carousels of San Francisco

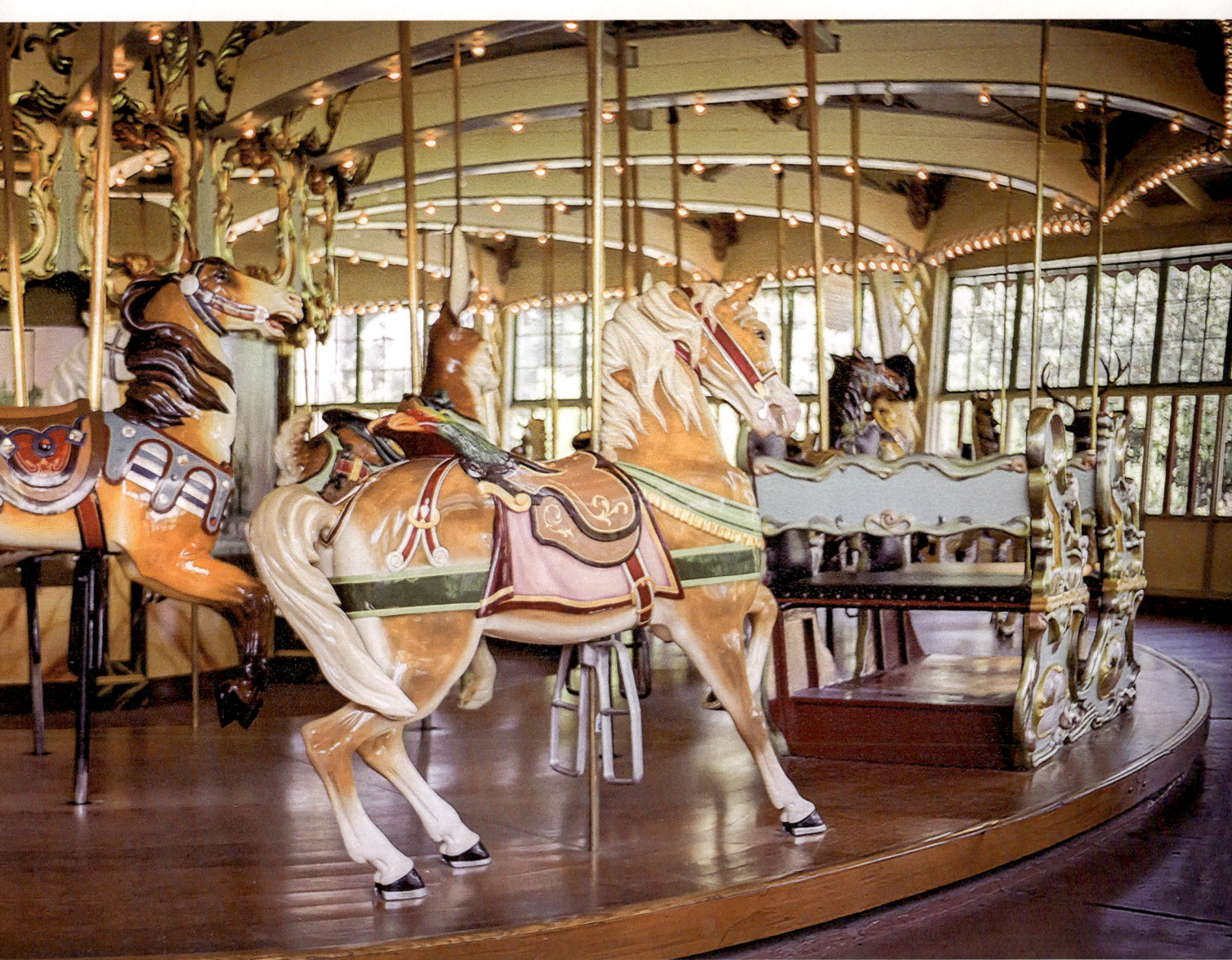

Shepard Publications • Bellingham, Washington

For Anne and Mirai

Library of Congress Control Number: 2016903223
Subject heading: Merry-go-round

The San Francisco Zoo Carousel was photographed on April 29, 2004, by permission of the San Francisco Zoo. The carousel at Yerba Buena Gardens was photographed on April 28, 2004, by permission of the Children's Creativity Museum (formerly Zeum). The Golden Gate Park Carousel was photographed on April 30, 2004, by permission of the San Francisco Recreation & Parks Department.

Historical details of Ruby Newman's restoration of the Golden Gate Park Carousel were gratefully drawn from "Ride a Painted Pony," by Lisa Schmidt, in *Golden State* magazine, Autumn 1984 (archived in the historical documents room of the San Francisco Public Library); and from "Wonderful Carousel Spins Again," by Allan Temko, in the *San Francisco Chronicle*, July 23, 1984. Newman, who has continued to restore carousel figures for private collectors, can be found at **www.rubynewman.com**.

Thanks to Patrick Wentzel of the National Carousel Association for help with carousel histories and figure identifications (though the author is solely responsible for their final forms). Thanks also to Gary Nance for encouragement through his posting early versions of these photos on the N.C.A. Web site.

Title page photo: San Francisco Zoo Carousel
This page photo: Golden Gate Park Carousel pavilion ceiling

Version 1.2

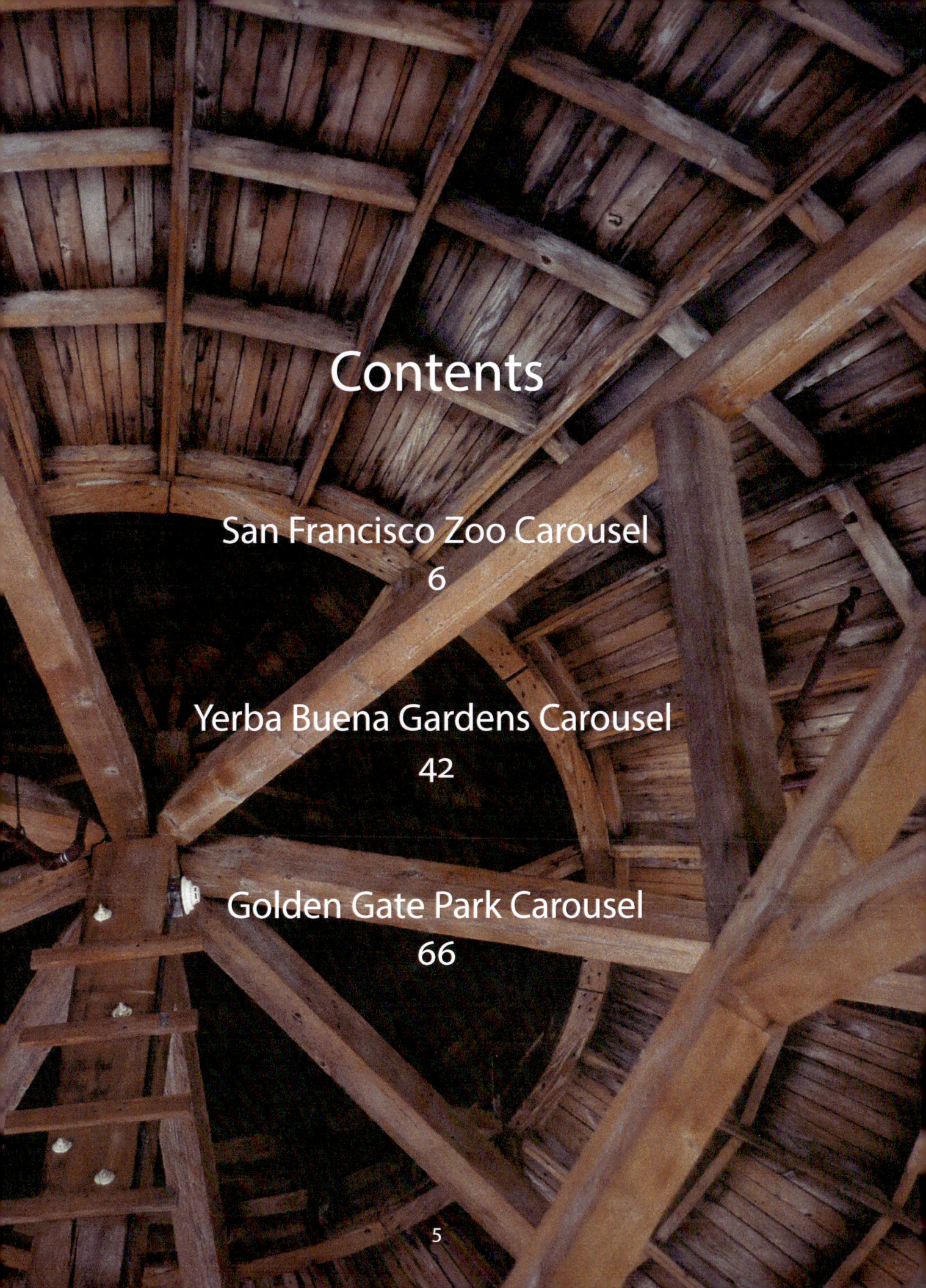

Contents

San Francisco Zoo Carousel

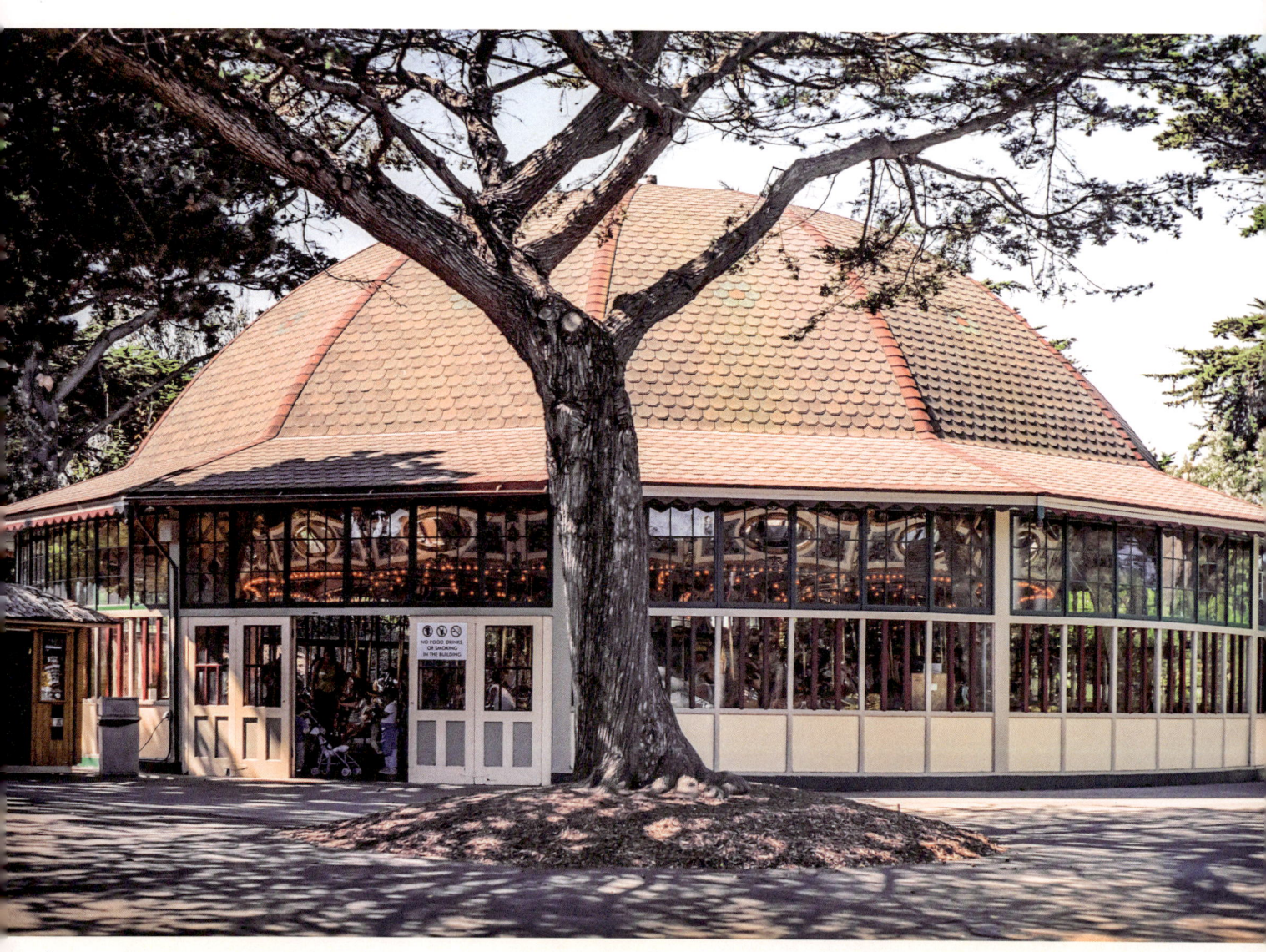

The San Francisco Zoo Carousel was built in 1921 in Philadelphia by the Dentzel Carousel Company under William Dentzel, son and heir of the company's founder, Gustav Dentzel. After a short stint at the Pacific City Amusement Park in Redwood City, California, it was installed in San Francisco in 1925, in what was then a children's park but is now part of the zoo. The carousel has been restored several times, most notably in 2000–2002.

Alongside its Dentzel carvings, the carousel features figures by the legendary craftsman M. C. Illions of Coney Island in Brooklyn, New York. Another of the horses is much older than the carousel itself—a "transitional Dentzel listener," so called because of the position of the ears. Carved between 1885 and 1890, it is said to be one of only two such figures in the world.

The carousel is today officially named the Eugene Friend Carousel, after a San Francisco civic leader and philanthropist.

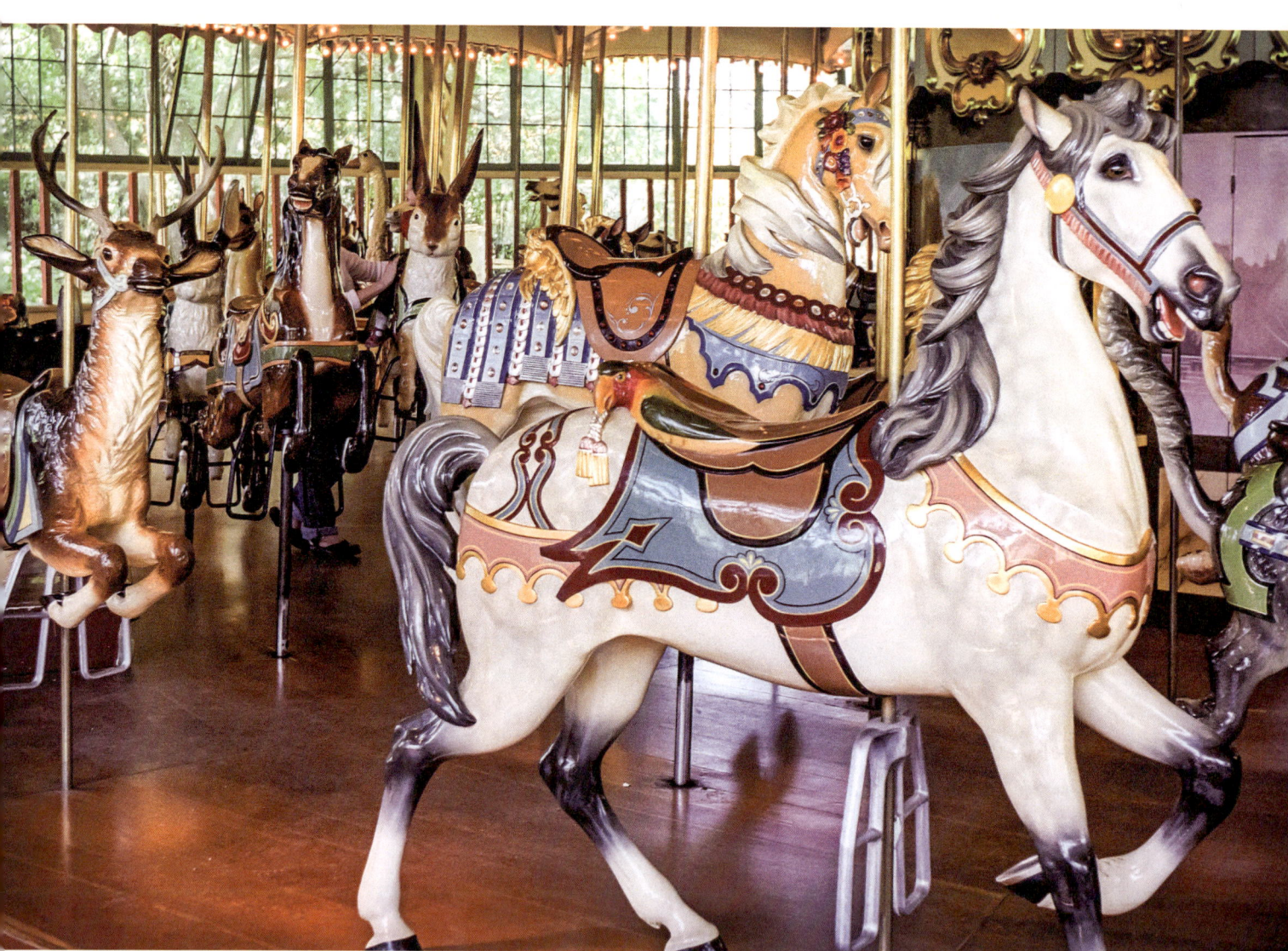

Carousel animals

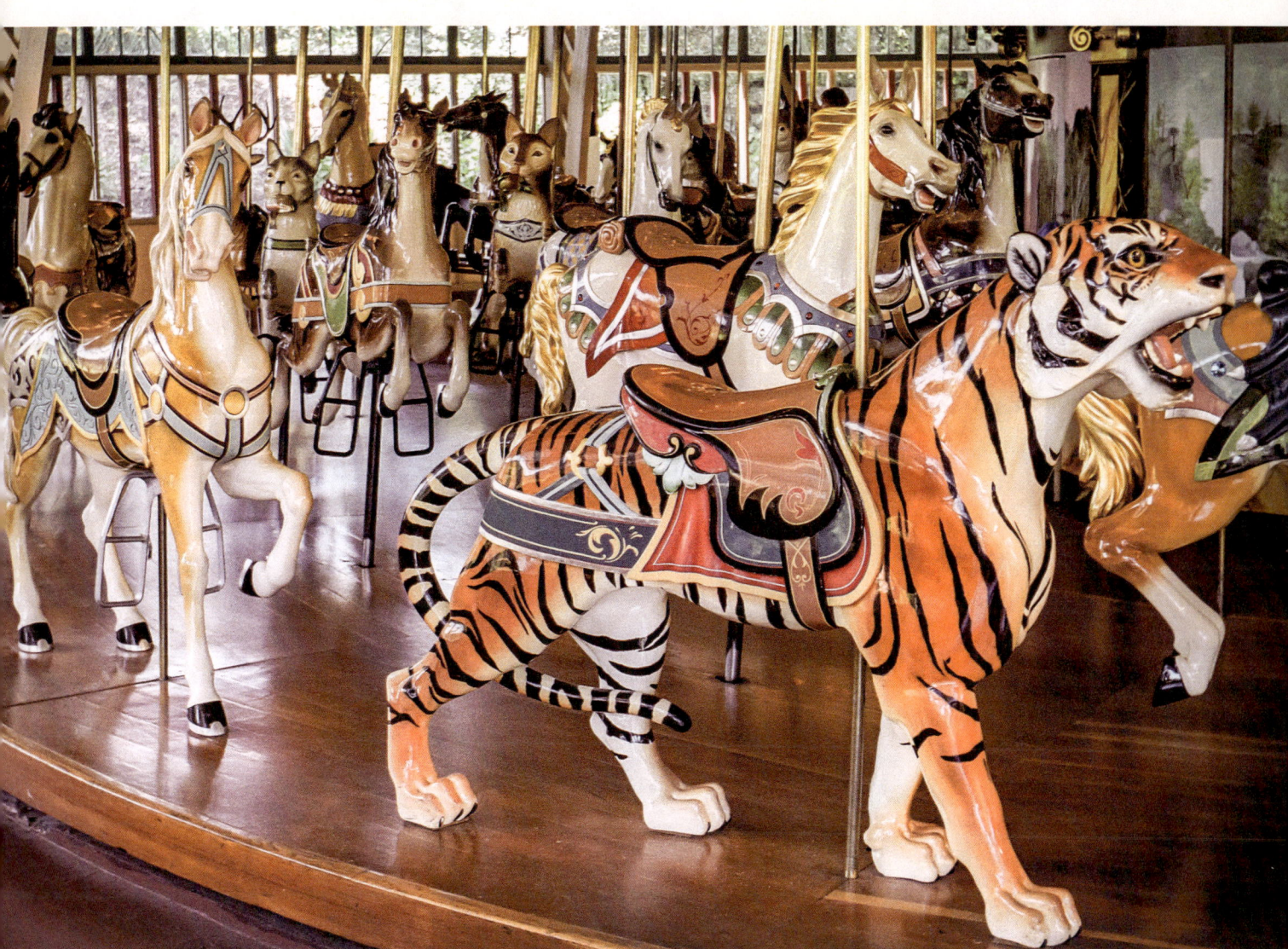

Carousel animals

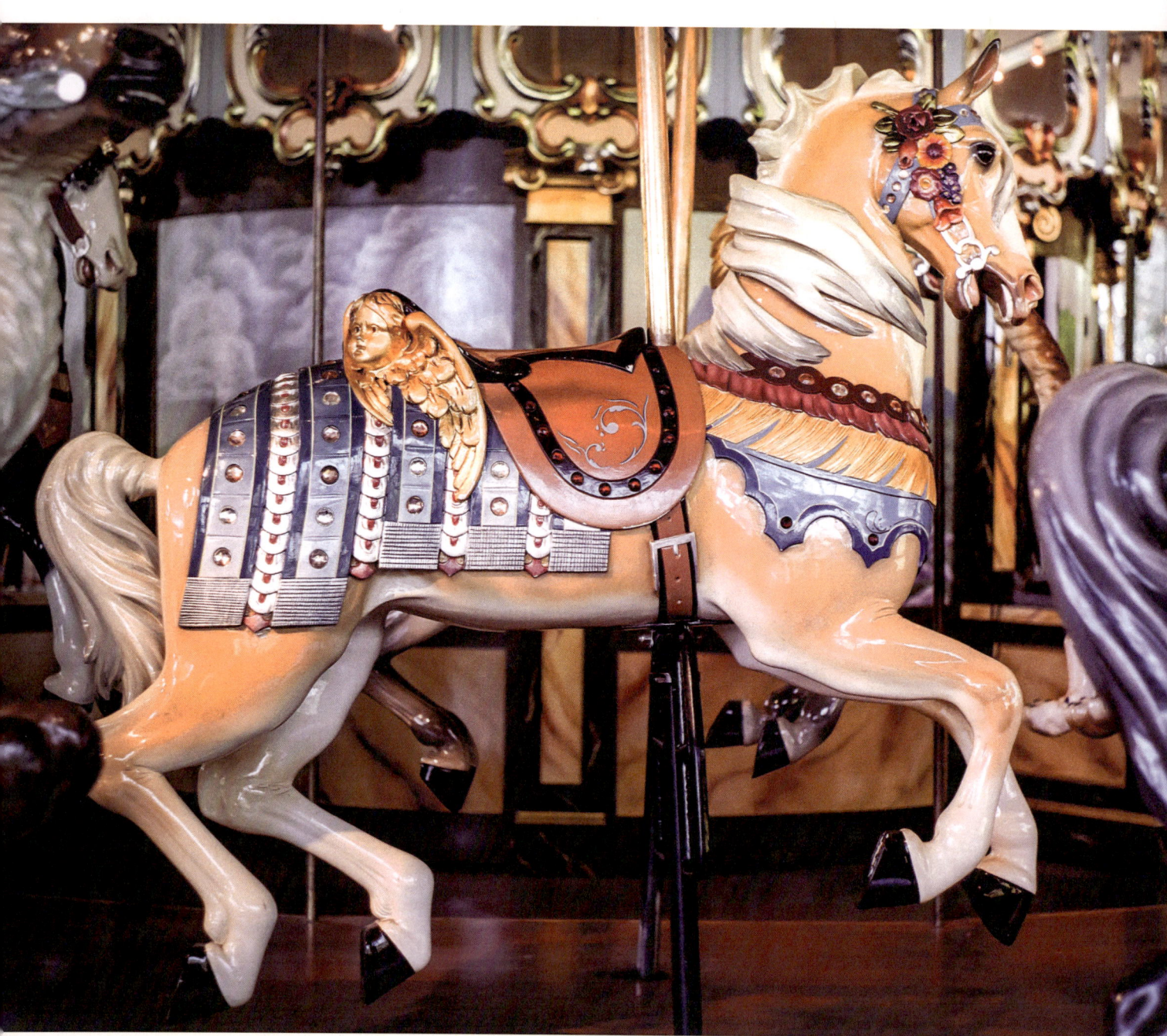

Jumper, "Rosie" (M. C. Illions)

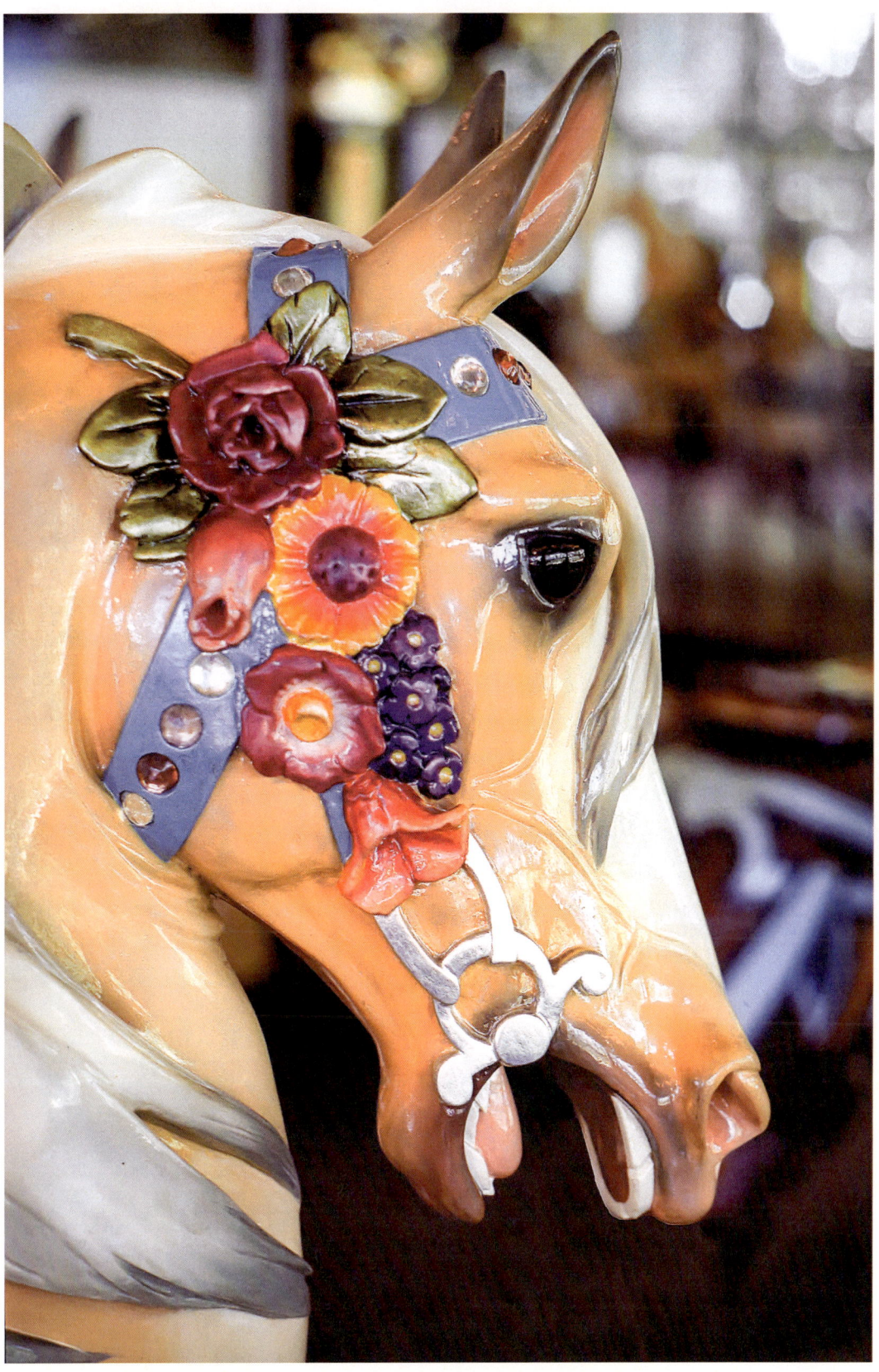

"Rosie" head

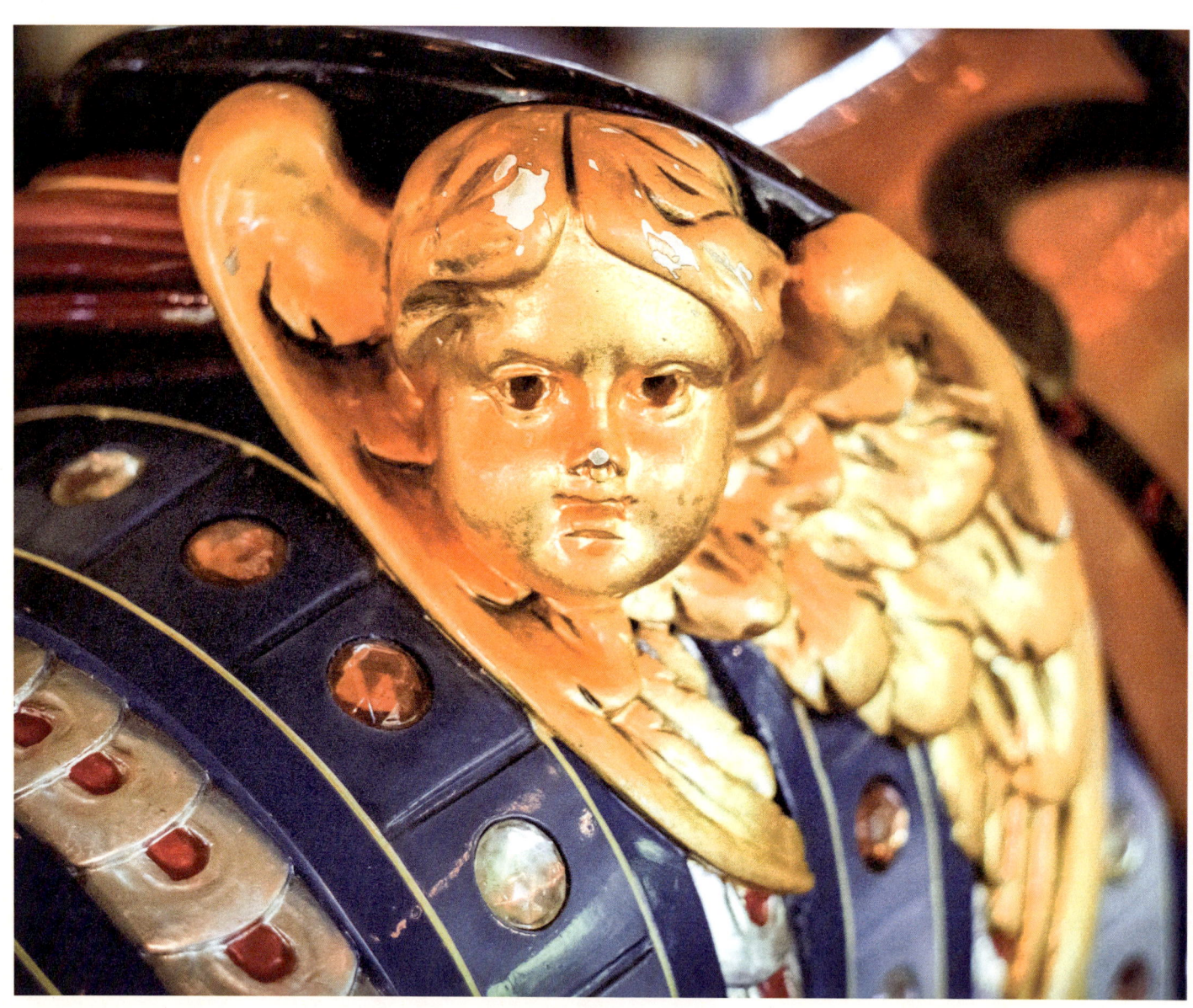

"Rosie" saddle detail

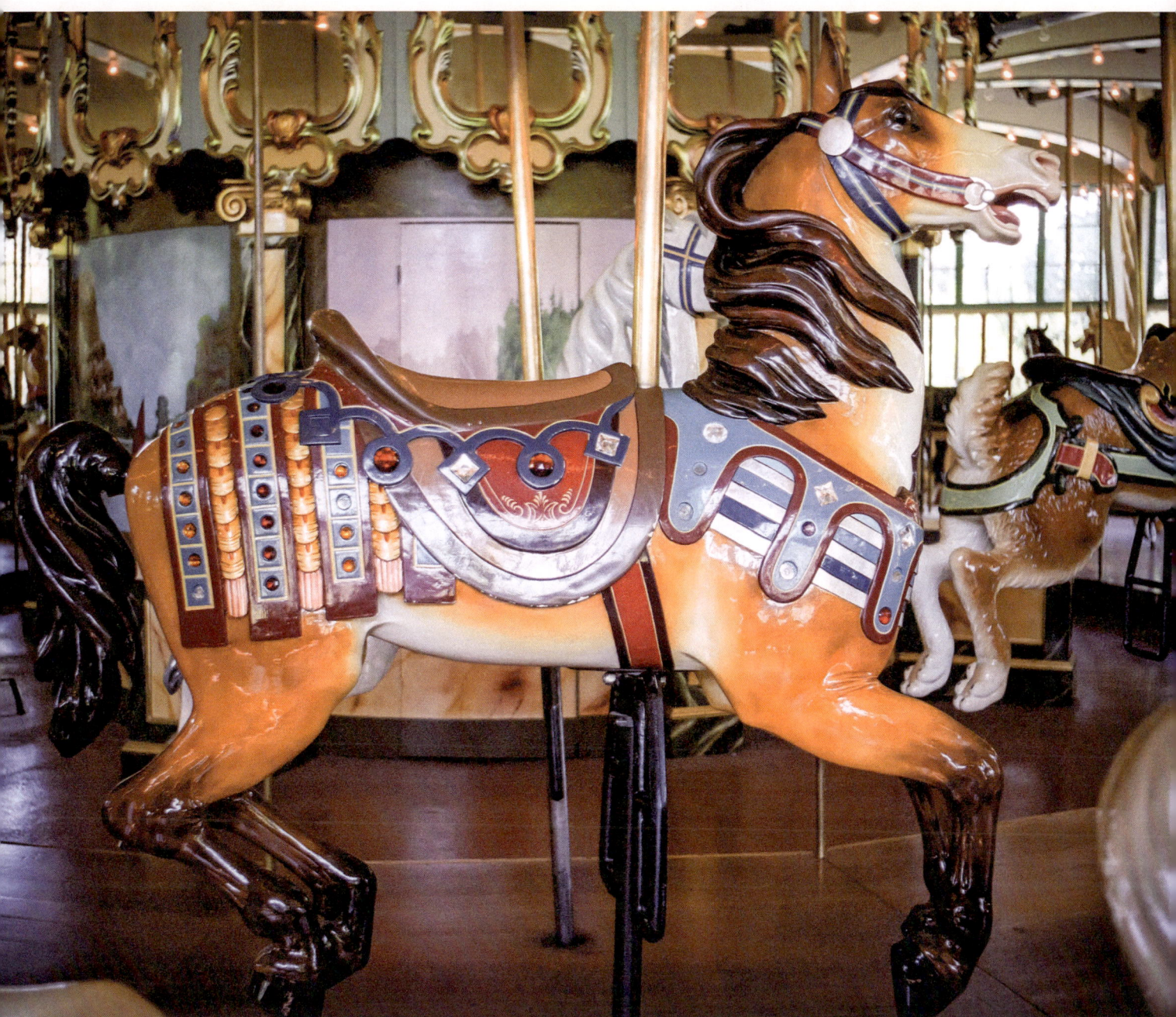

Jumper (M. C. Illions)

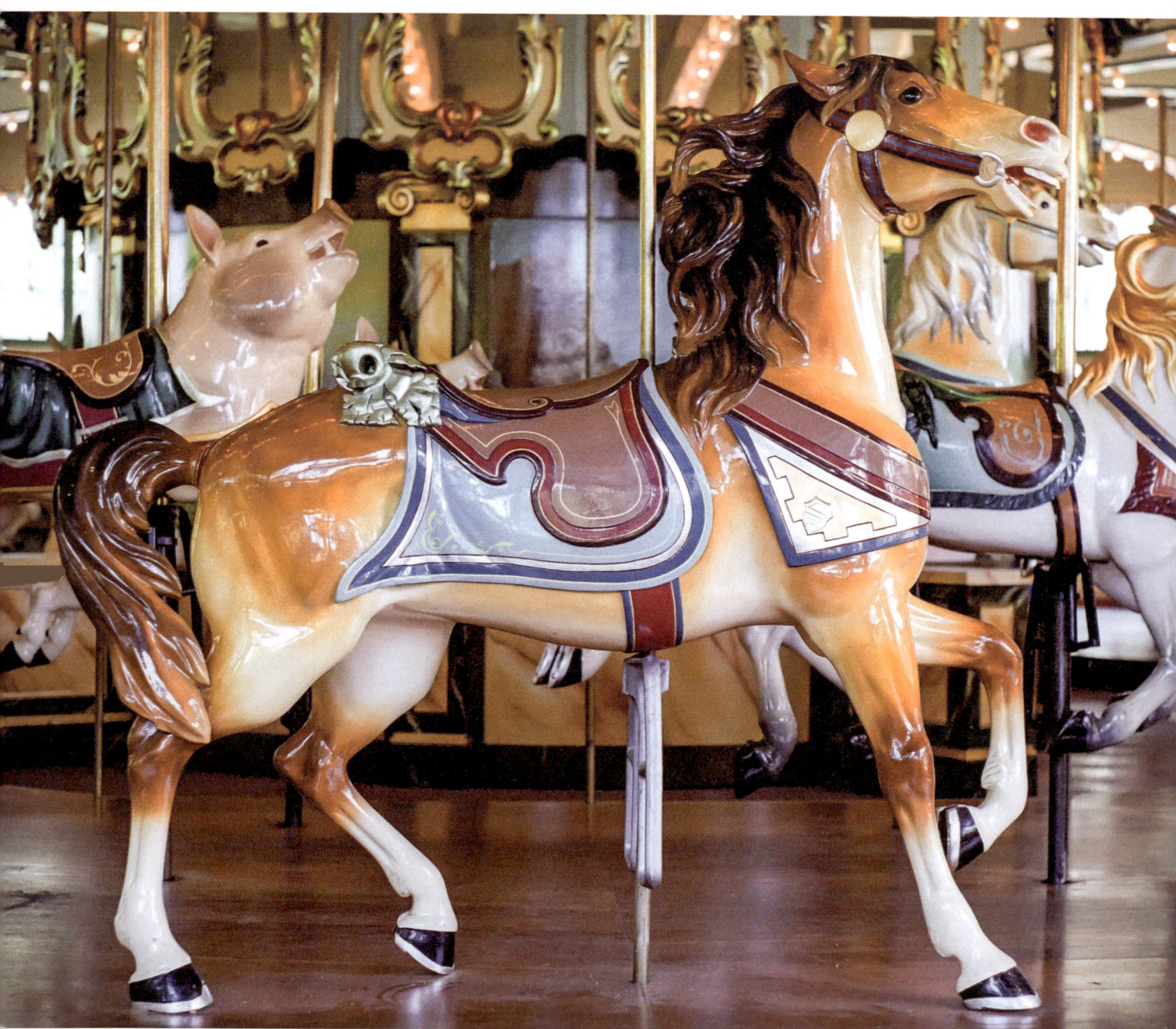

Stander, "Listener" style

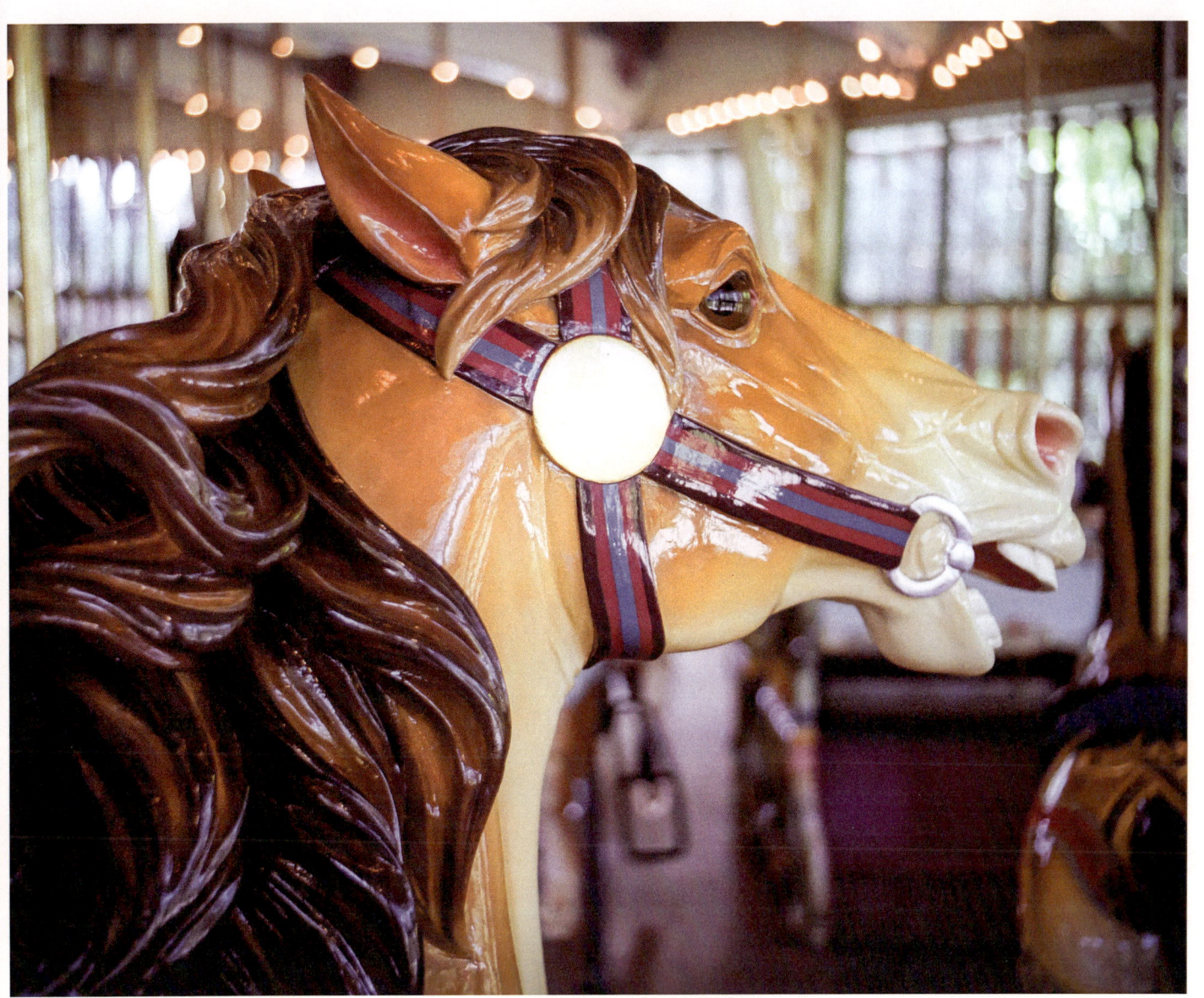

"Listener" stander head

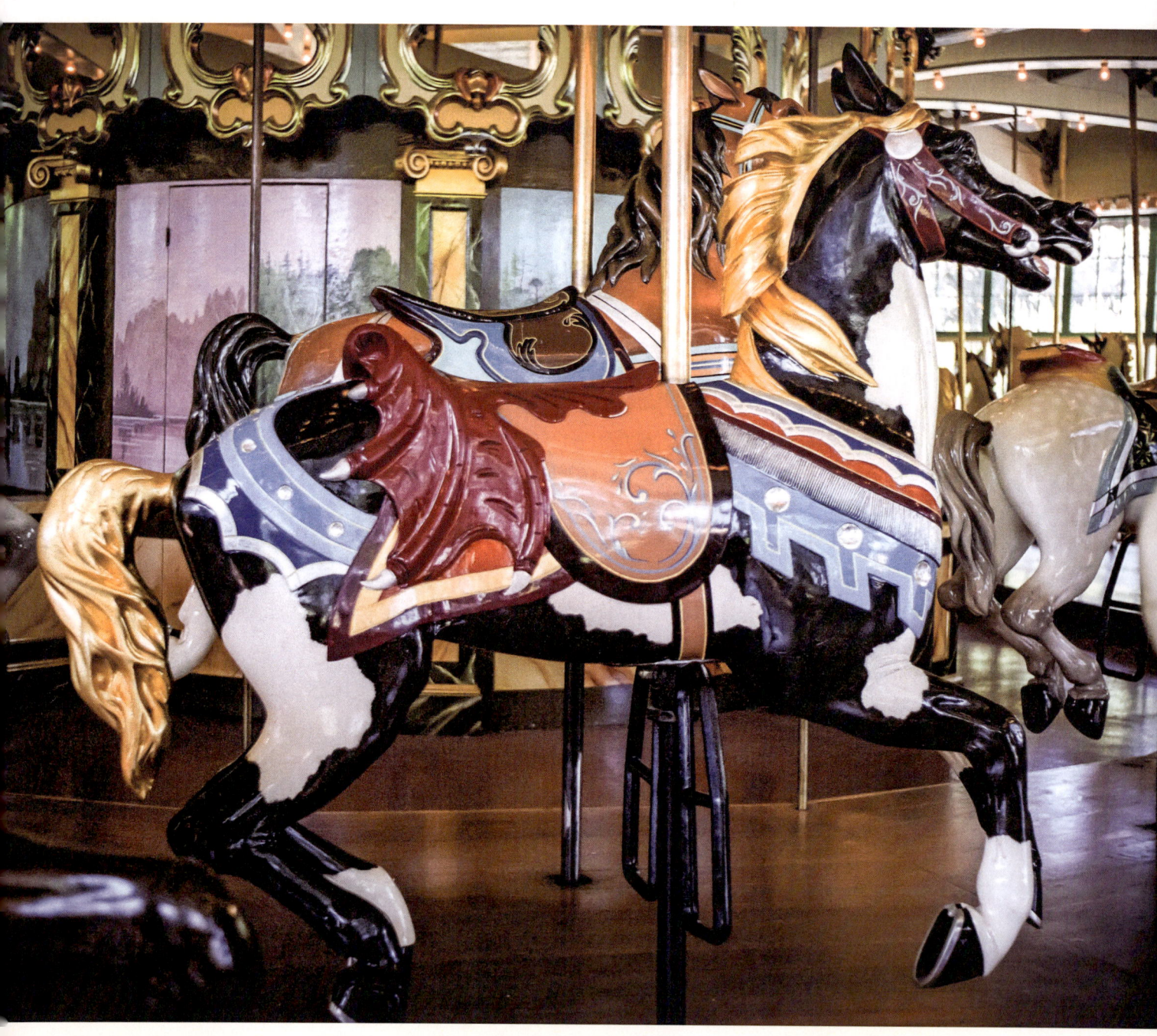

Jumper (M. C. Illions)

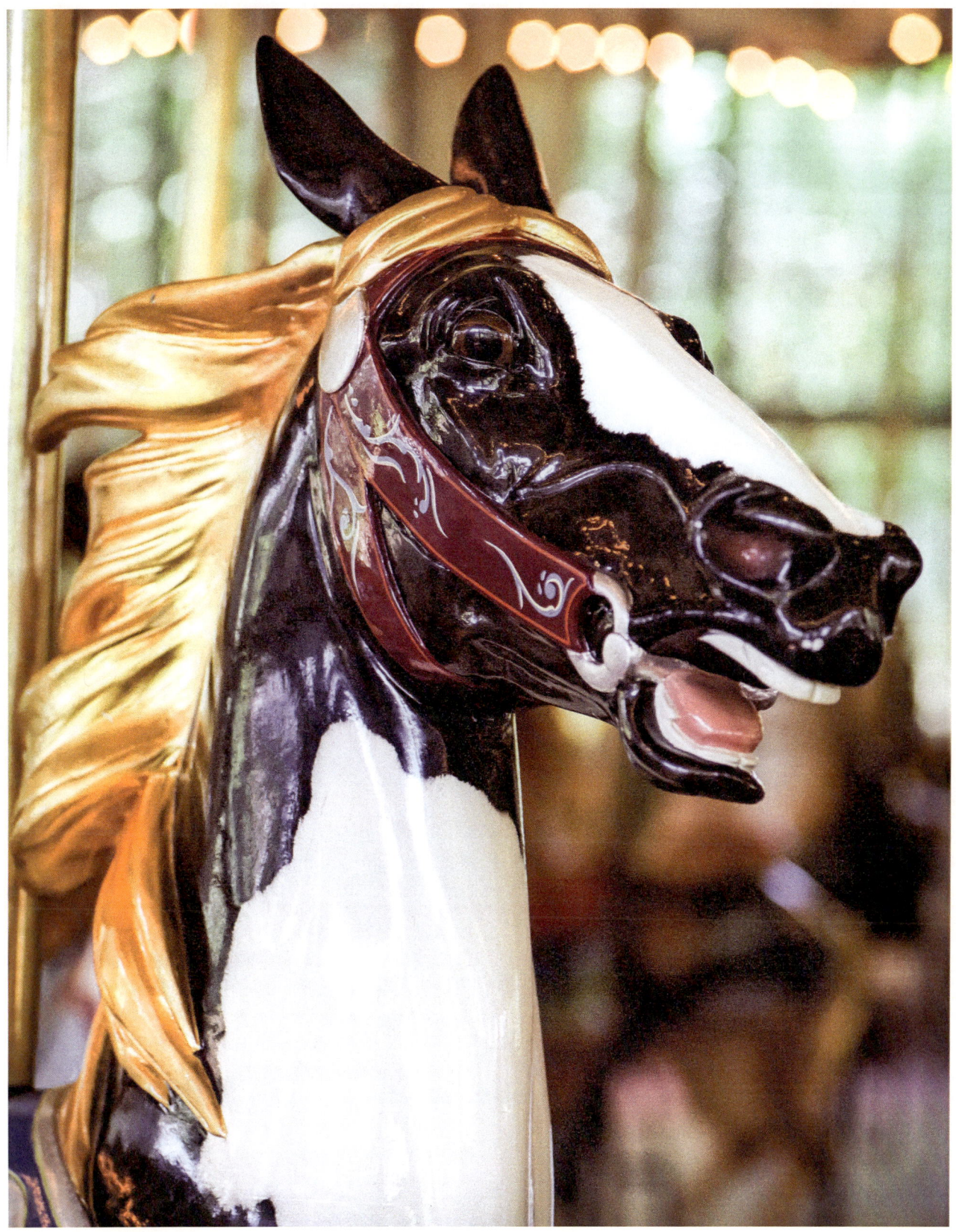

Jumper head

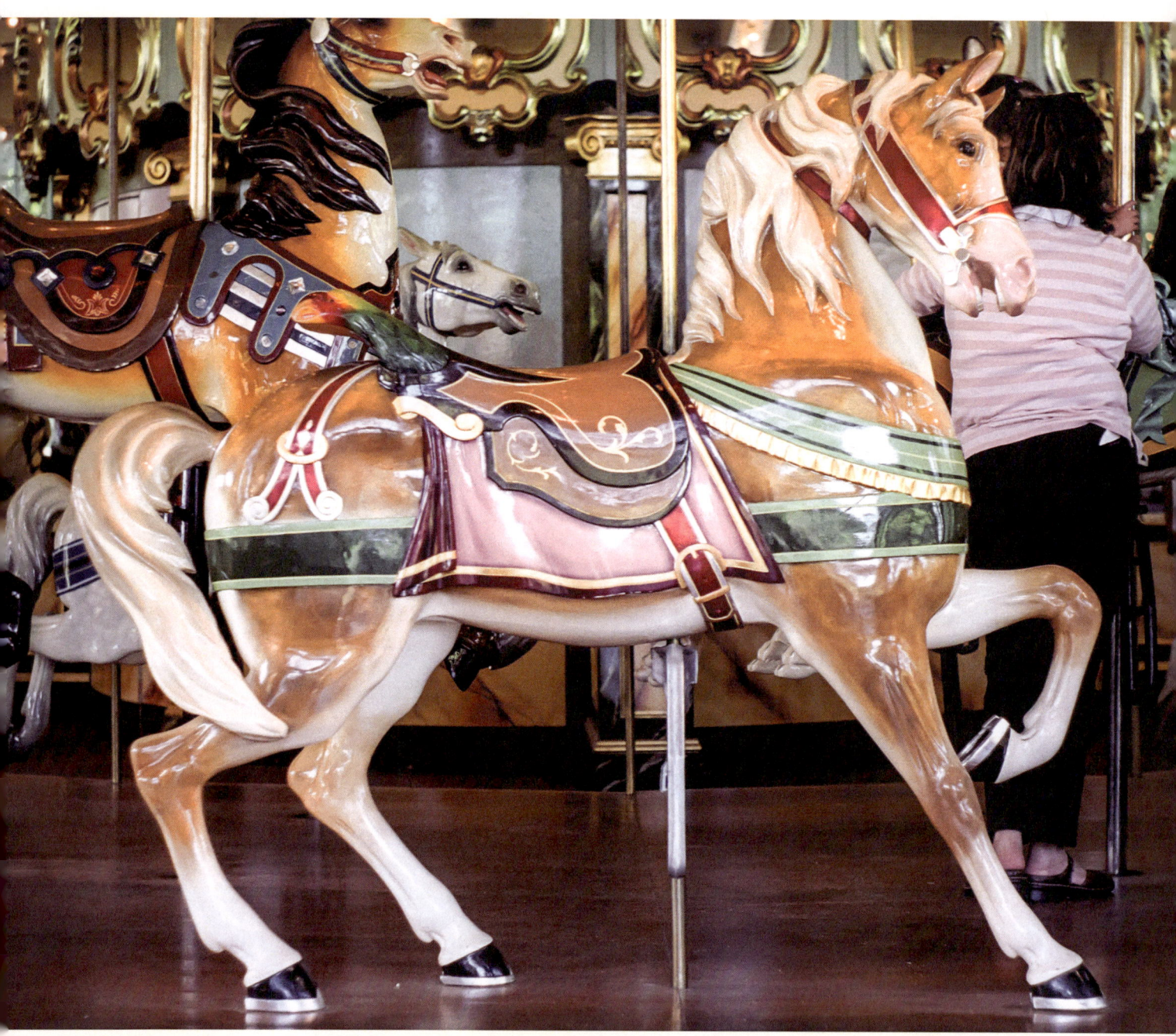

Stander

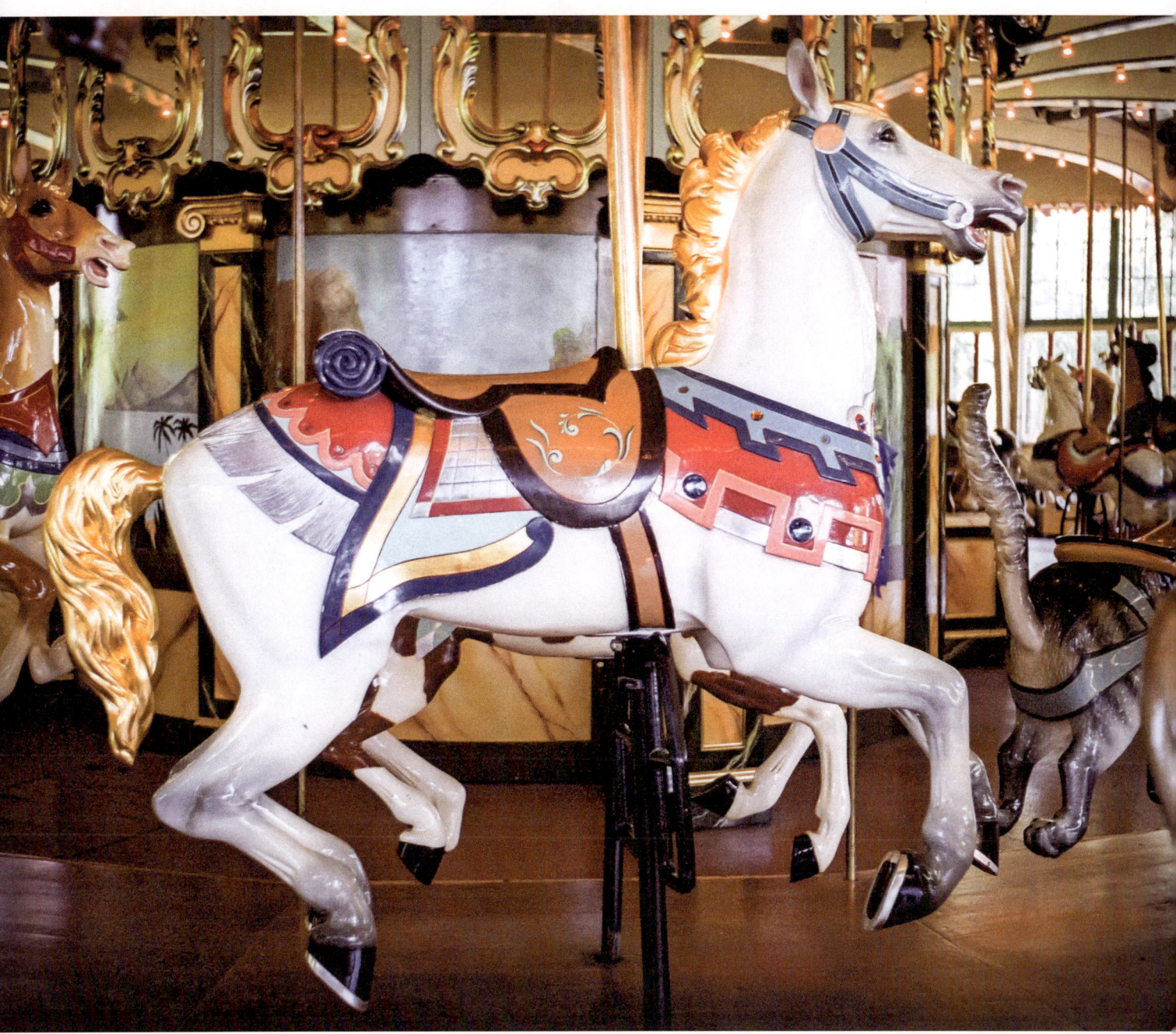

Jumper (M. C. Illions)

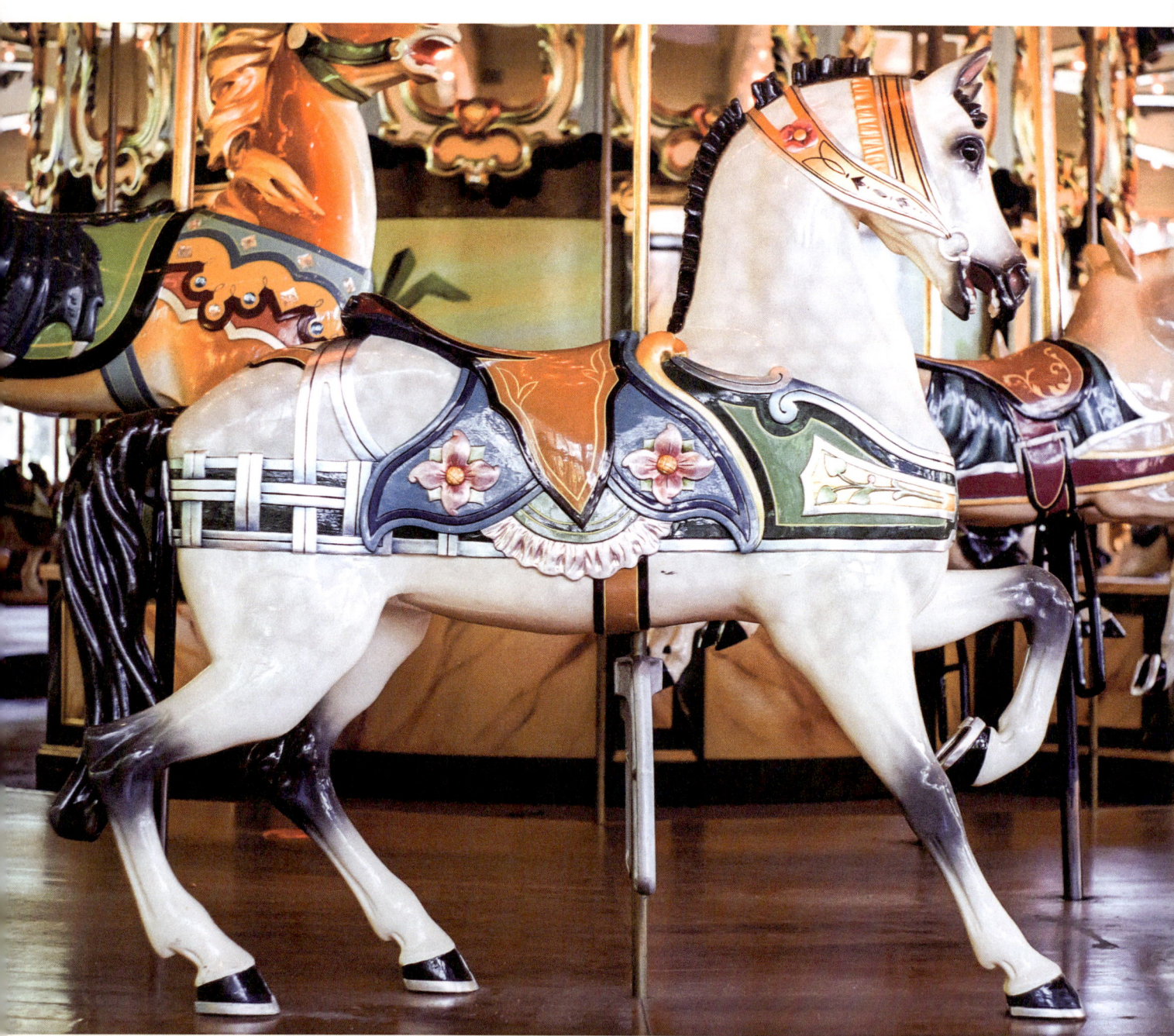

Stander, "Roached Mane" style

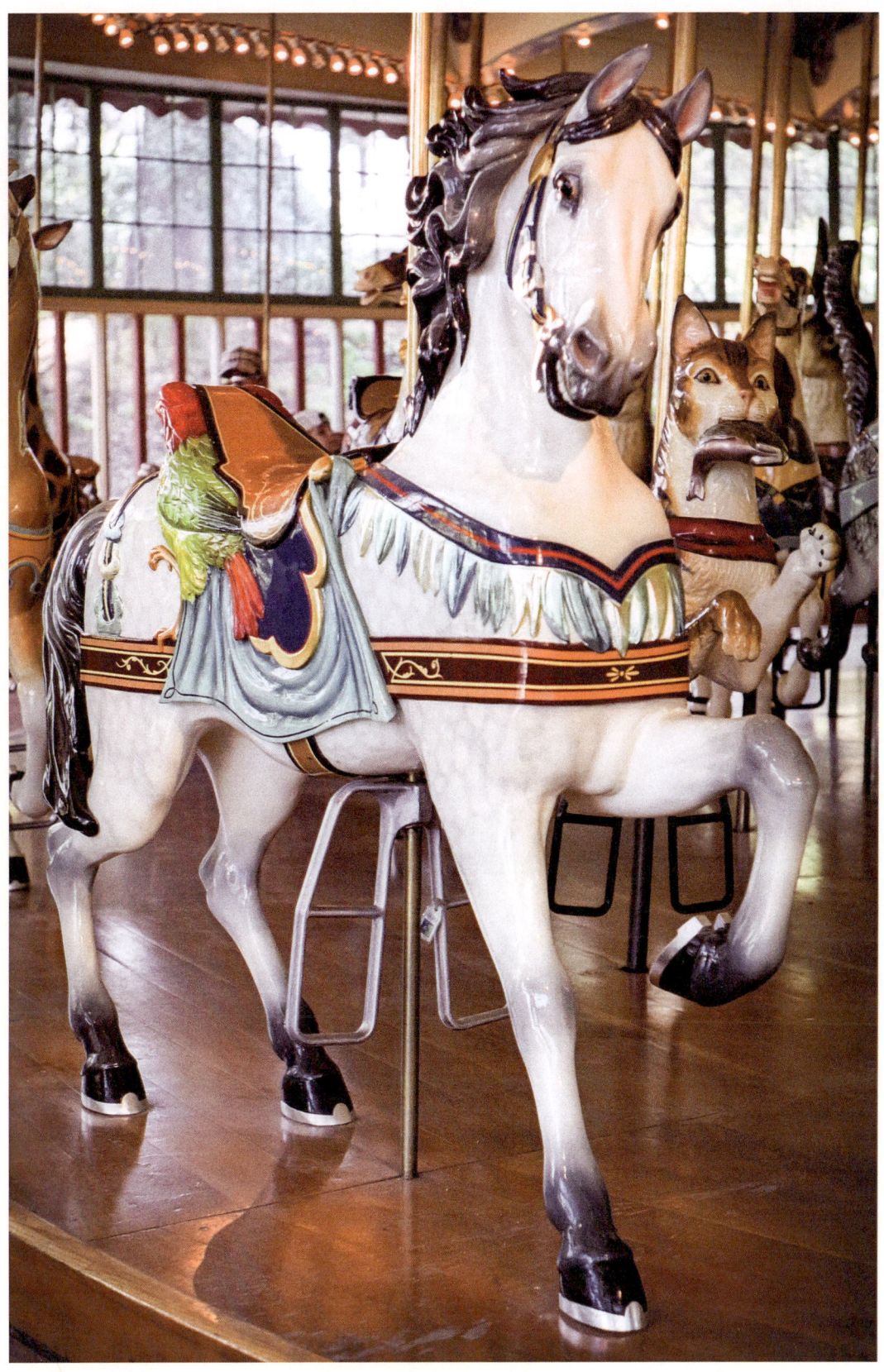

Stander

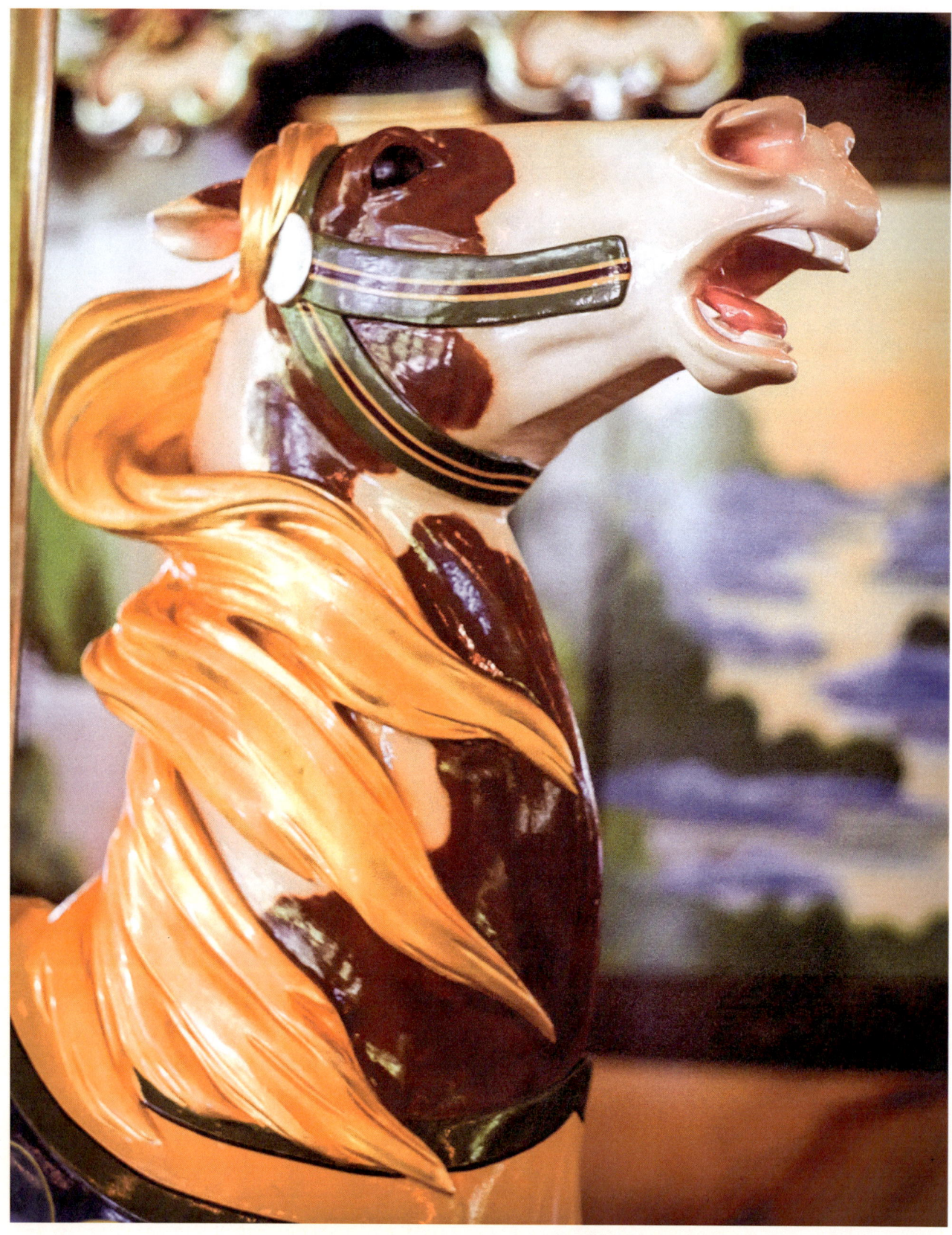

Jumper head (M. C. Illions)

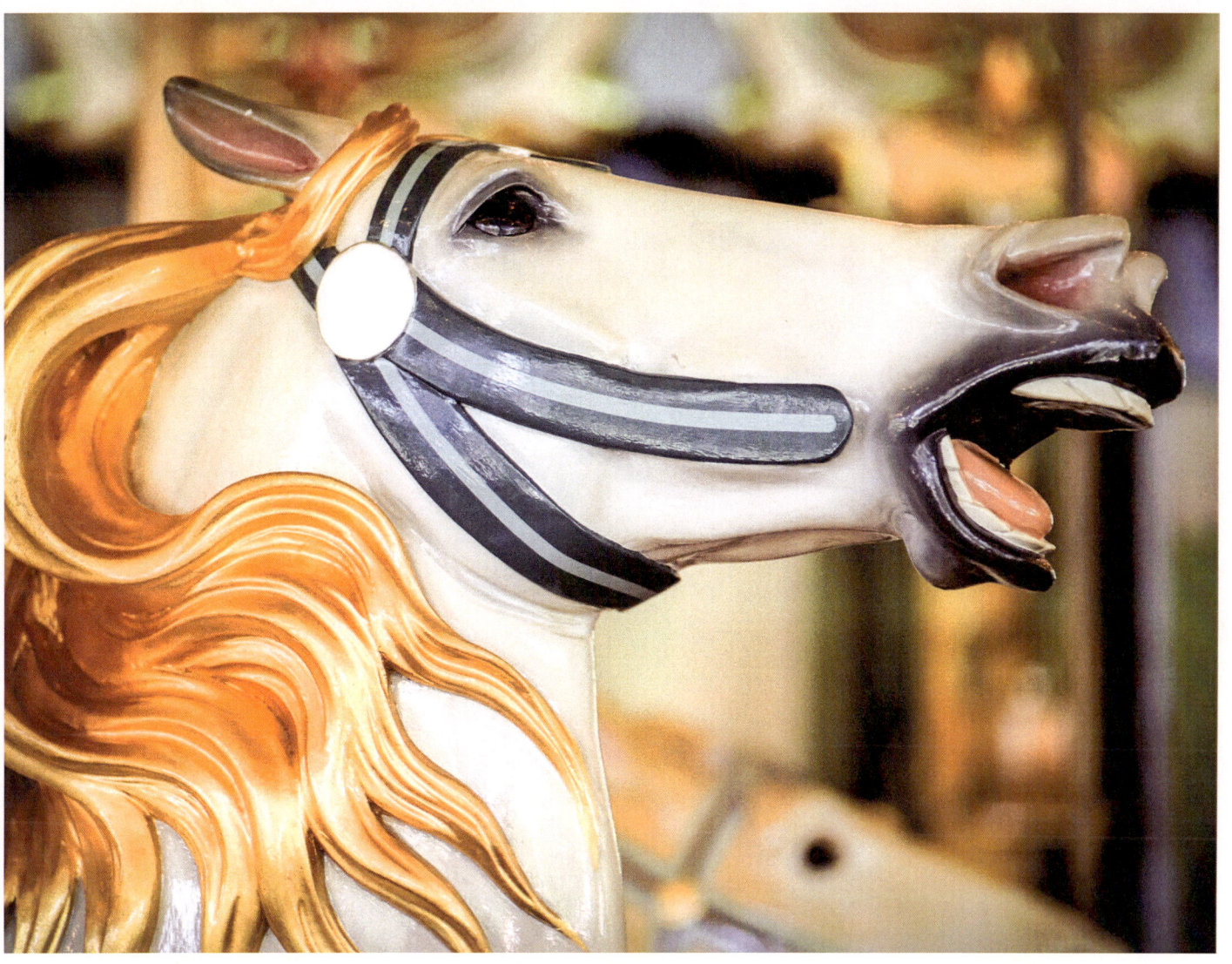

Jumper head (M. C. Illions)

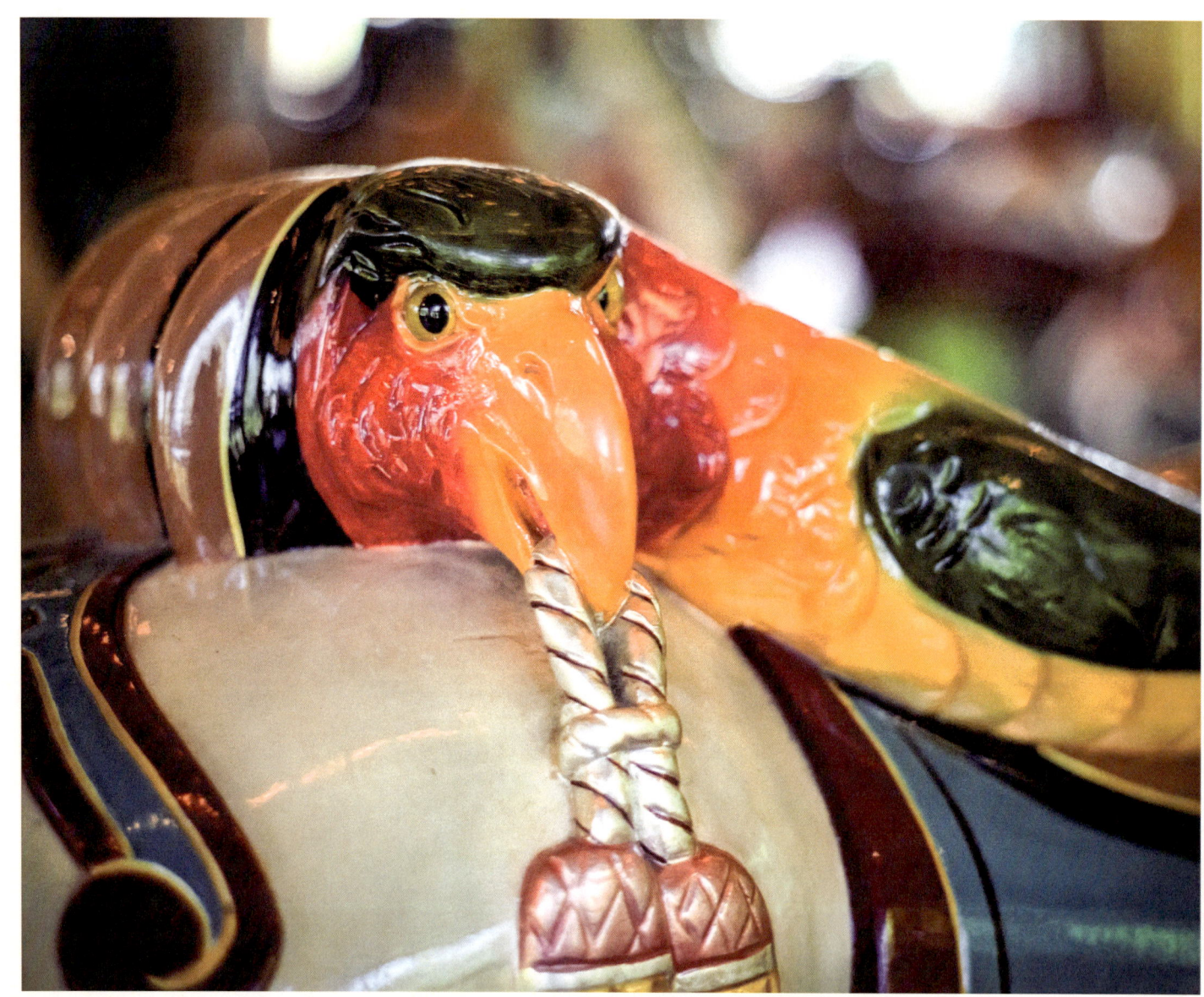

Saddle detail

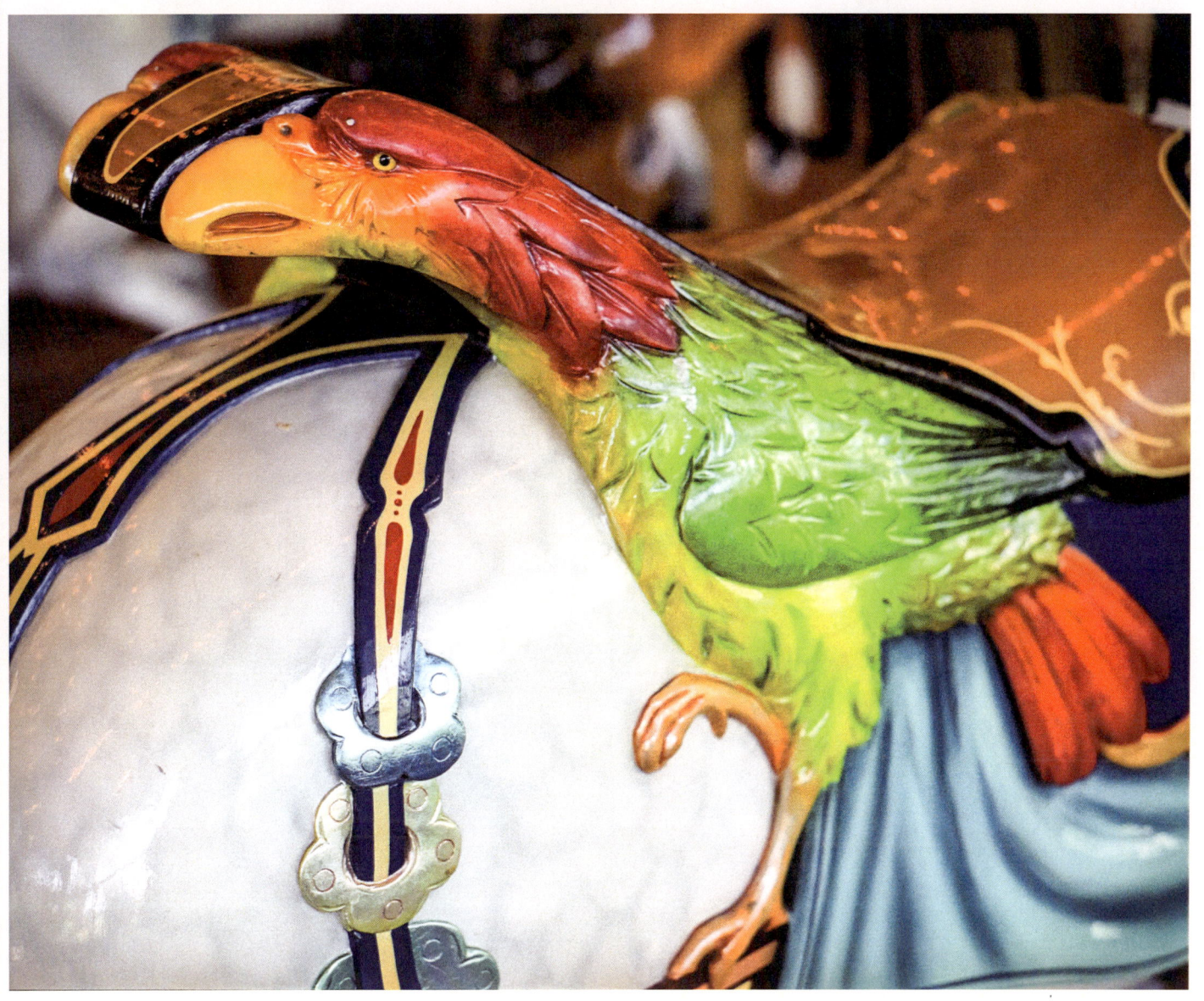

Saddle detail

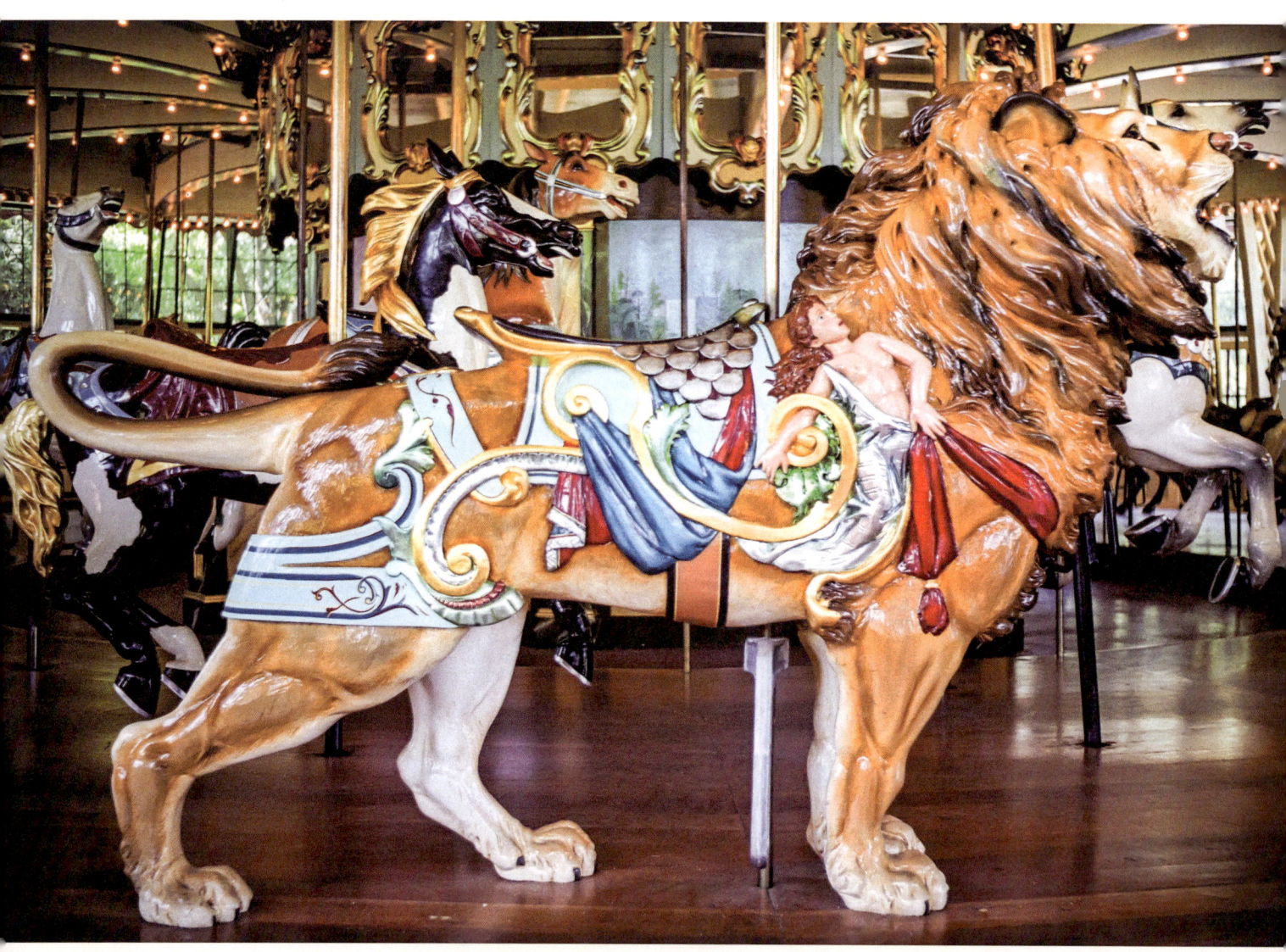

Standing lion

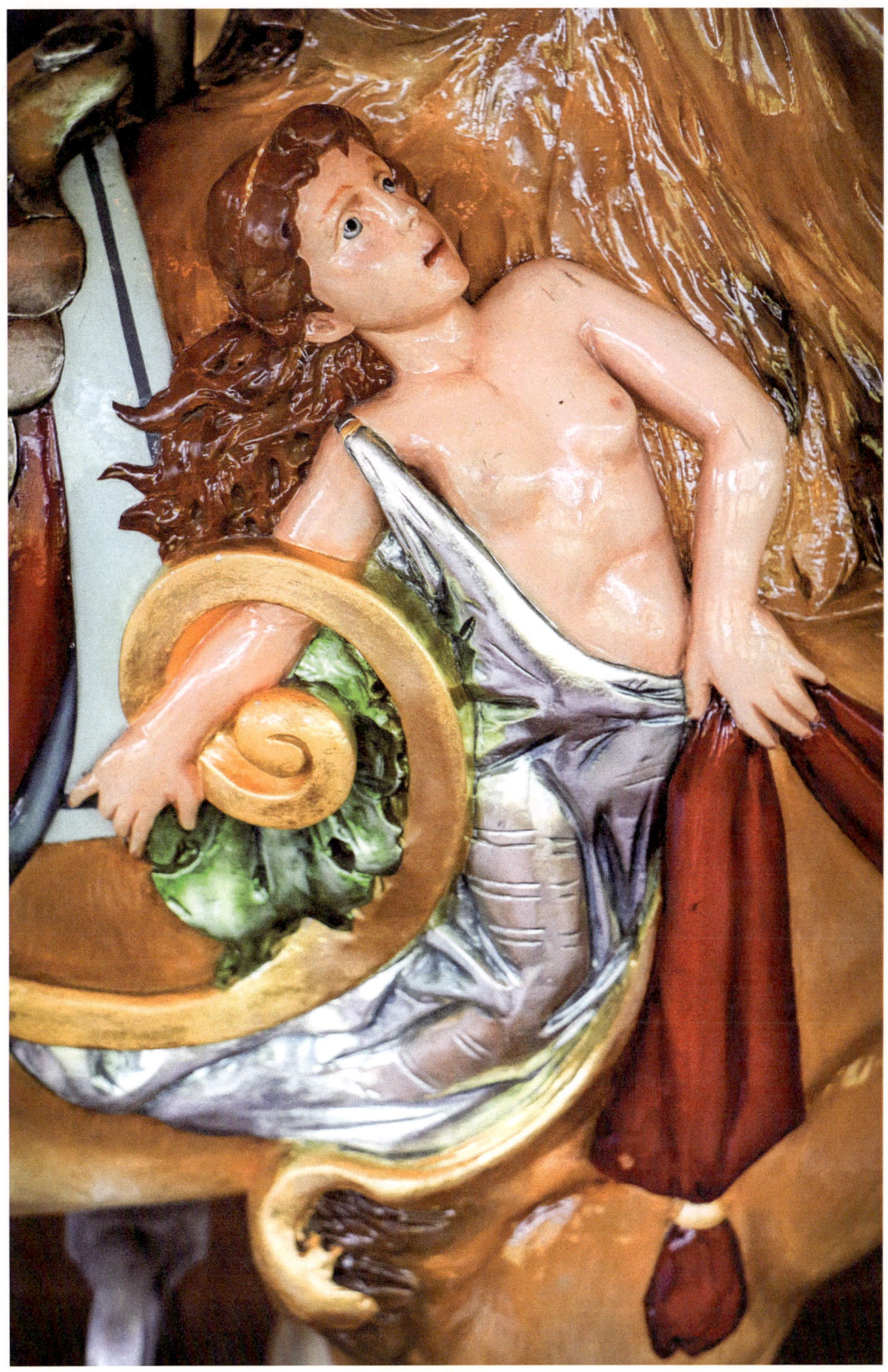

Lion detail

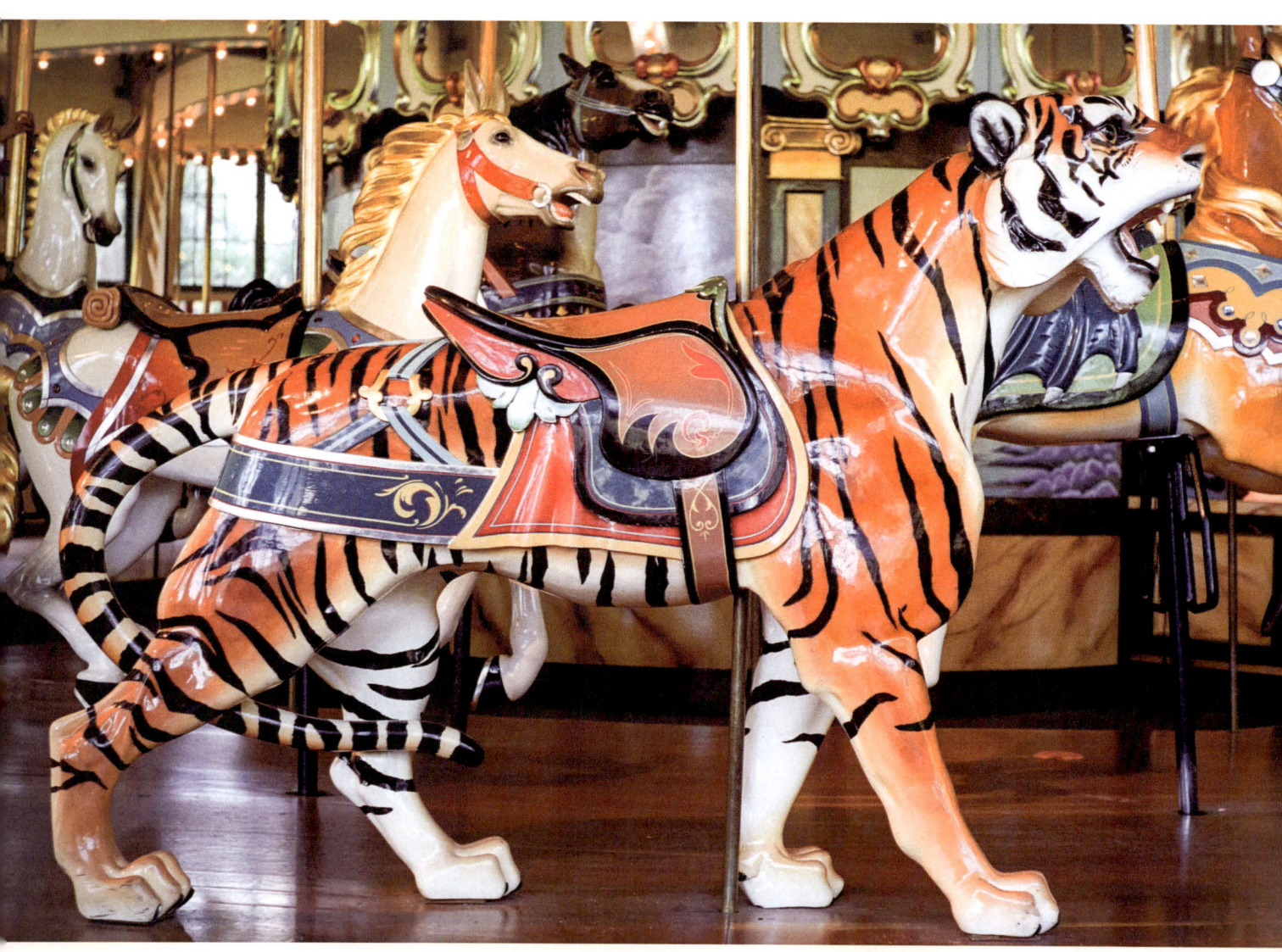

Standing tiger

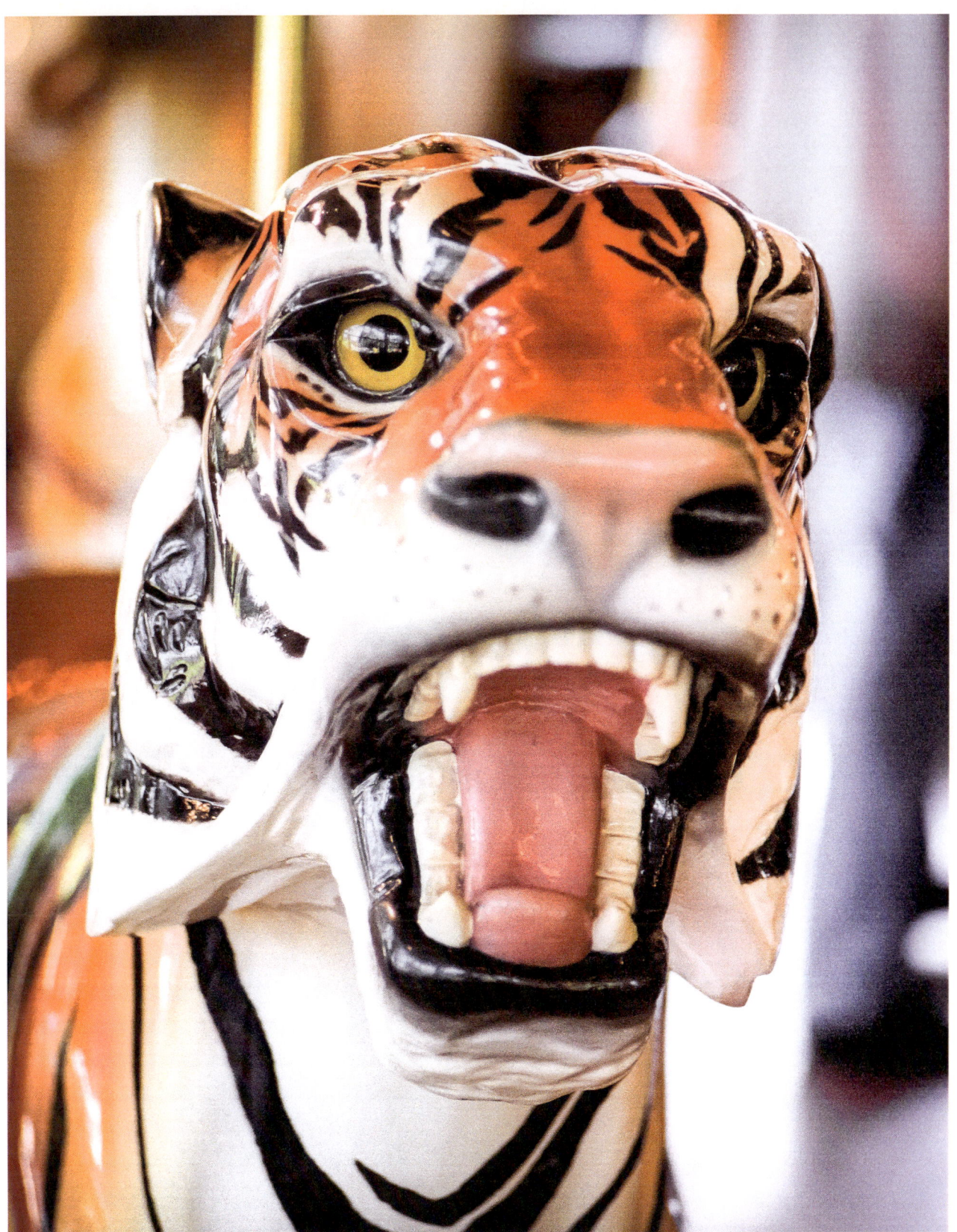

Tiger head

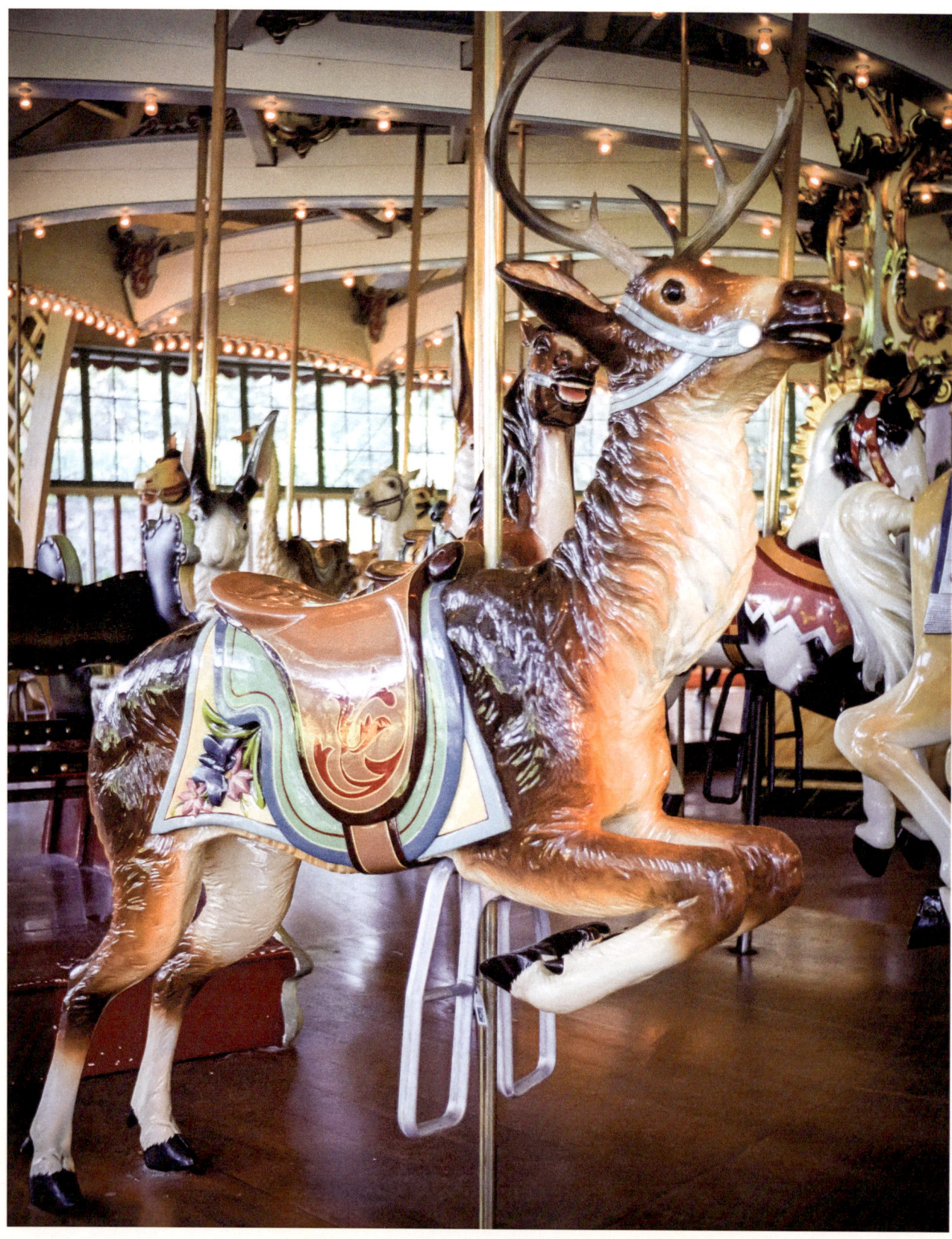

Standing stag

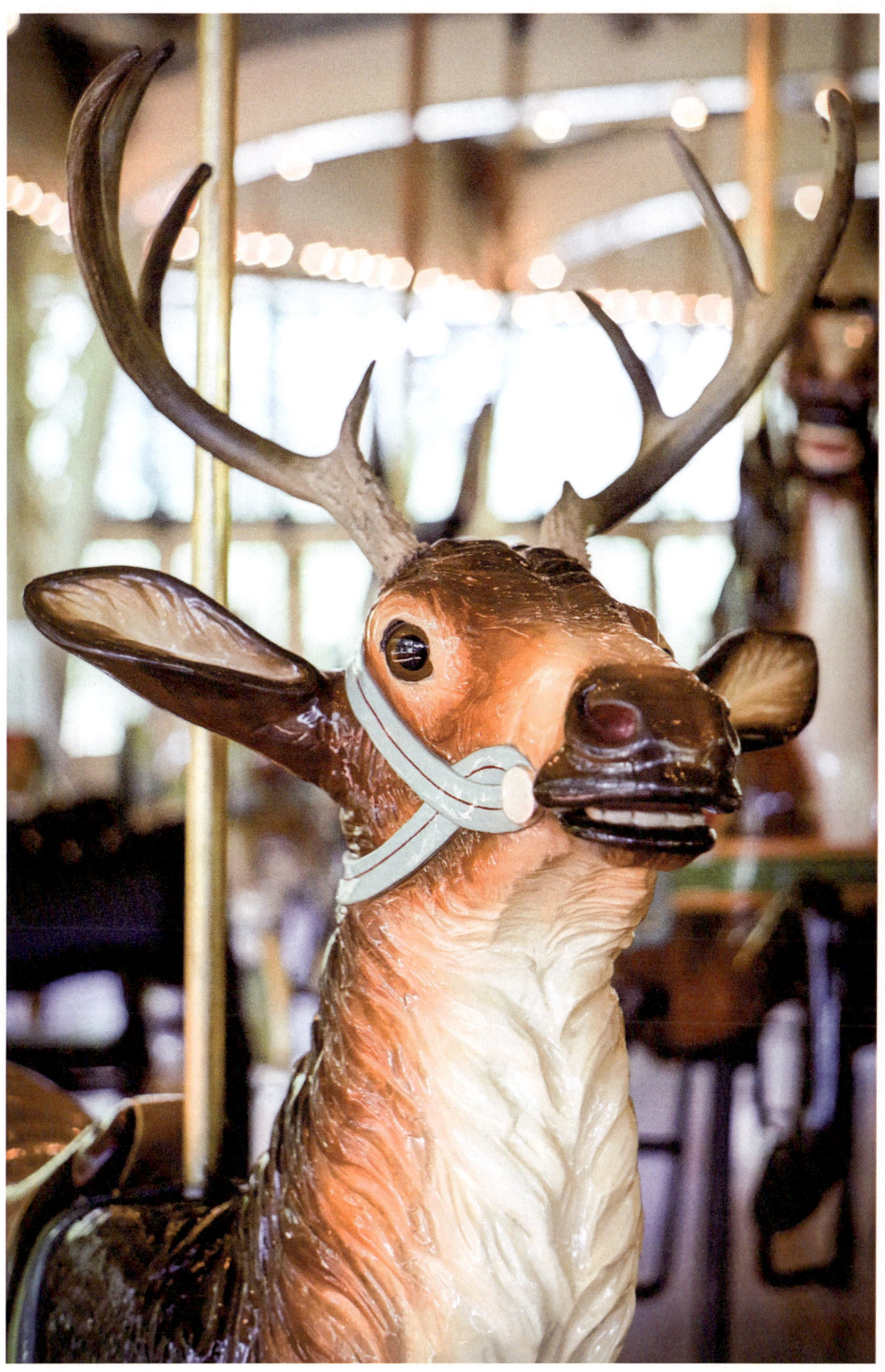

Stag head

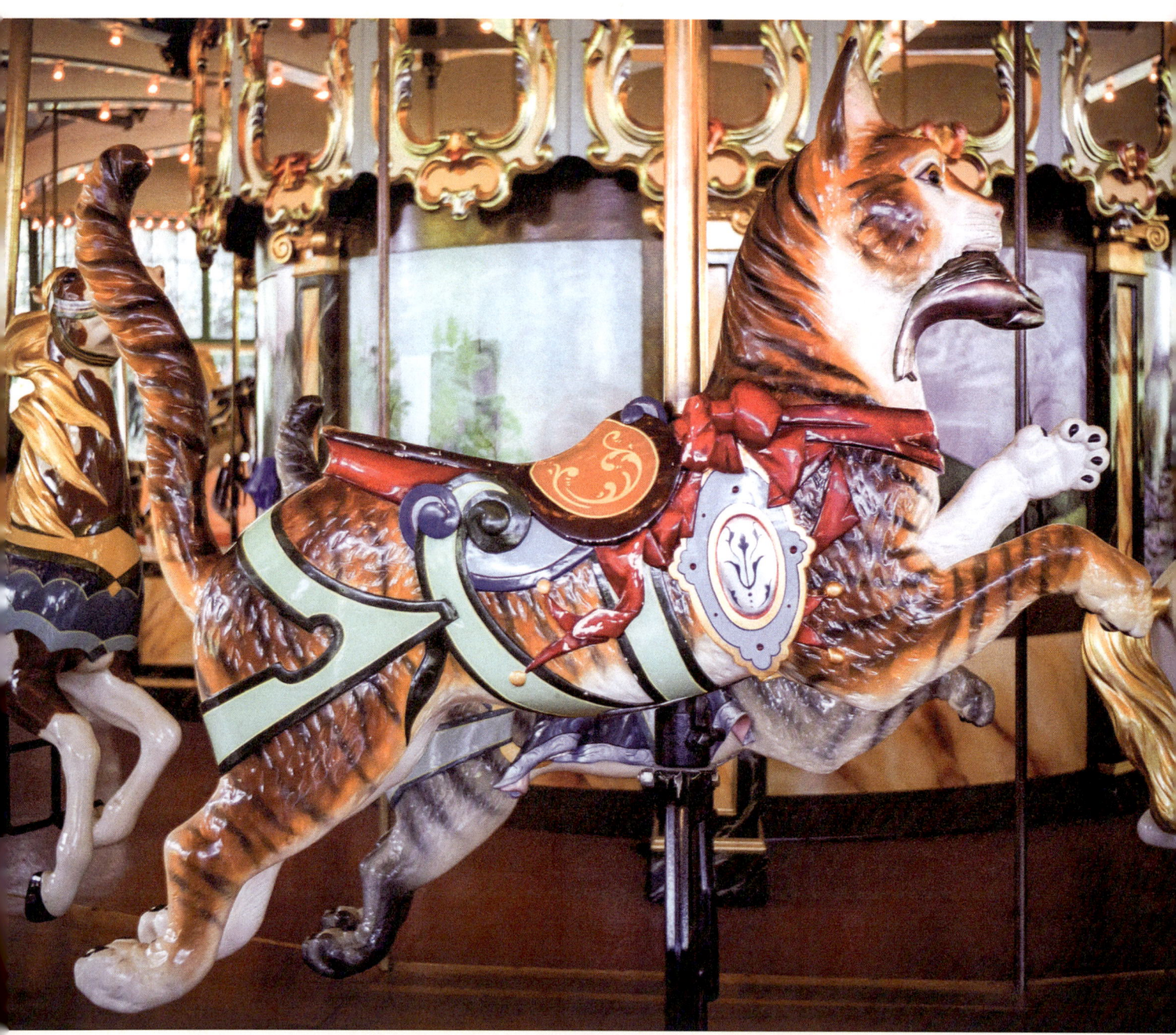

Jumping cat

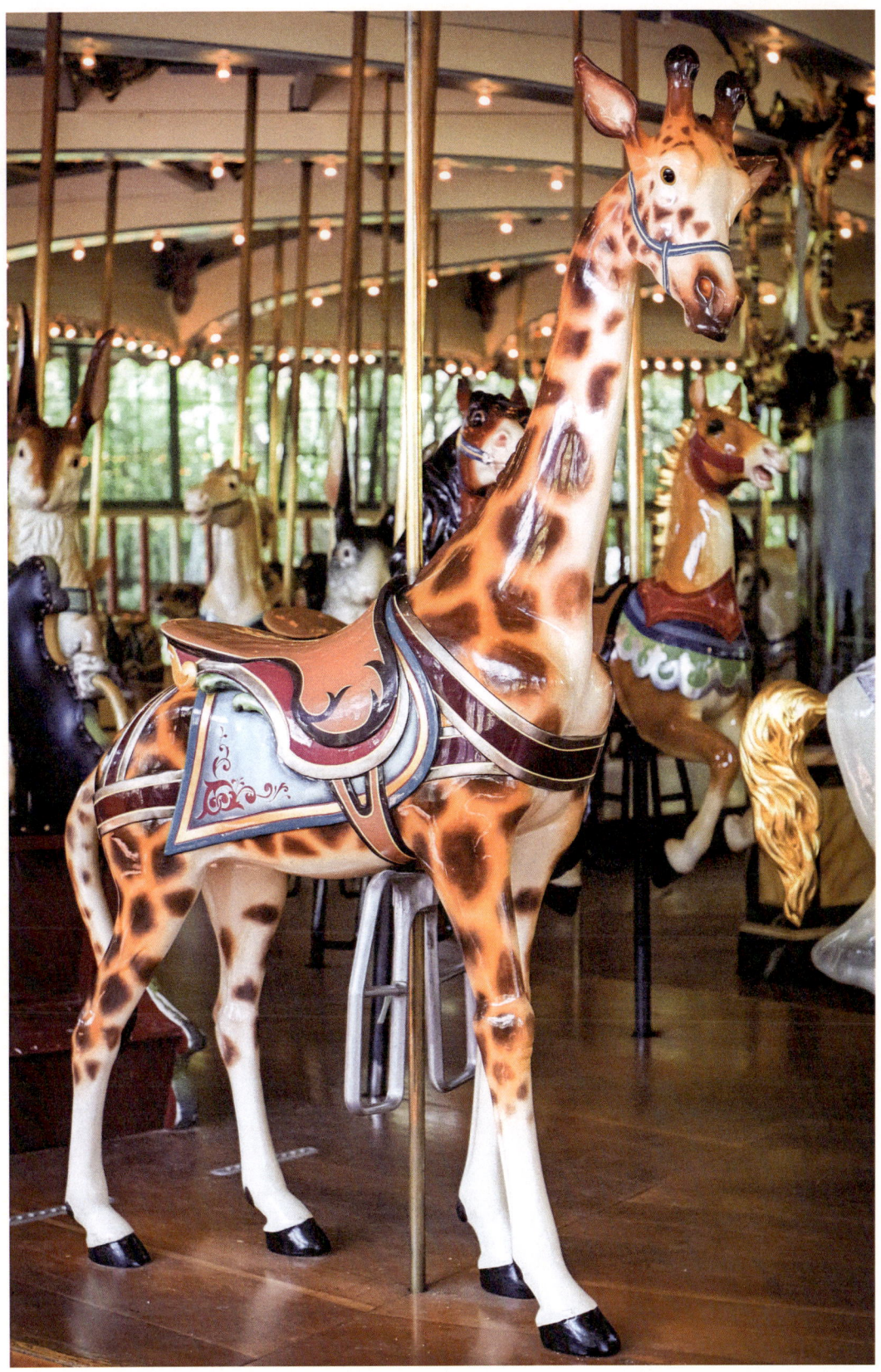

Standing giraffe

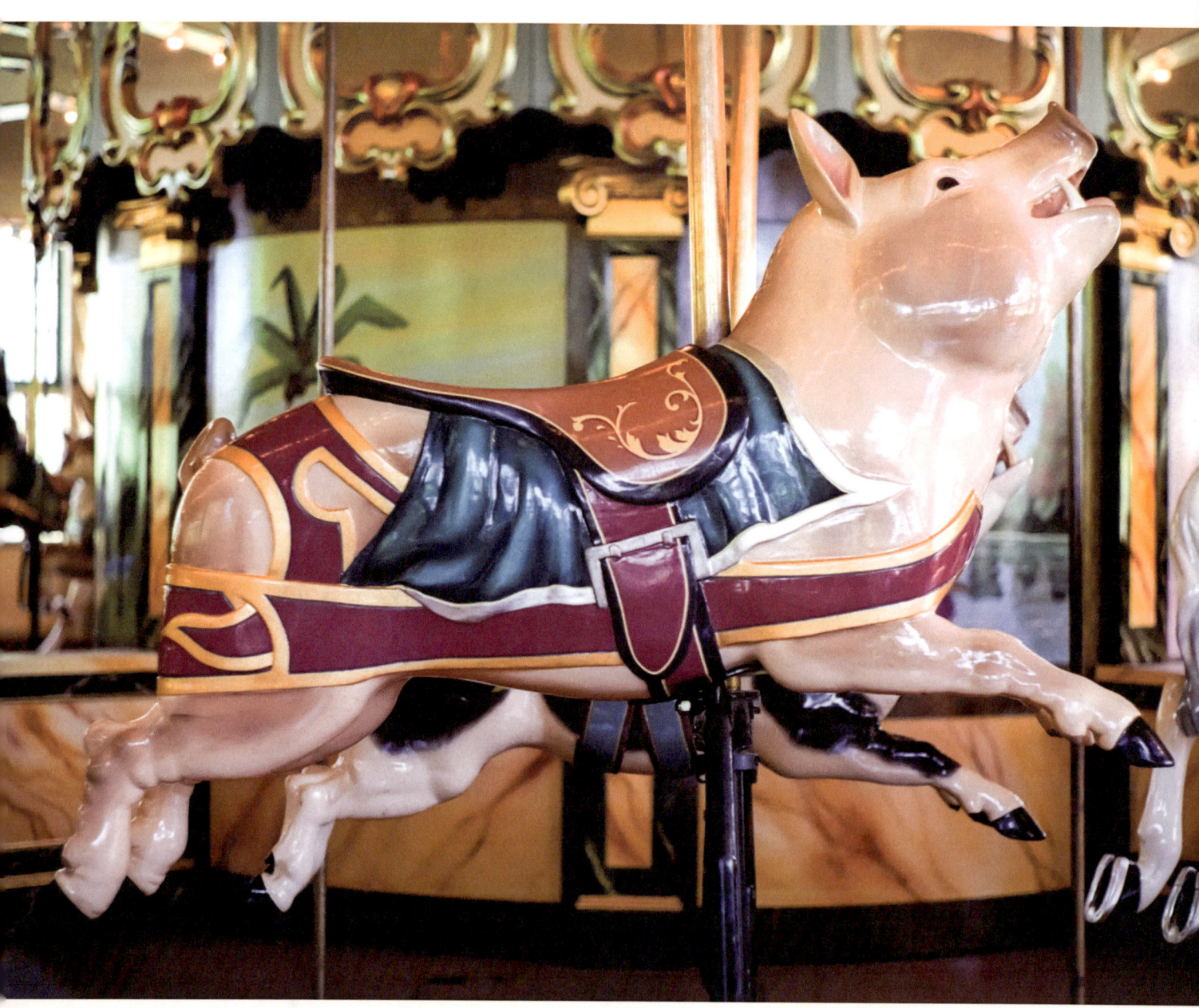

Jumping pig

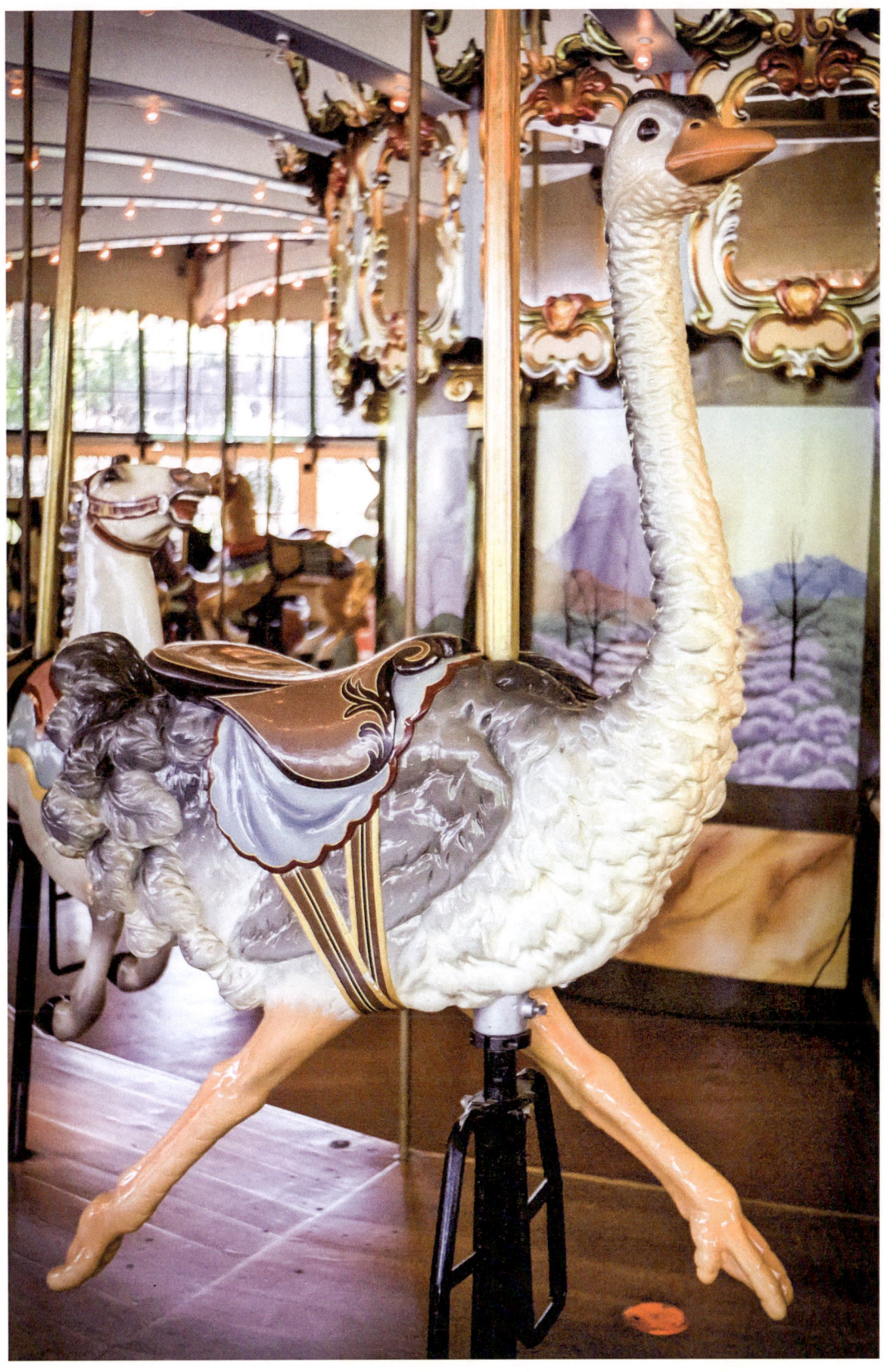

Jumping ostrich

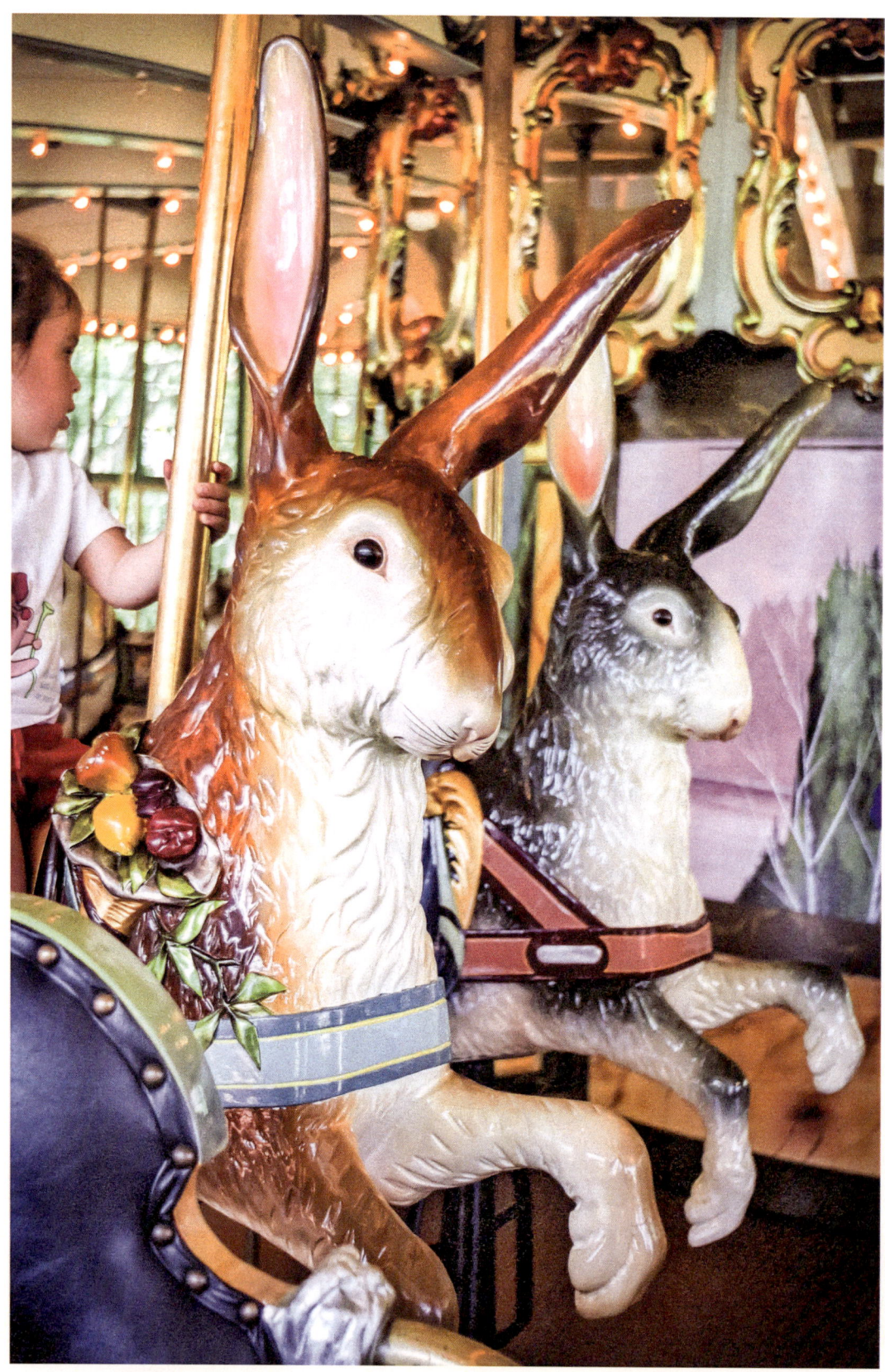

Jumping rabbits

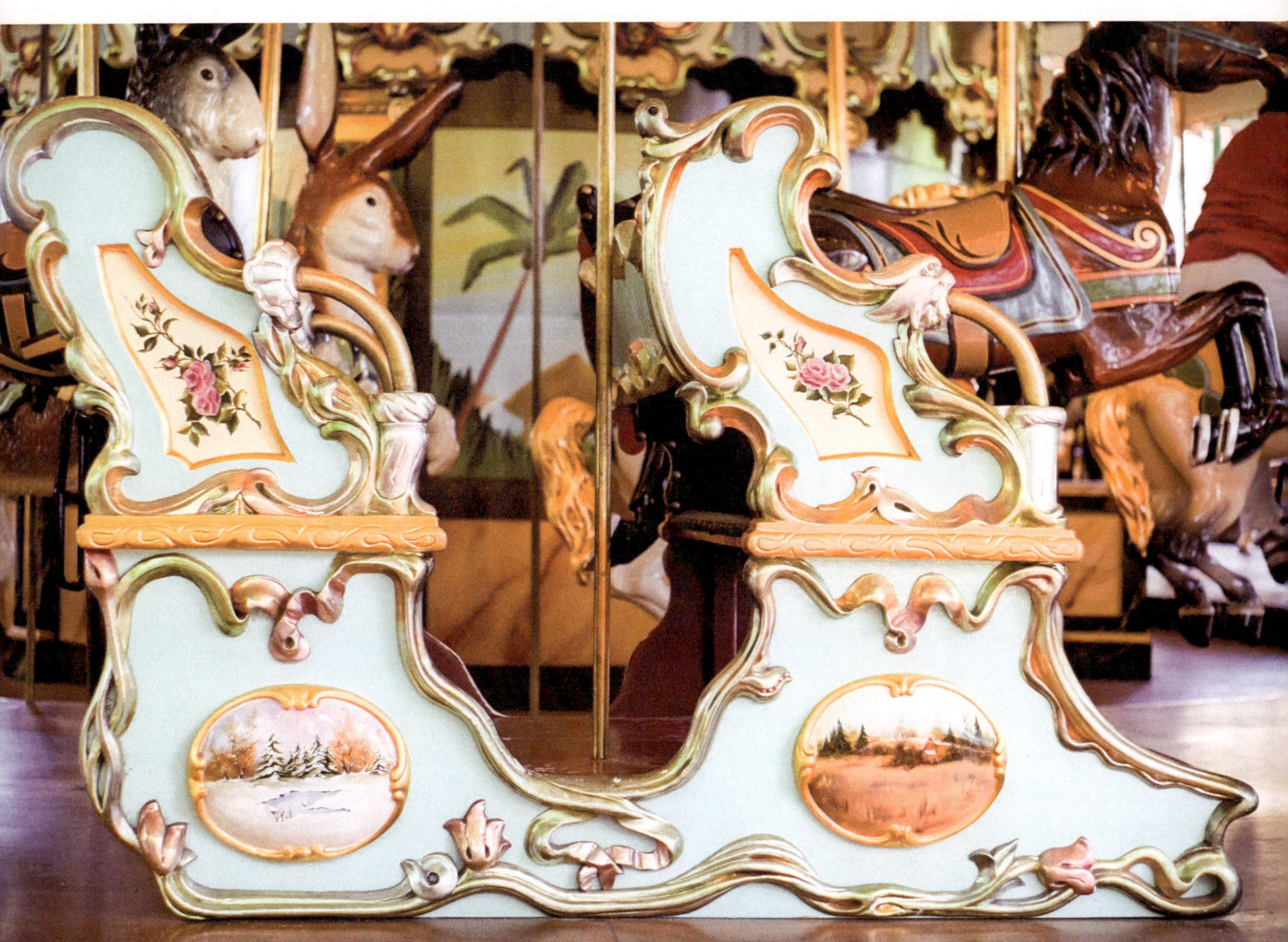

Chariot

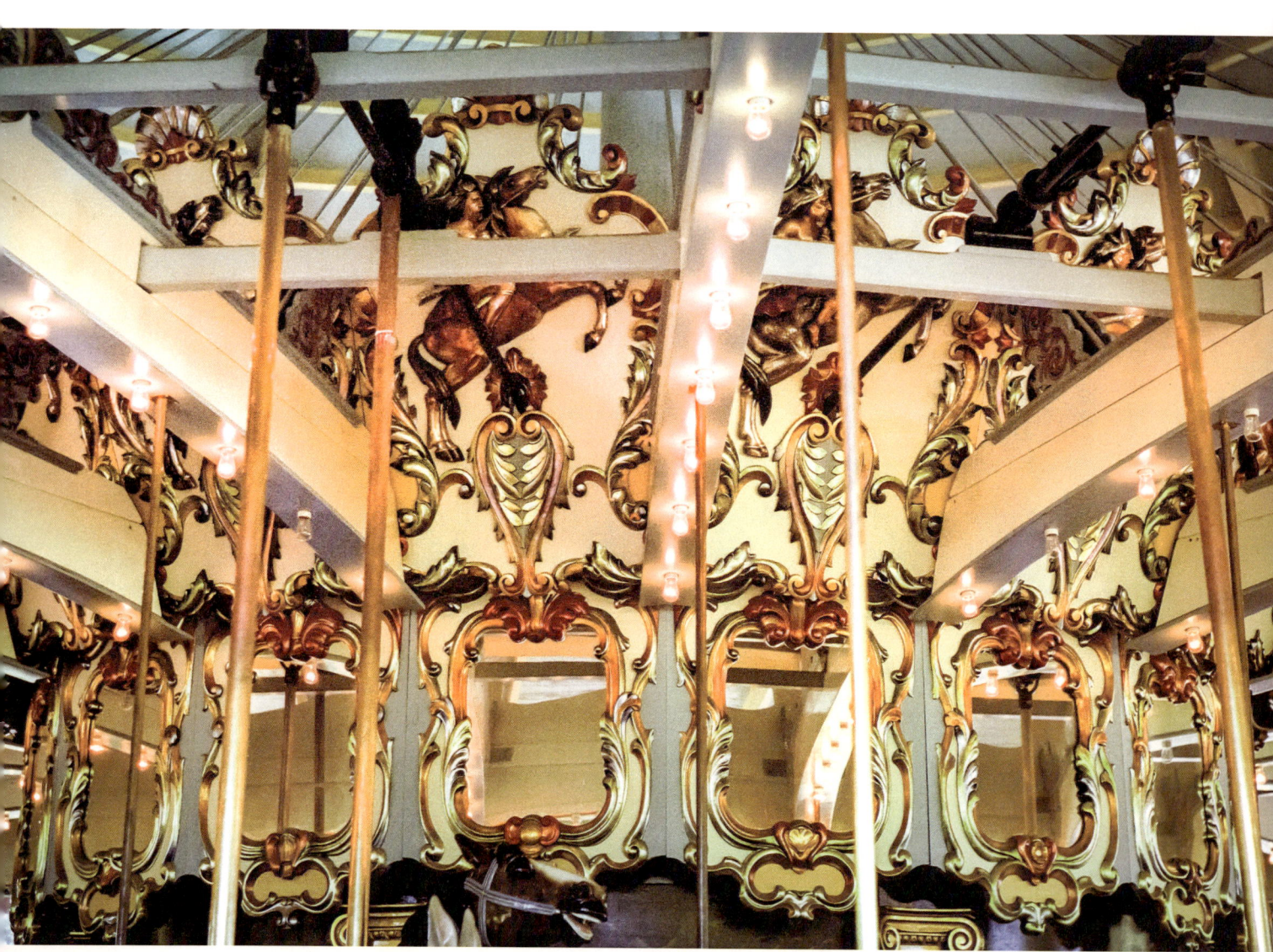

Scenery panels

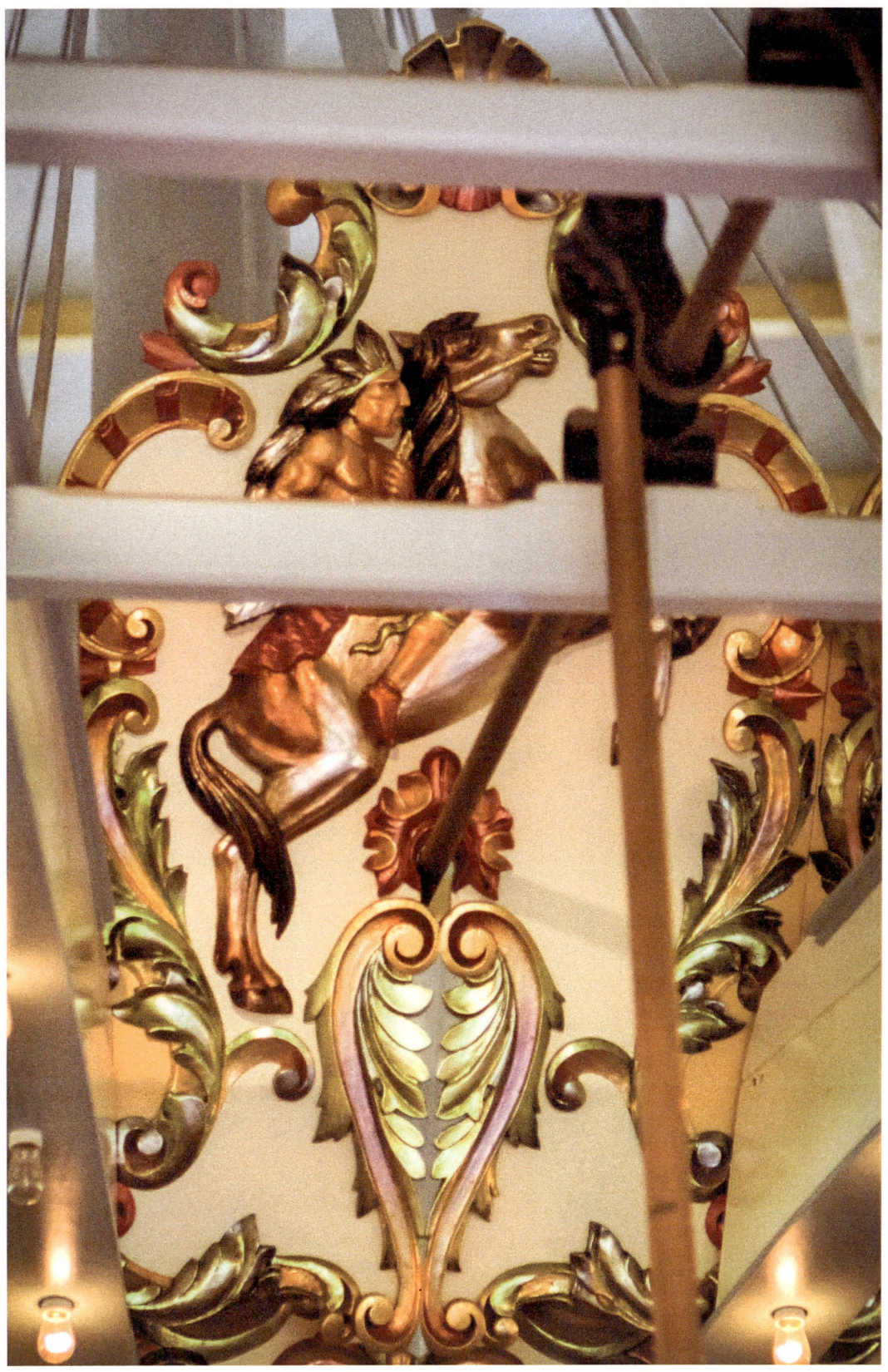

Scenery panel

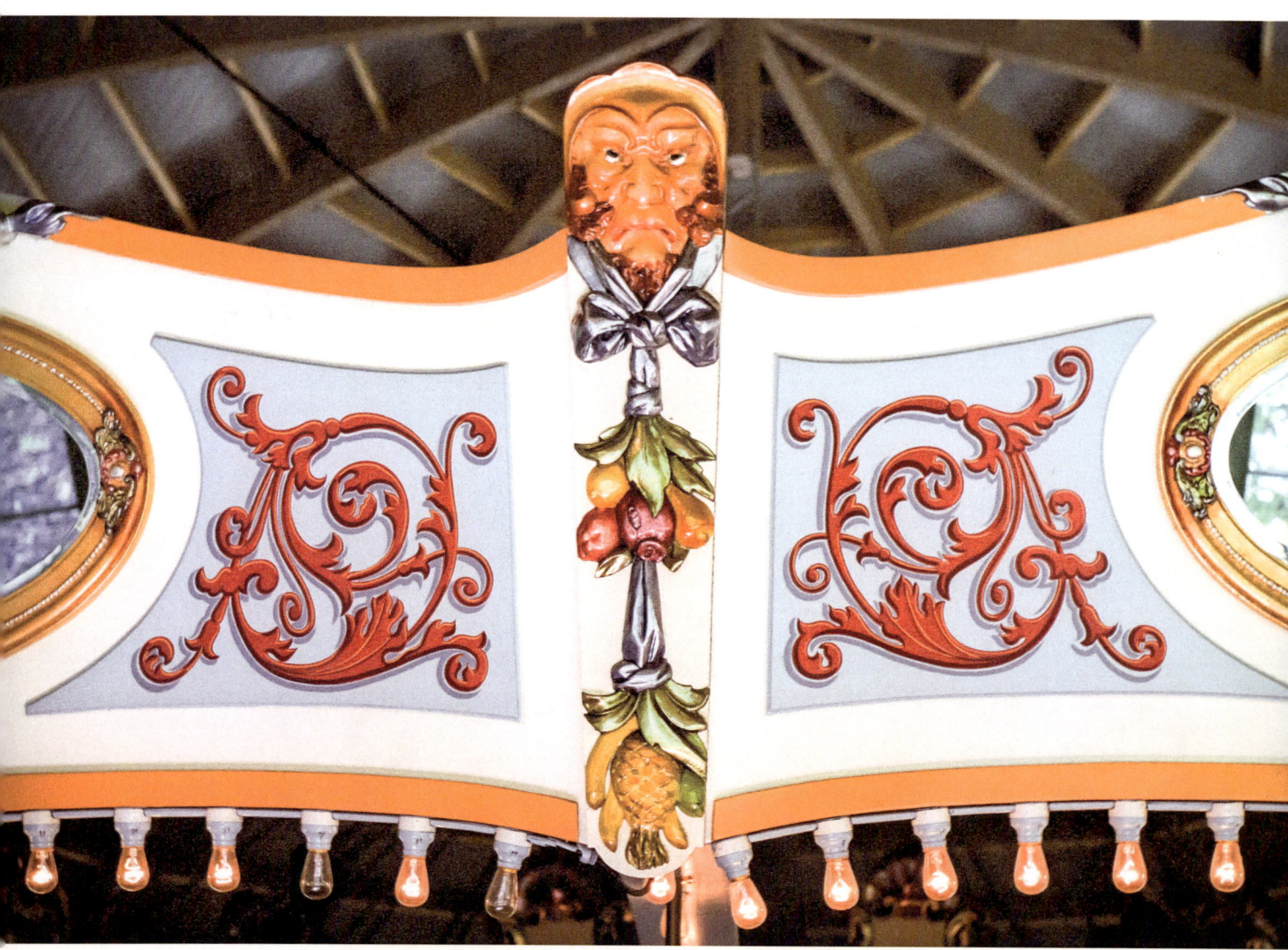

Rounding boards and shield

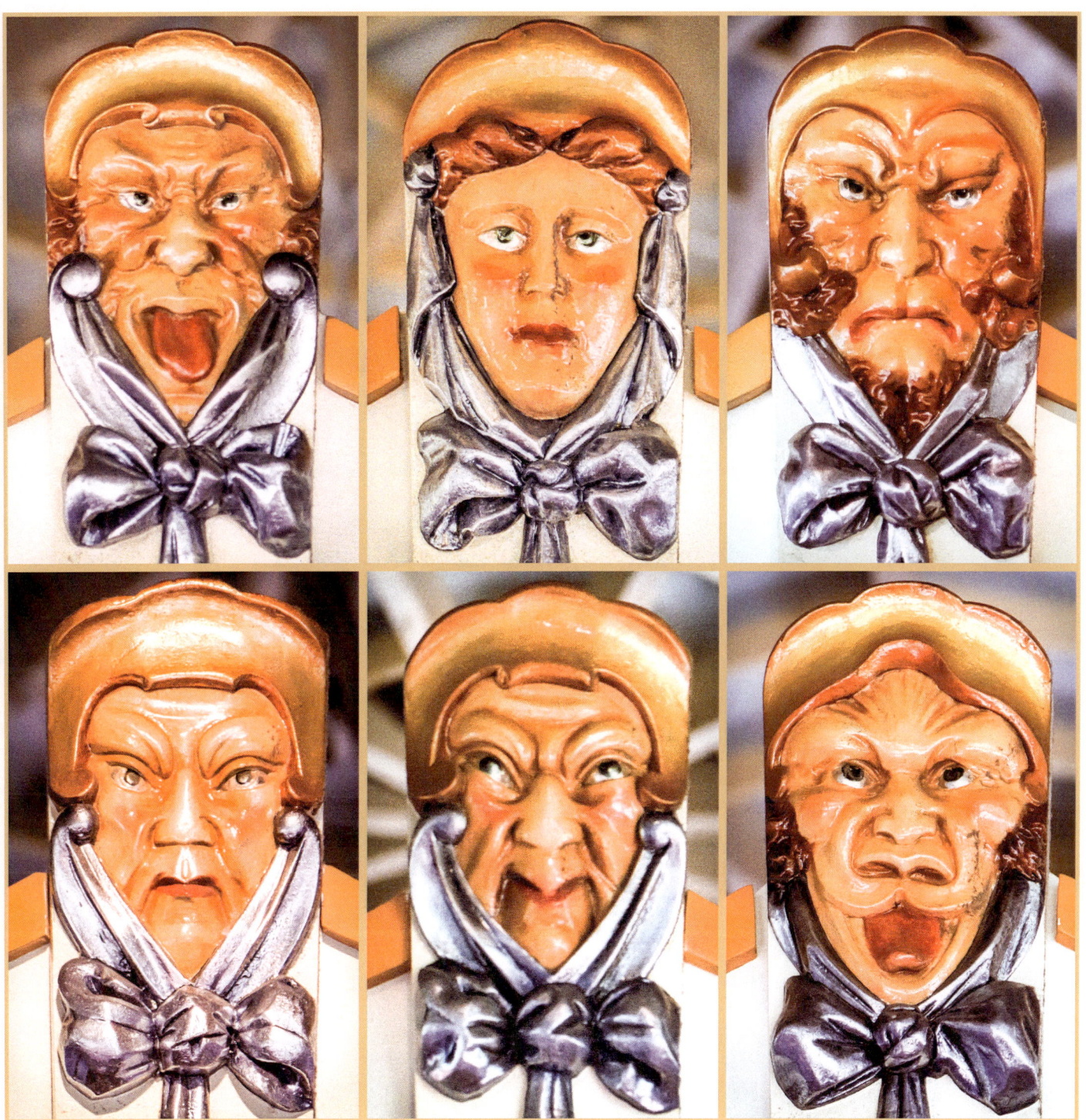

Shield details

Yerba Buena Gardens Carousel

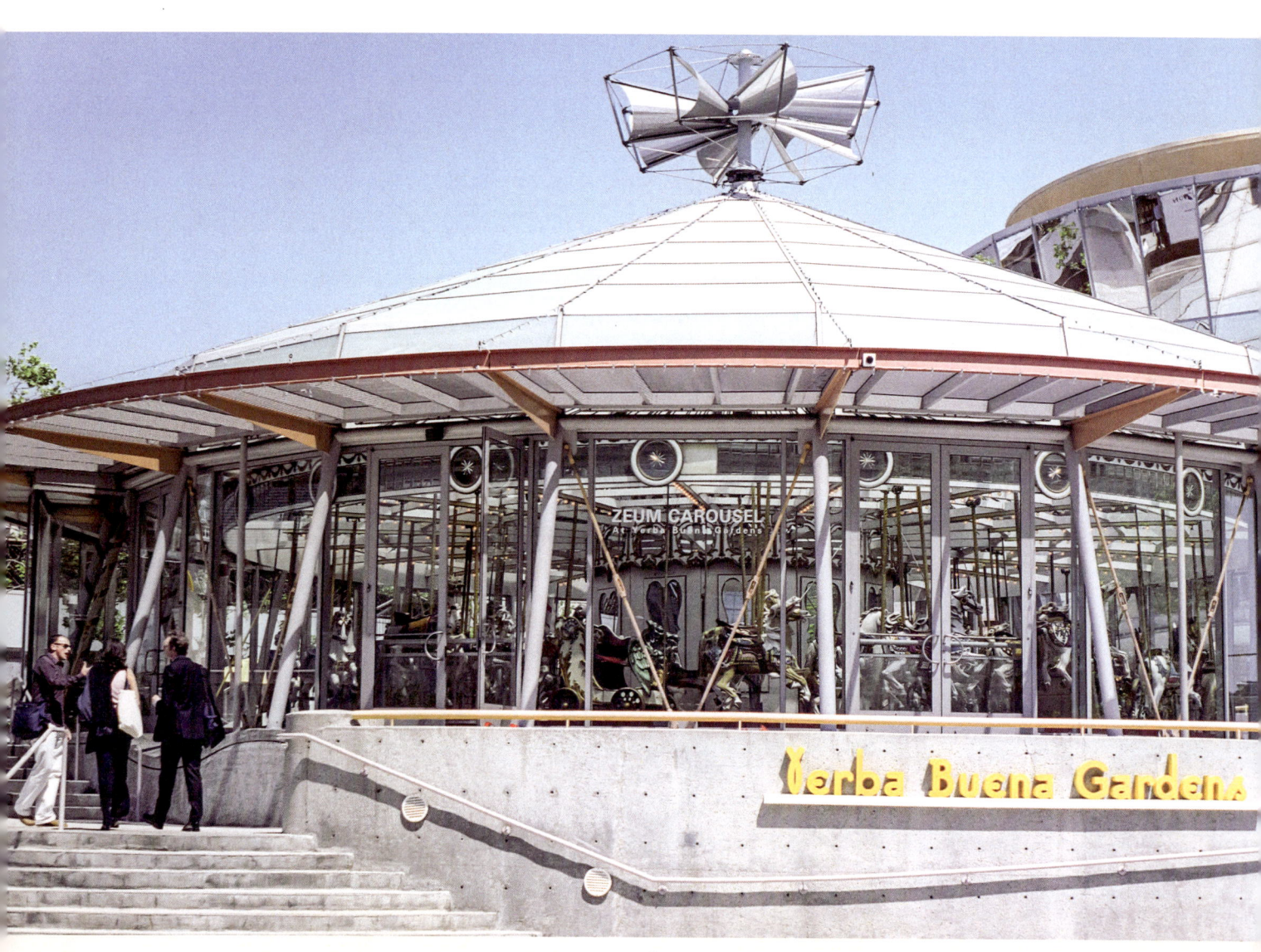

The carousel at Yerba Buena Gardens is located beside the Children's Creativity Museum—named Zeum at the time of these photos—near the entrance to the Moscone Convention Center. (The carousel is operated by the museum on behalf of the city.) It was built by Charles Looff in 1906 in East Providence, Rhode Island.

San Francisco was the original destination of the carousel when built, but because of the 1906 earthquake and fire, it was diverted to Seattle's Luna Park. A few years later, though, it was sent on to Playland-at-the-Beach in San Francisco, where it operated from 1914 to 1973.

After the amusement park closed, a private purchaser took the carousel to New Mexico for restoration. The carousel then operated from 1984 to 1998 in southern California at Long Beach's Shoreline Village, near the Queen Mary. But it returned in 1998 to San Francisco, where it was restored further and installed at its present home. Additional restoration took place in 2013–2014.

The carousel is housed in a glass pavilion, which bathes it in light much brighter than enjoyed by most carousels. Music is supplied by recordings. It has had a variety of names in this location—Zeum Carousel, Children's Creativity Carousel, and since its 2014 reopening, LeRoy King Carousel. King was a redevelopment commissioner, civil rights activist, and labor leader who led the effort to bring the carousel back to San Francisco. His inspiration for that effort? He and his future wife rode this carousel at Playland-at-the-Beach on their very first date.

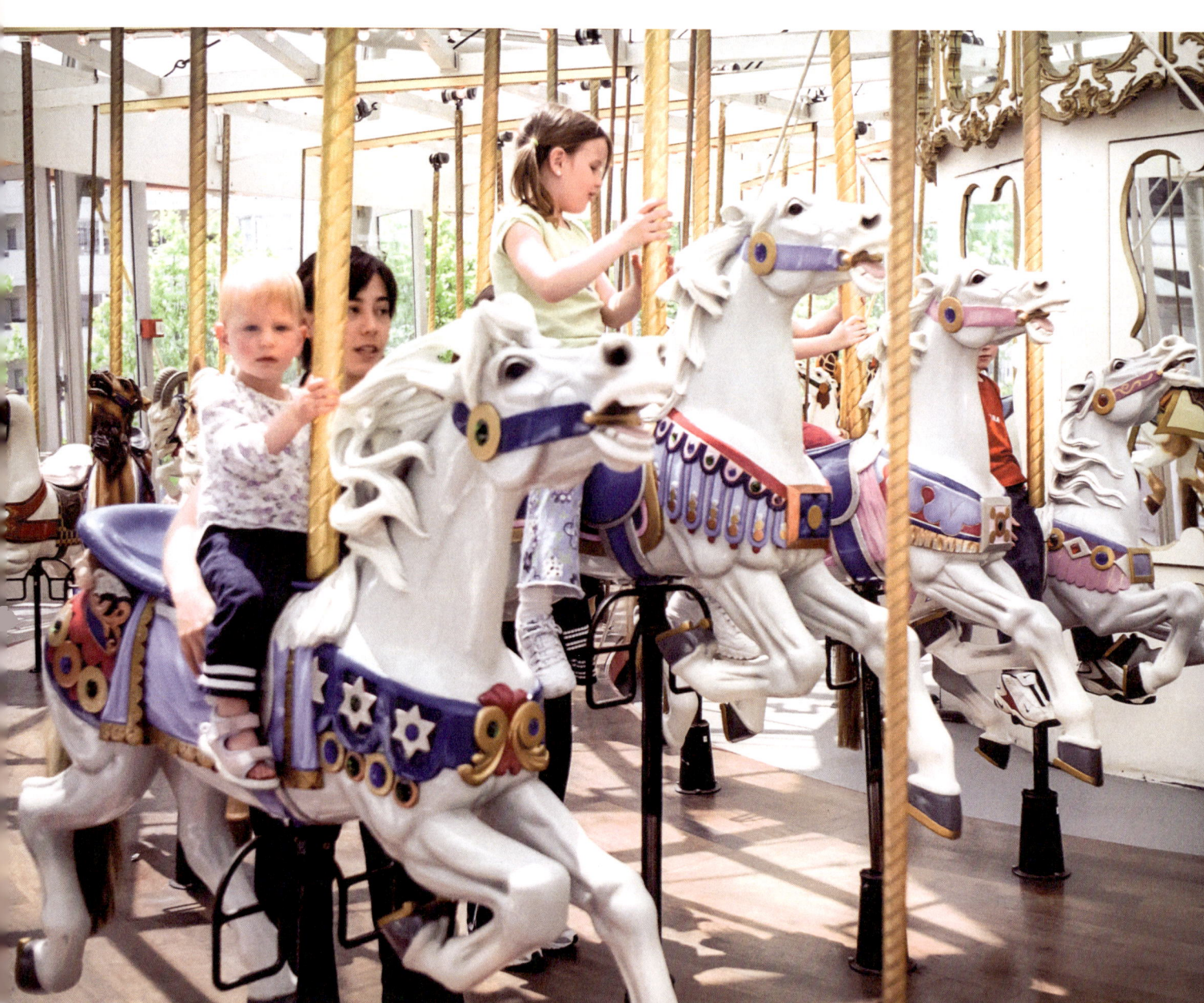

Jumpers

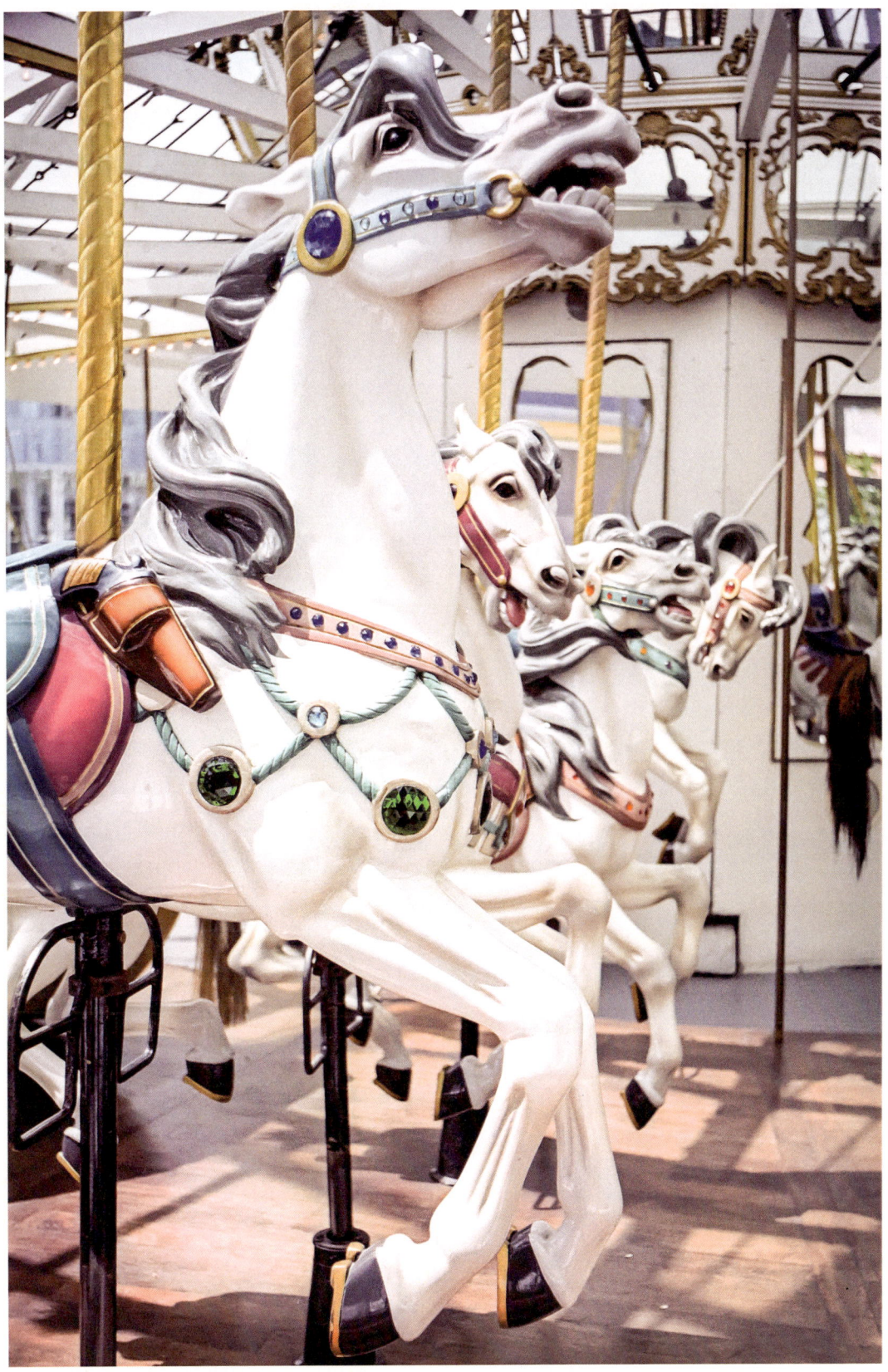

Jumpers

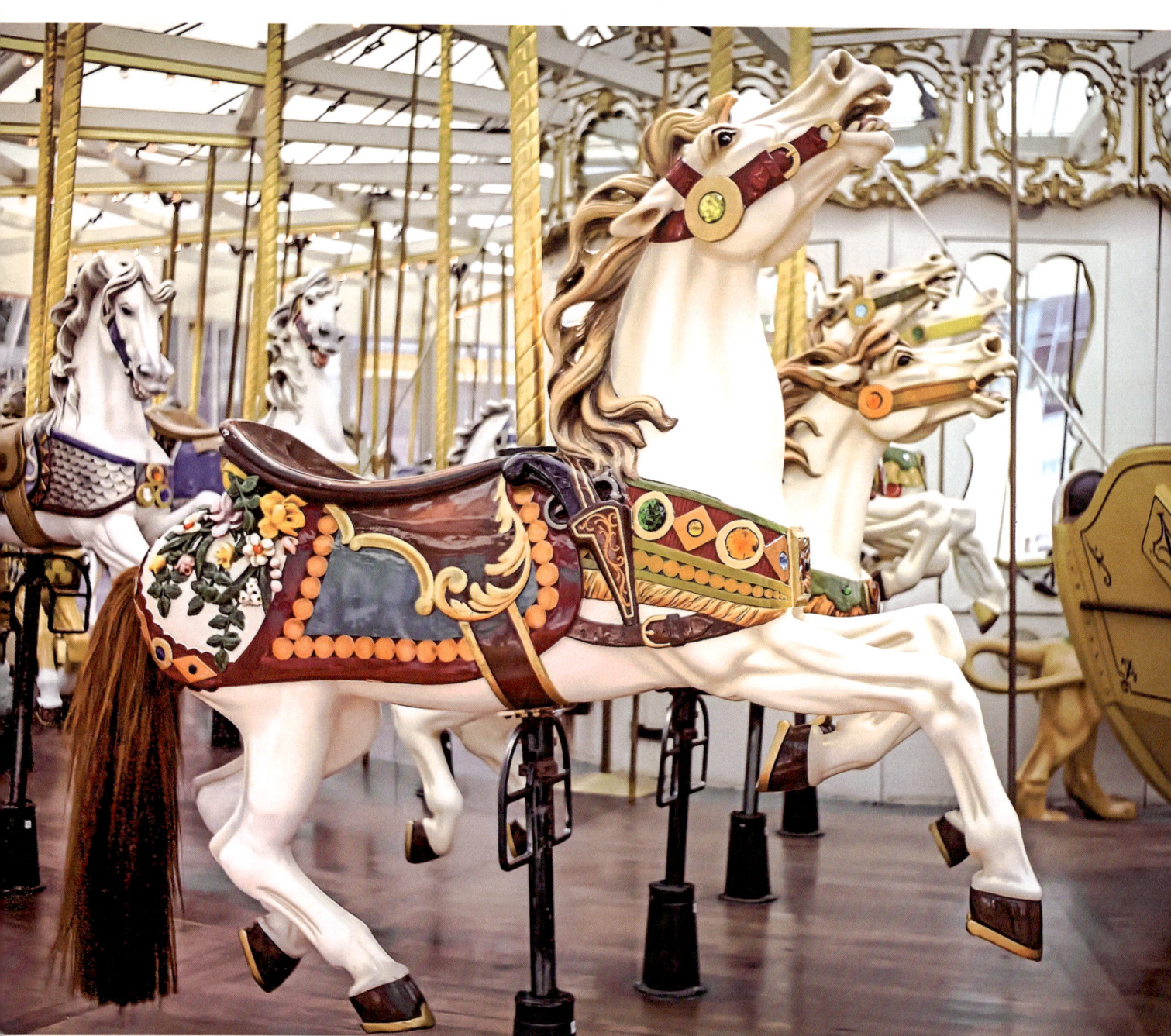

Jumpers

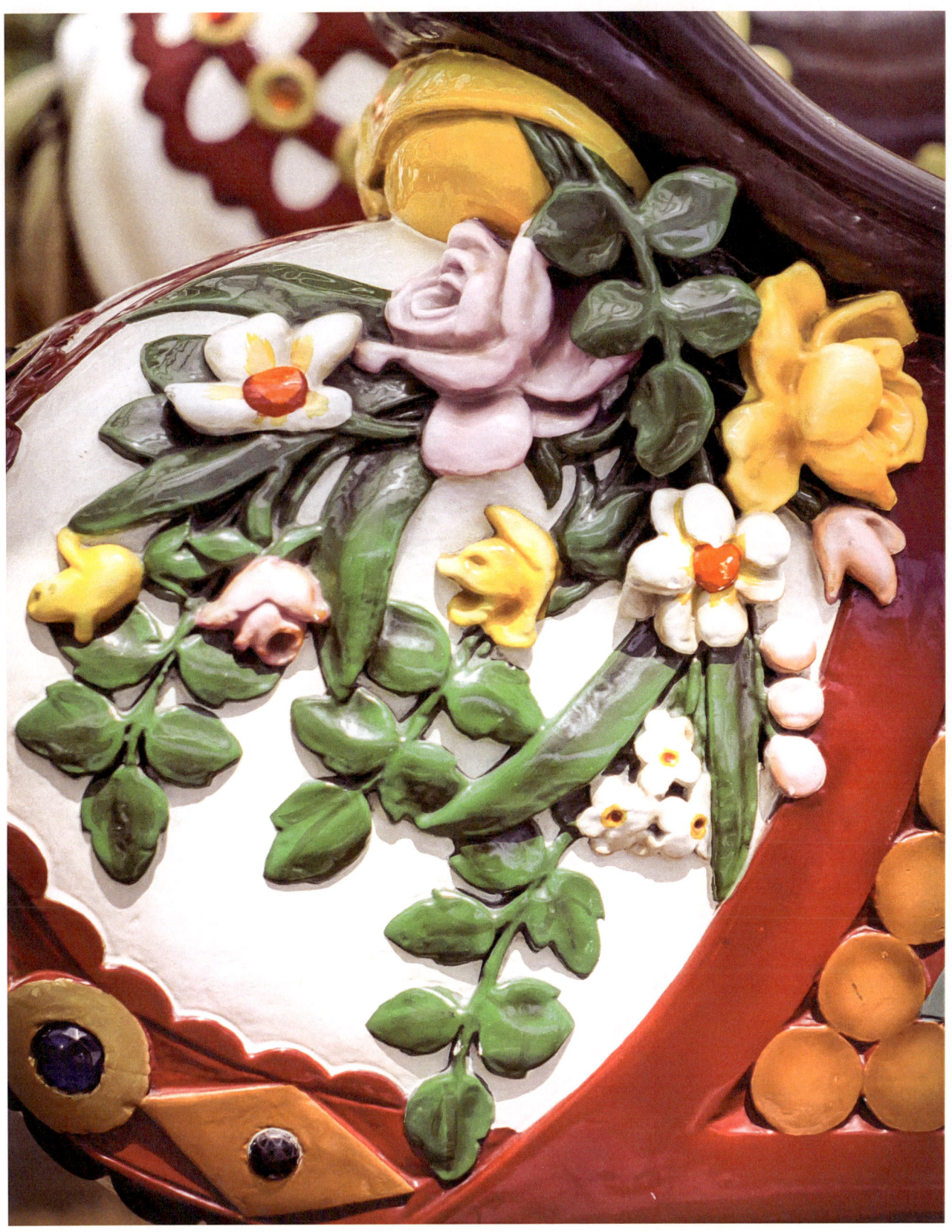

Jumper detail

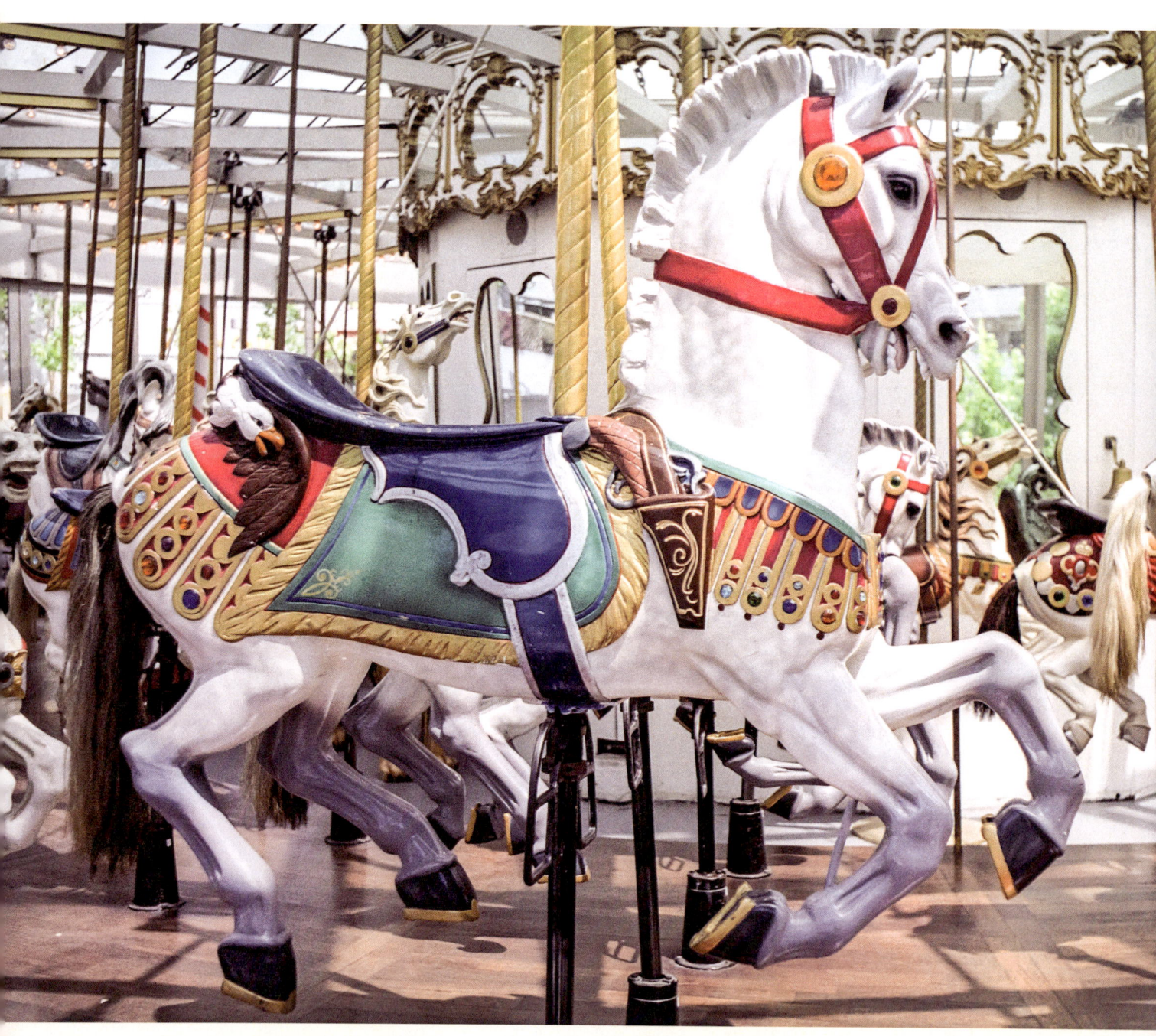

Jumper

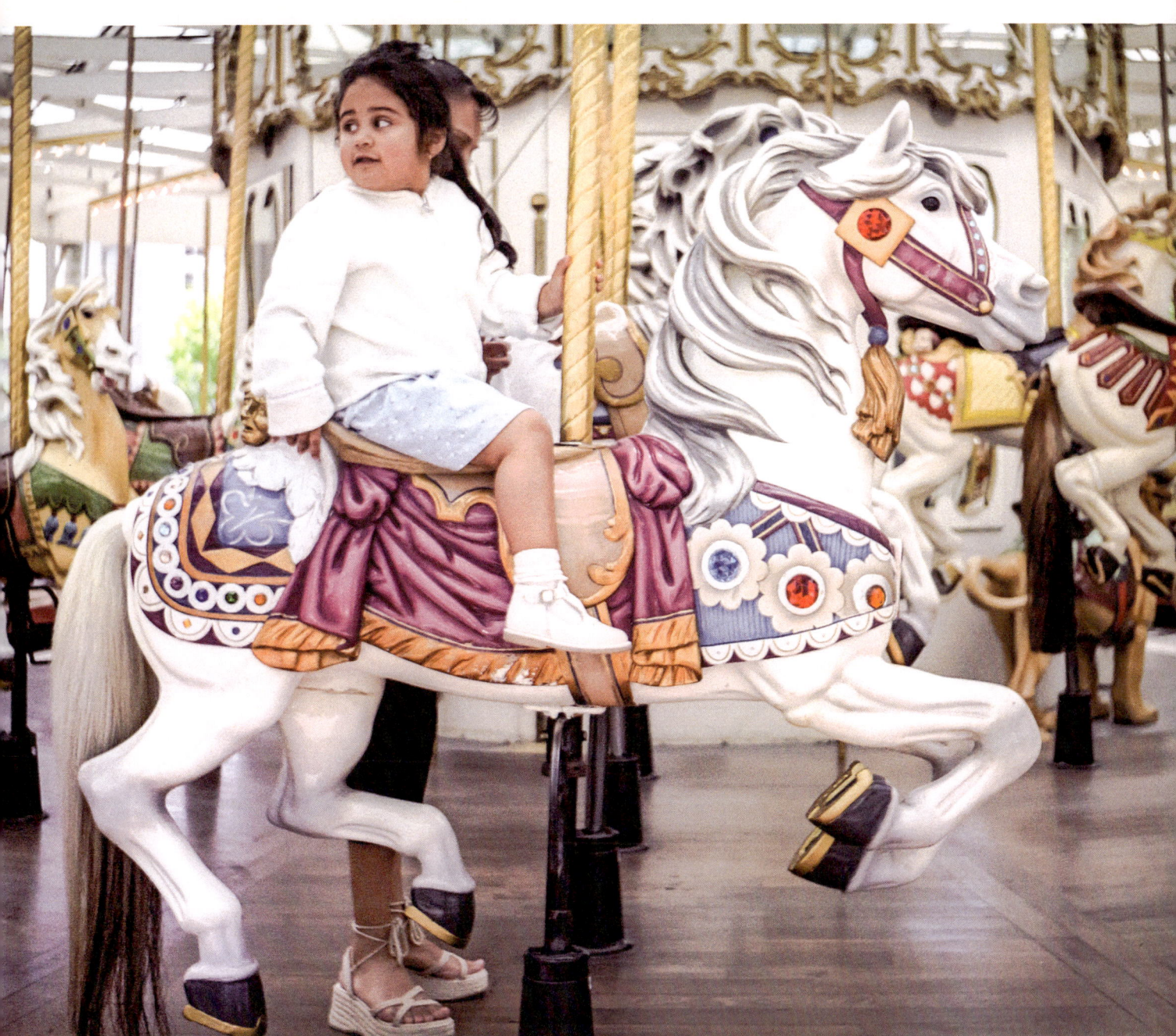

Jumper, "Closed Mouth" style

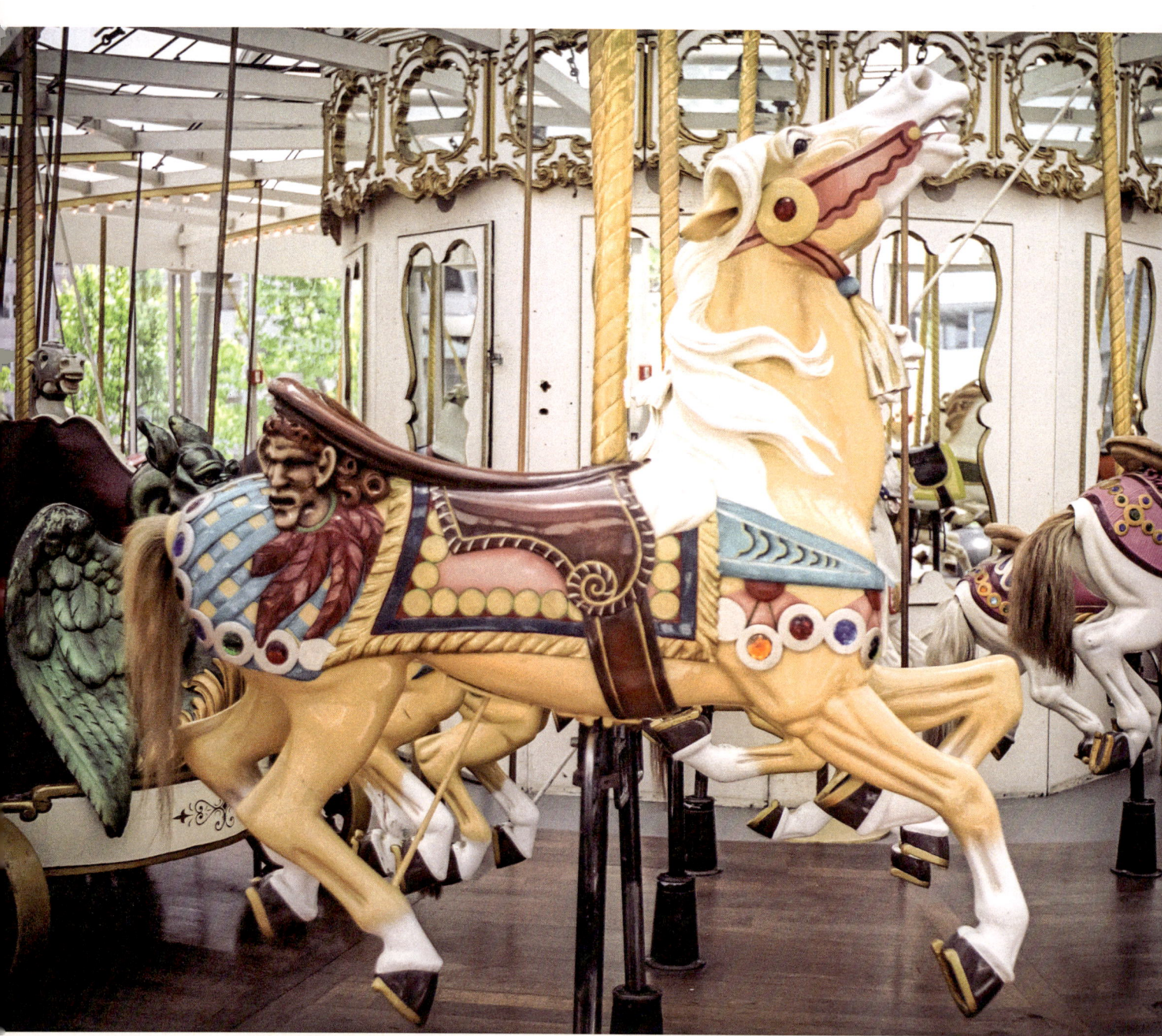

Jumper

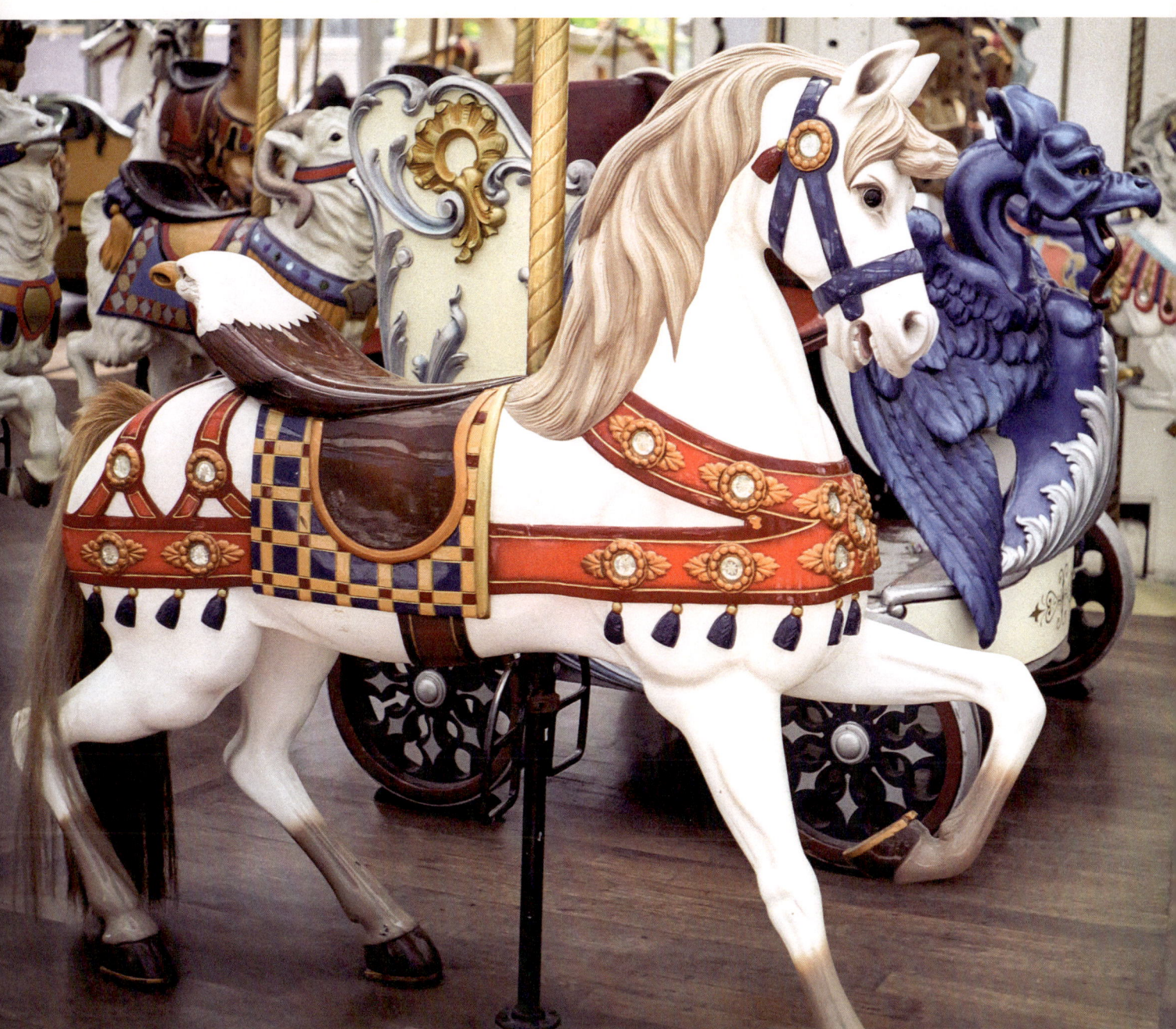

Stander

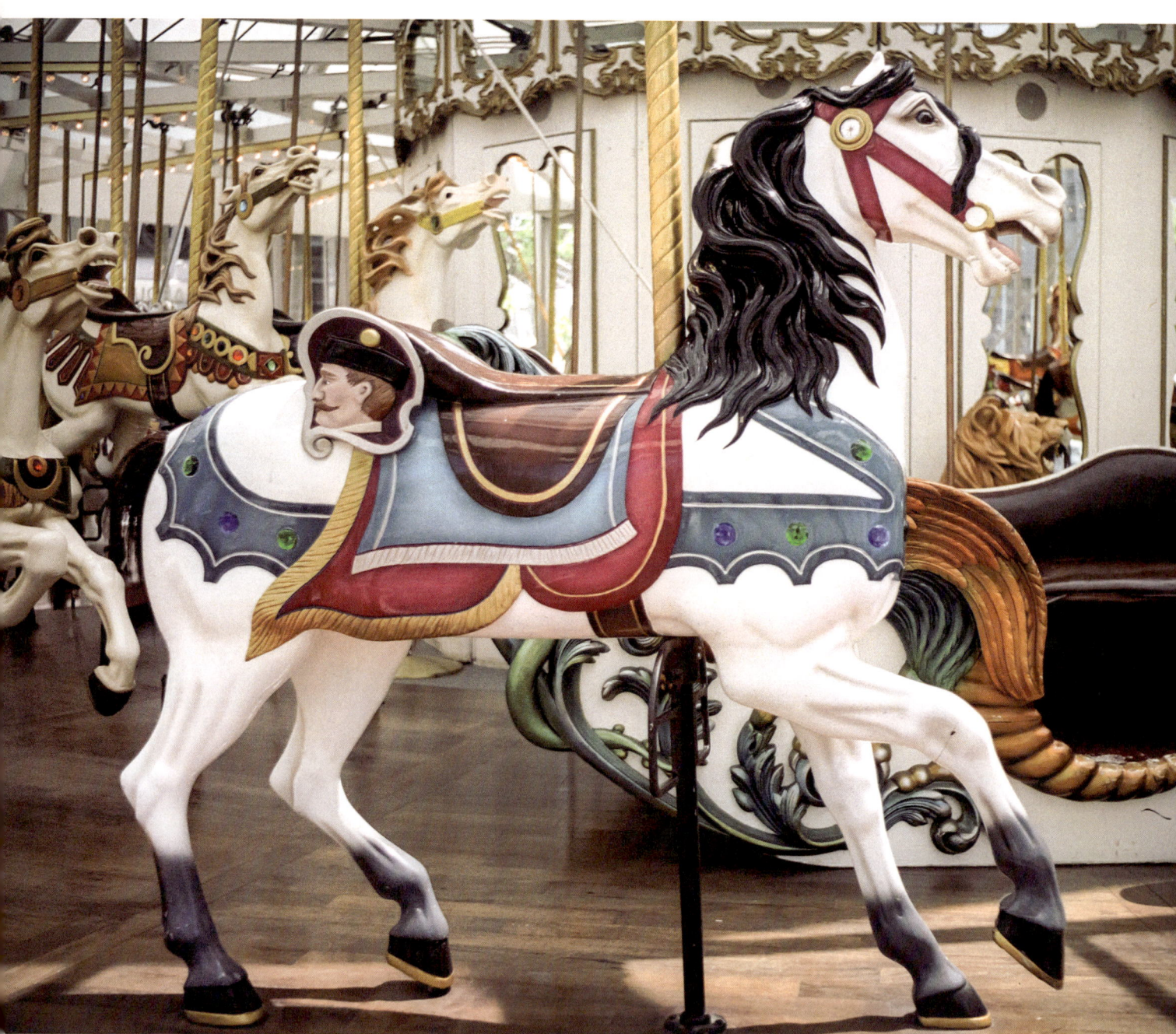

Stander

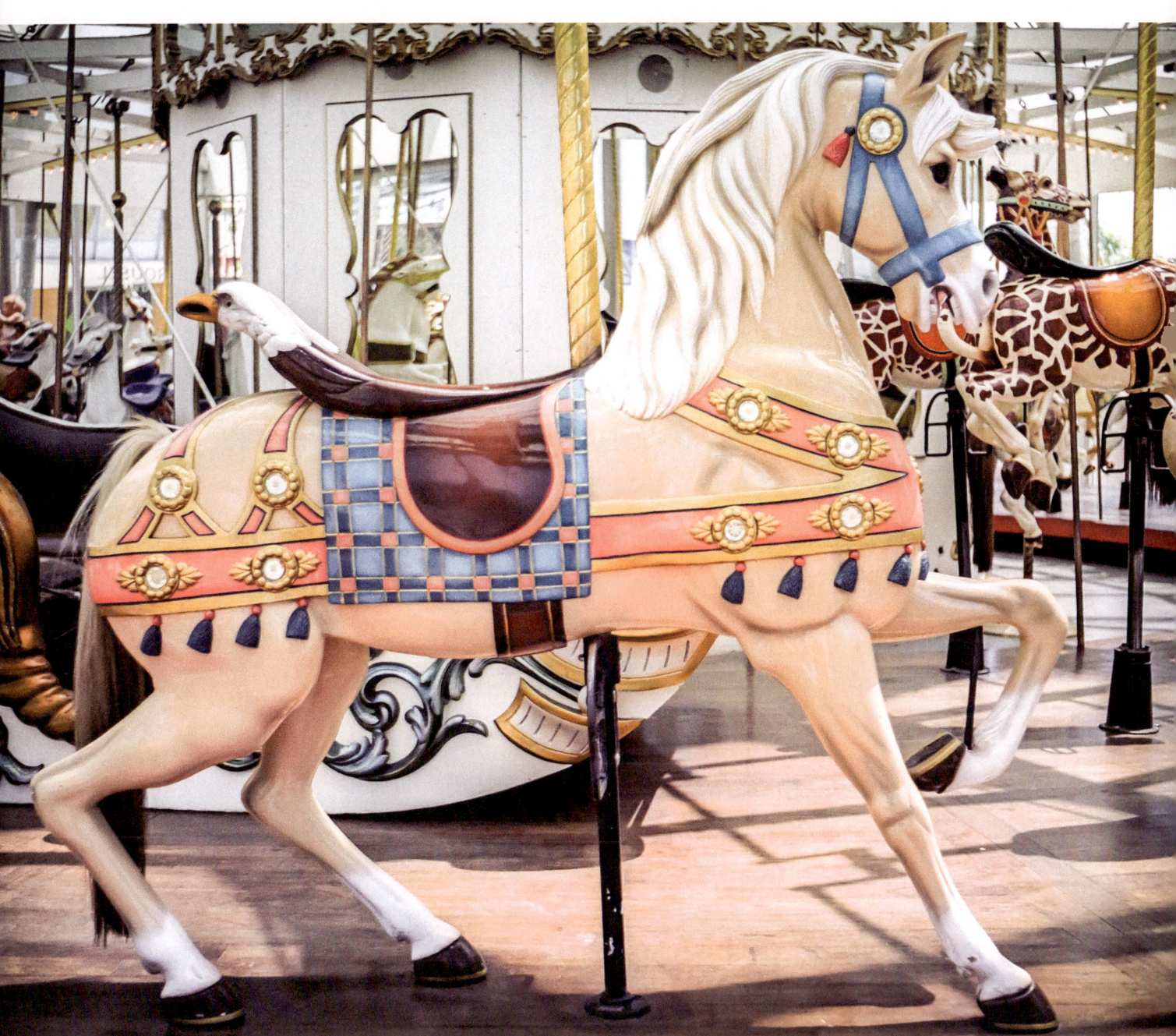

Stander

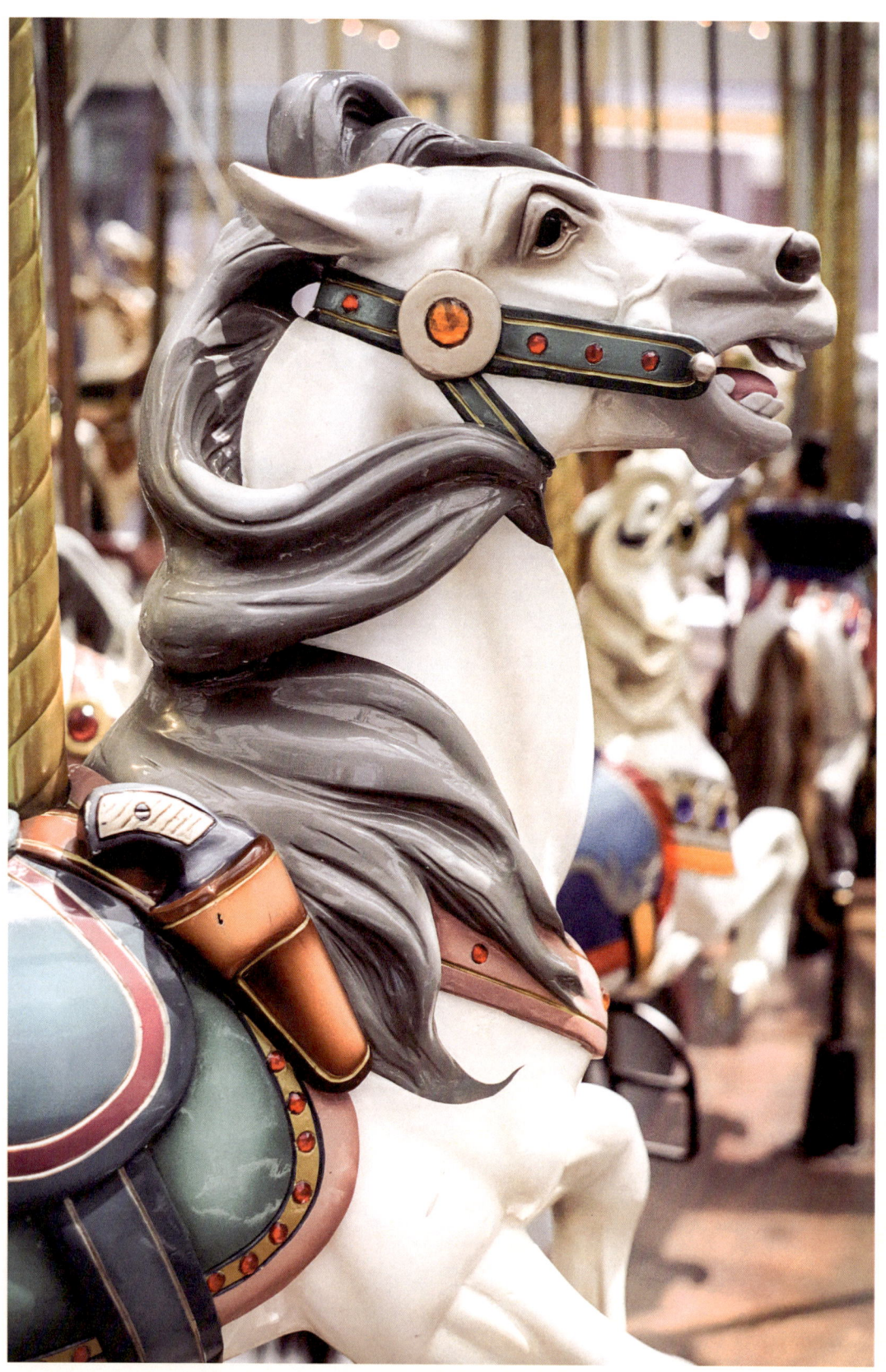

Jumper head

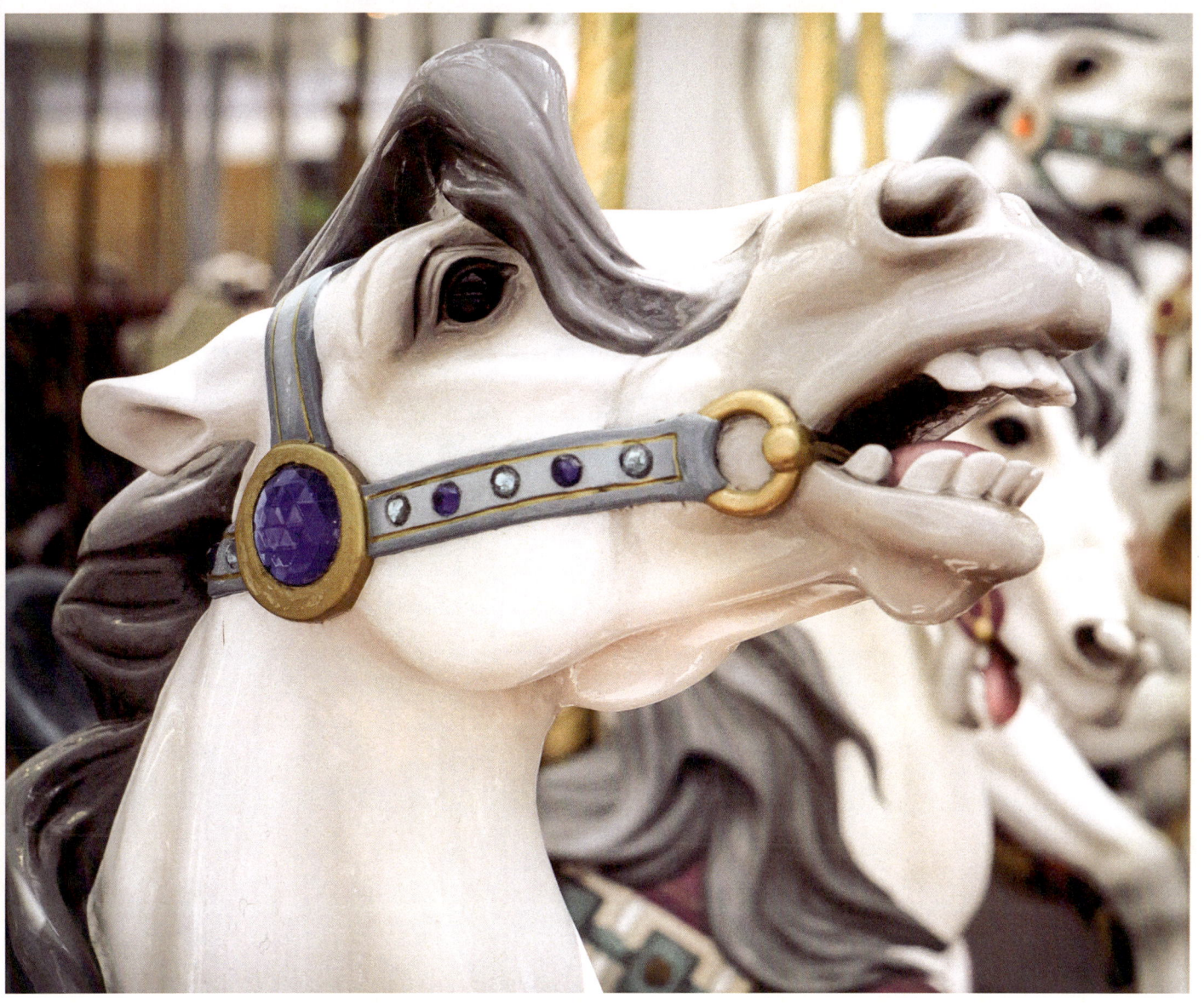

Jumper head

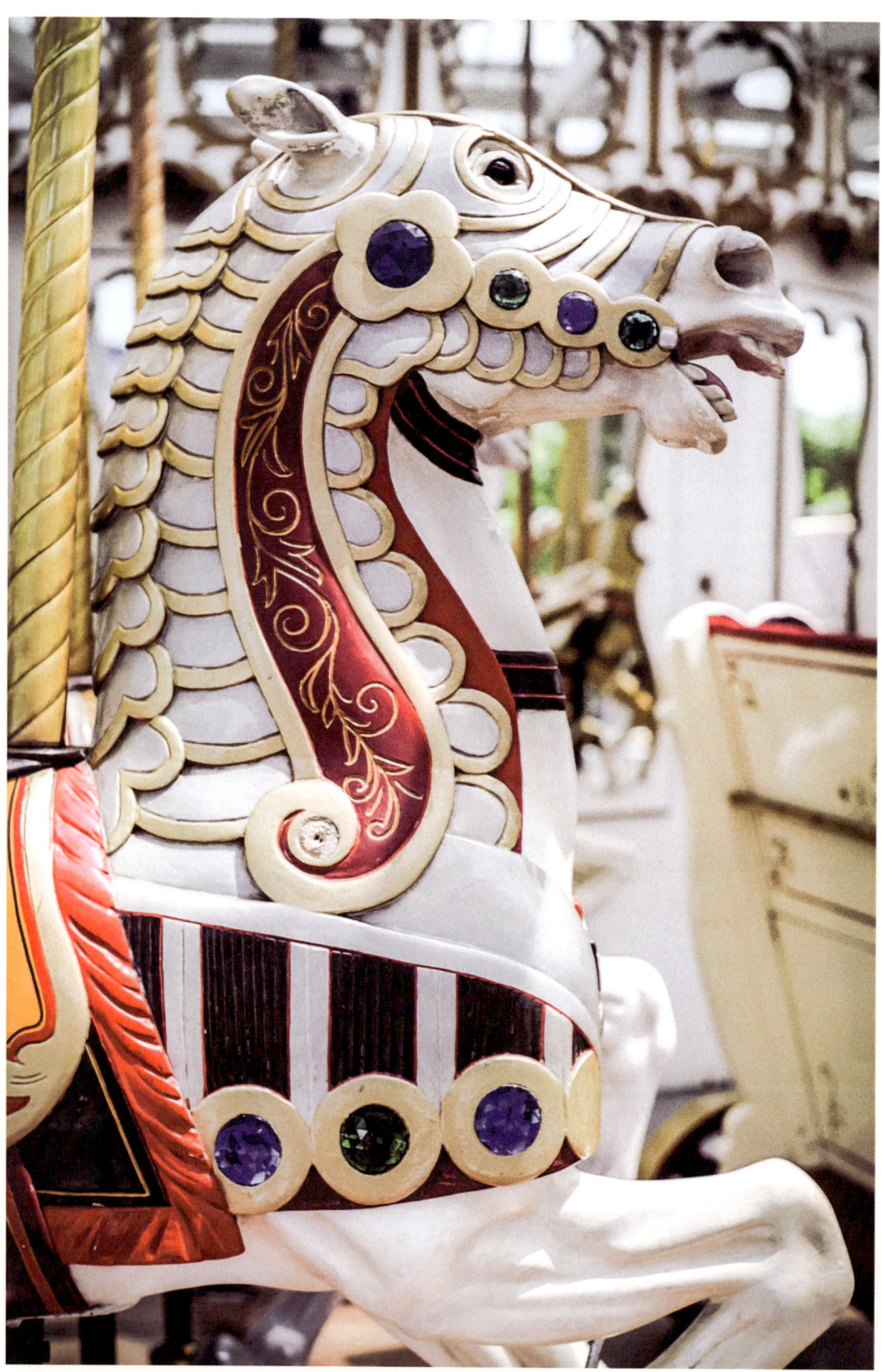

Jumper head, "Armored" style

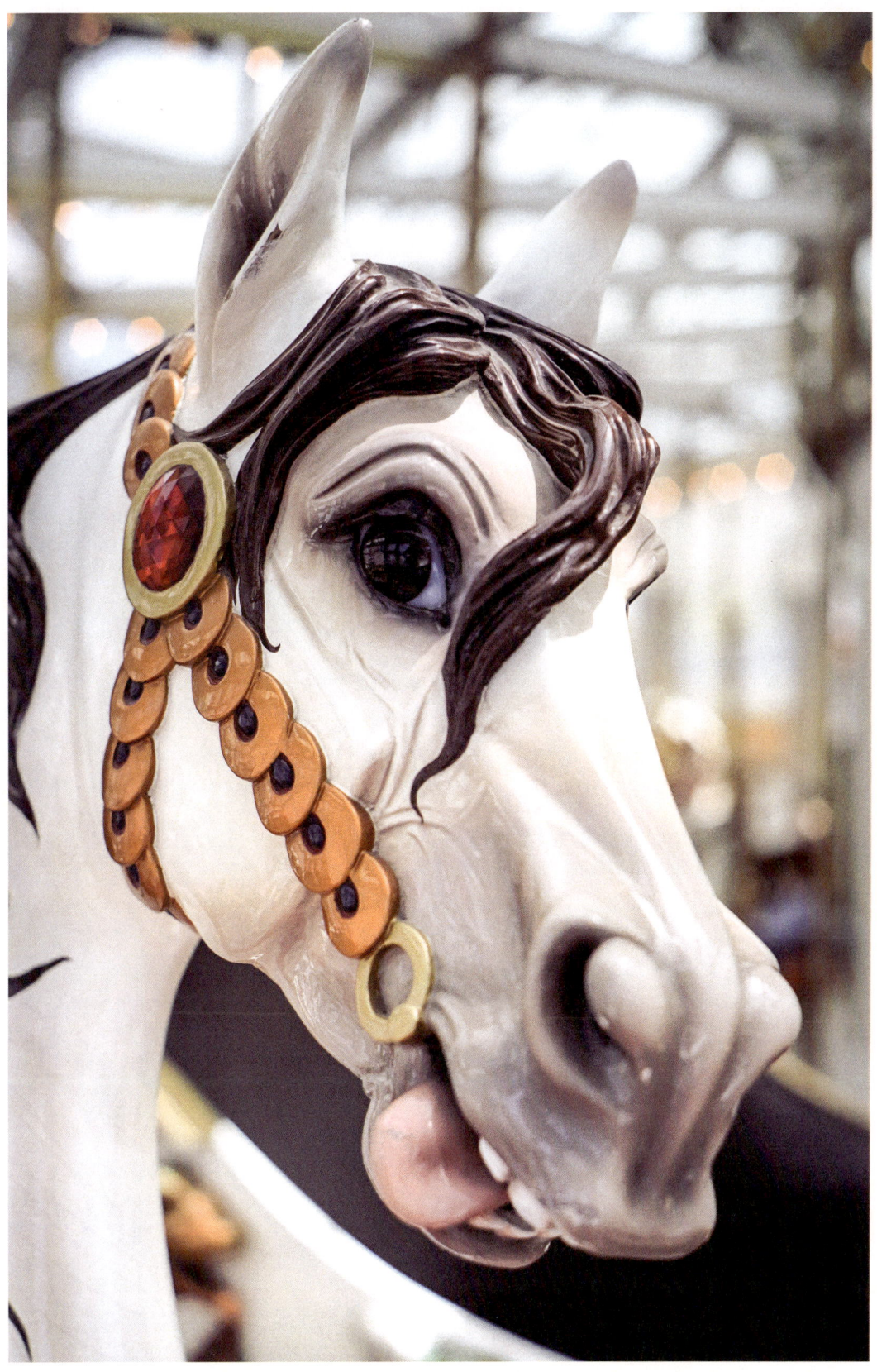

Jumper head, "Lolling Tongue" style

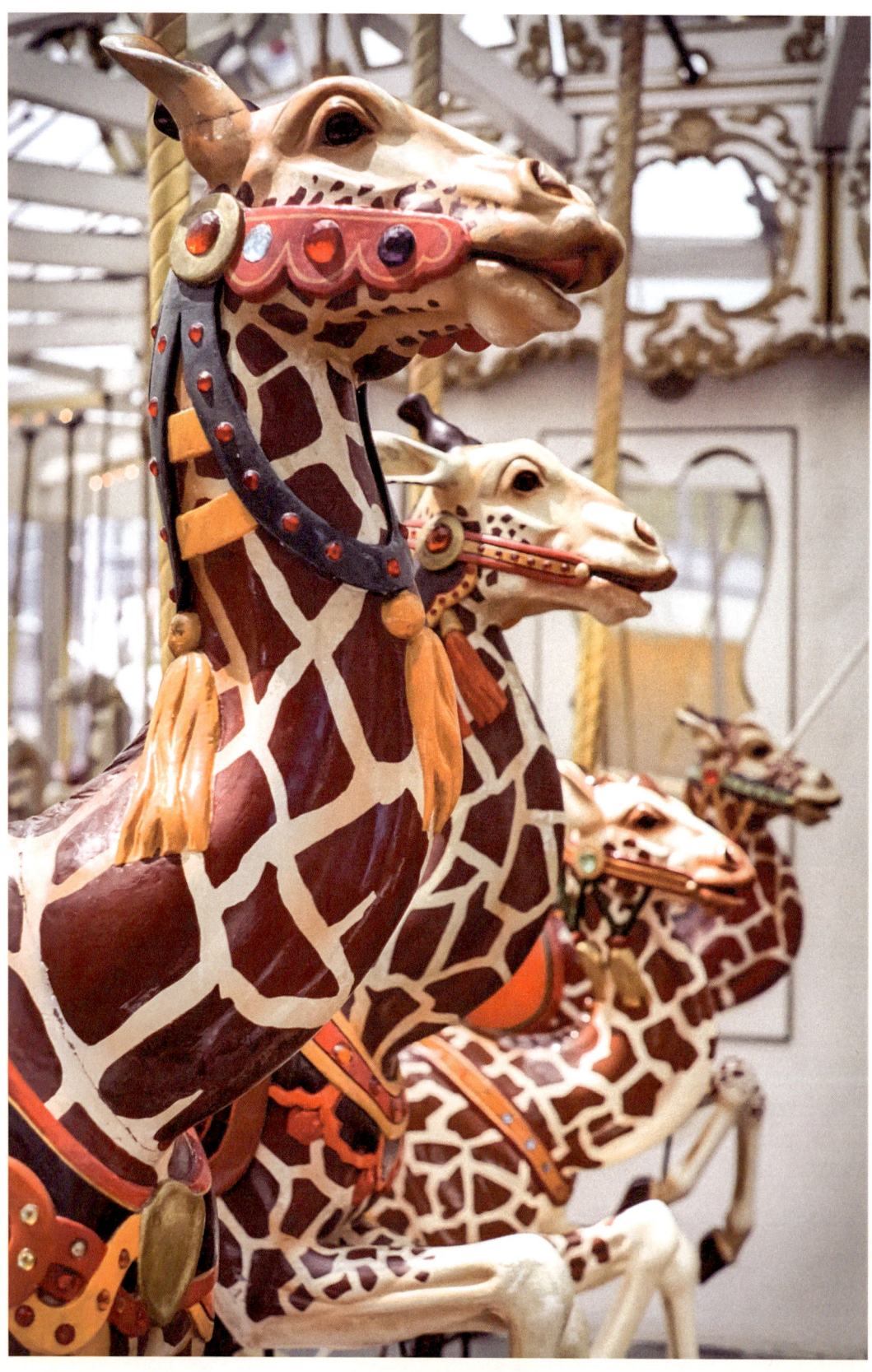

Jumping giraffes

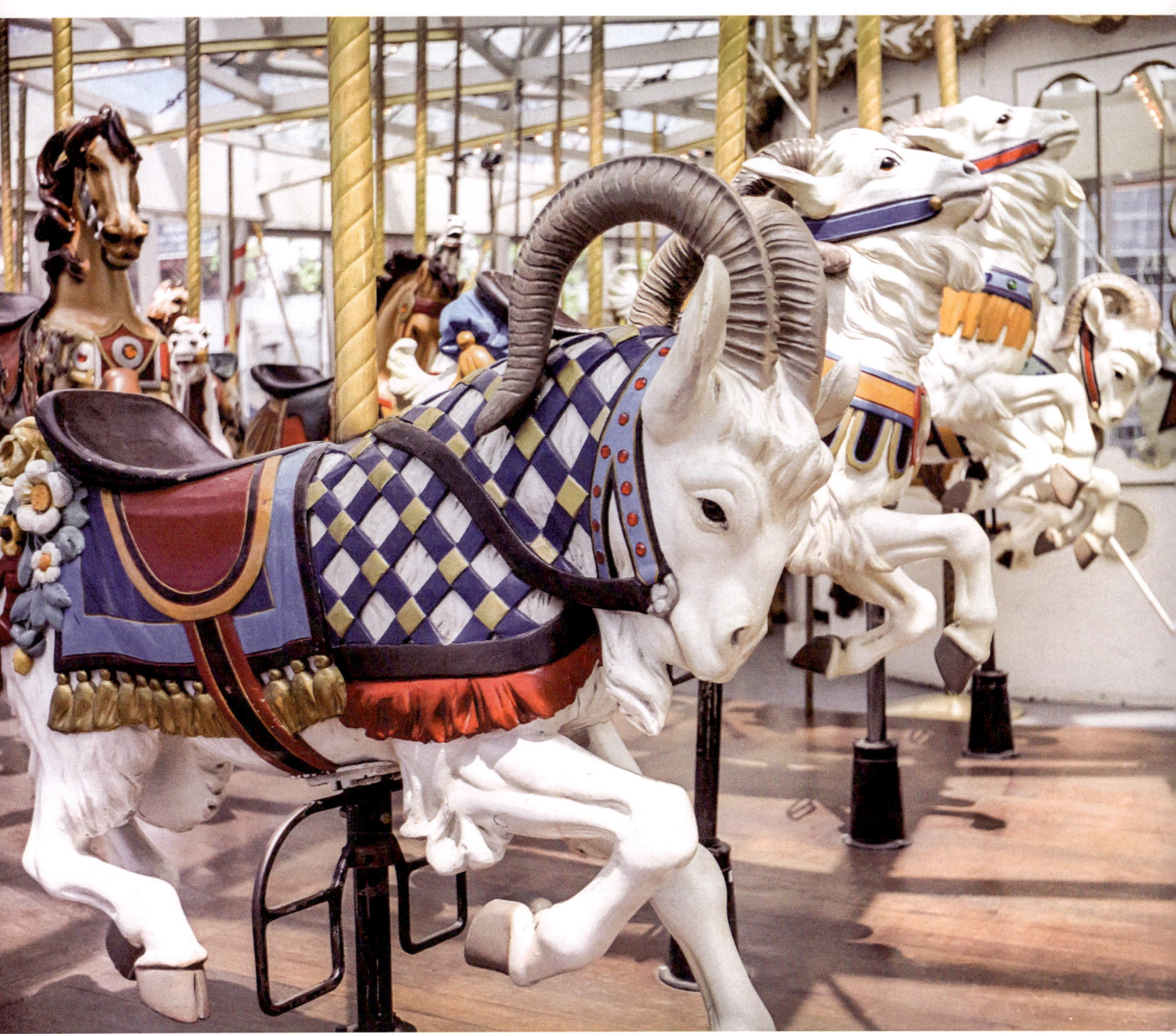

Jumping rams

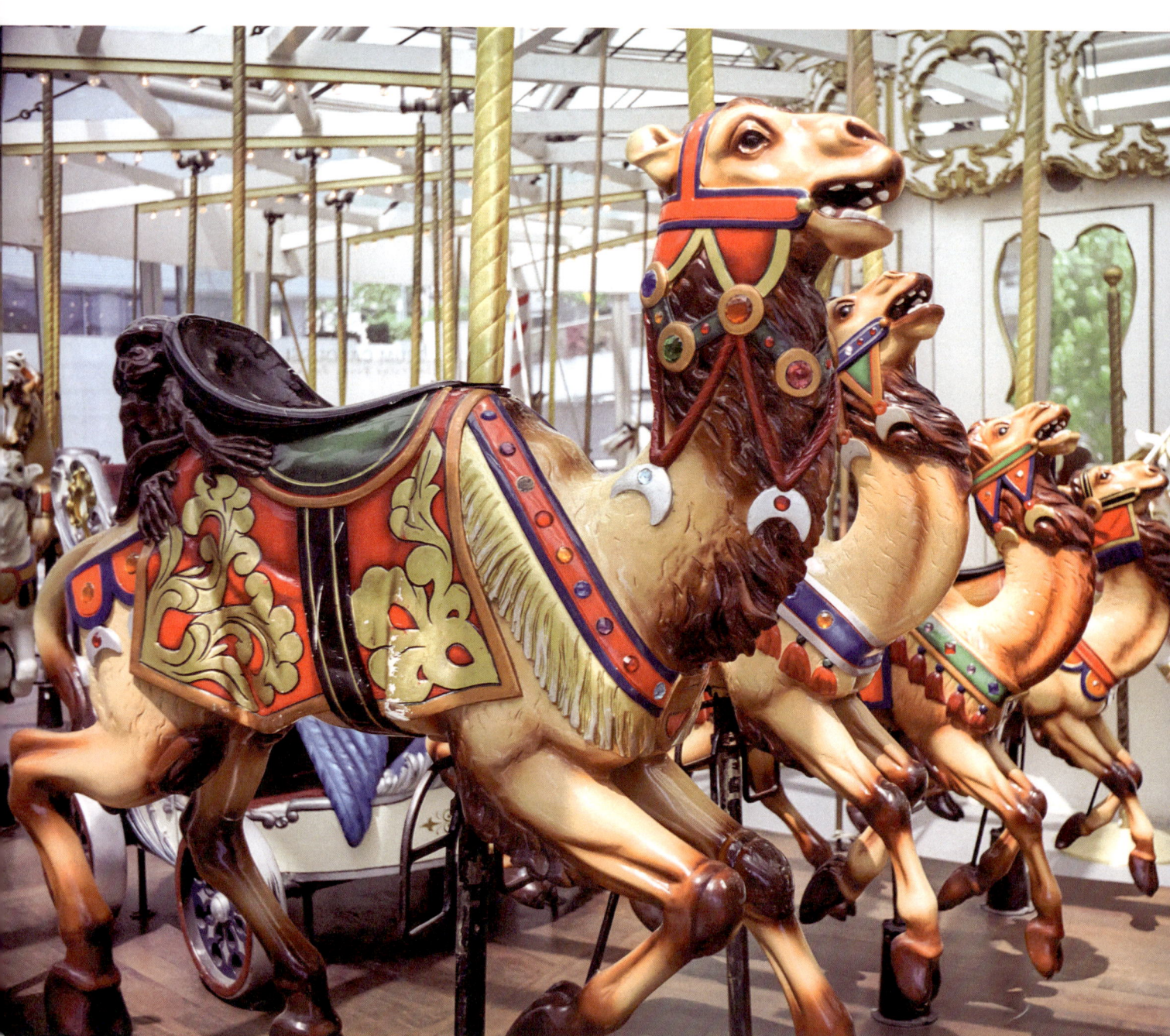

Jumping camels

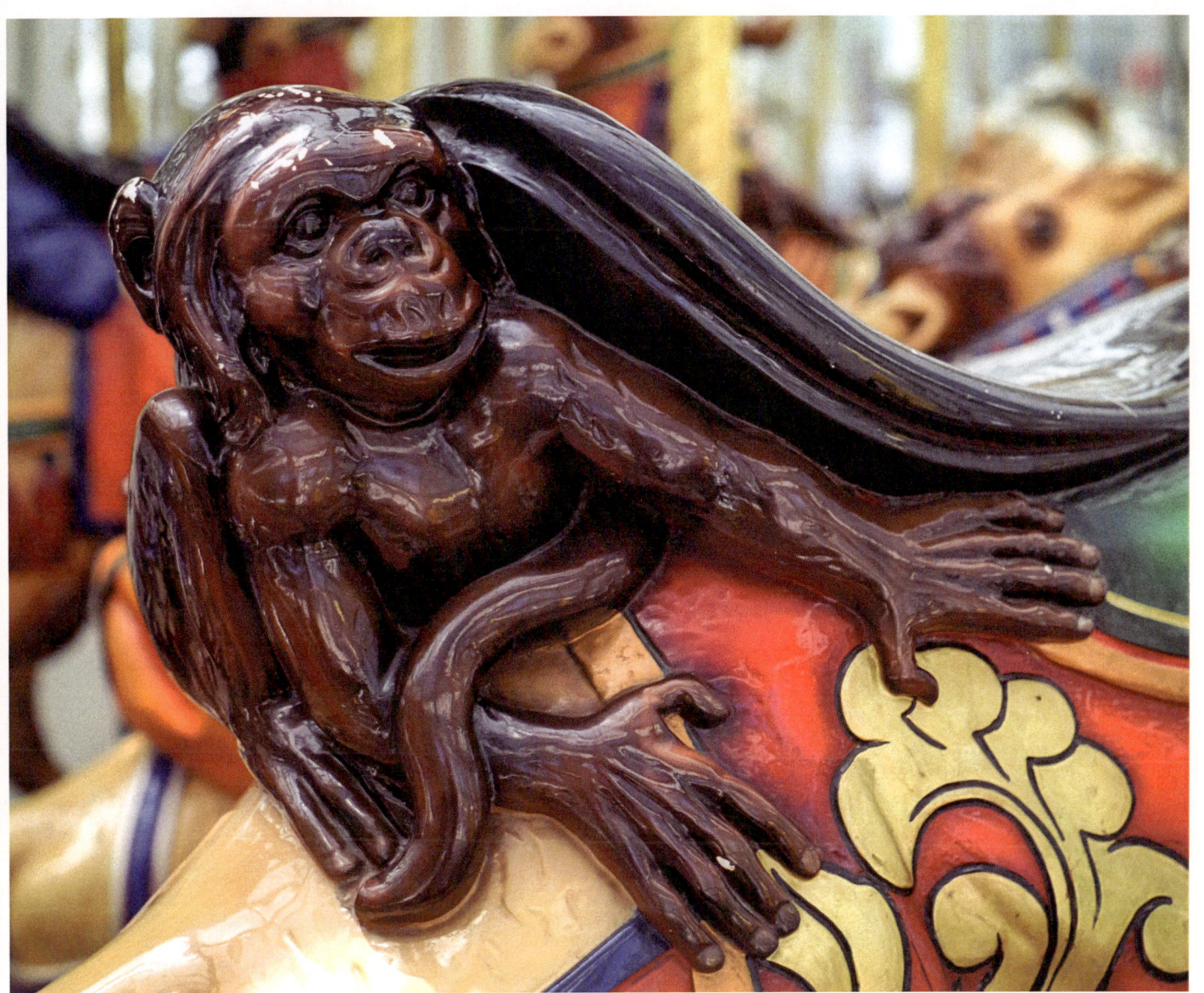

Camel saddle detail

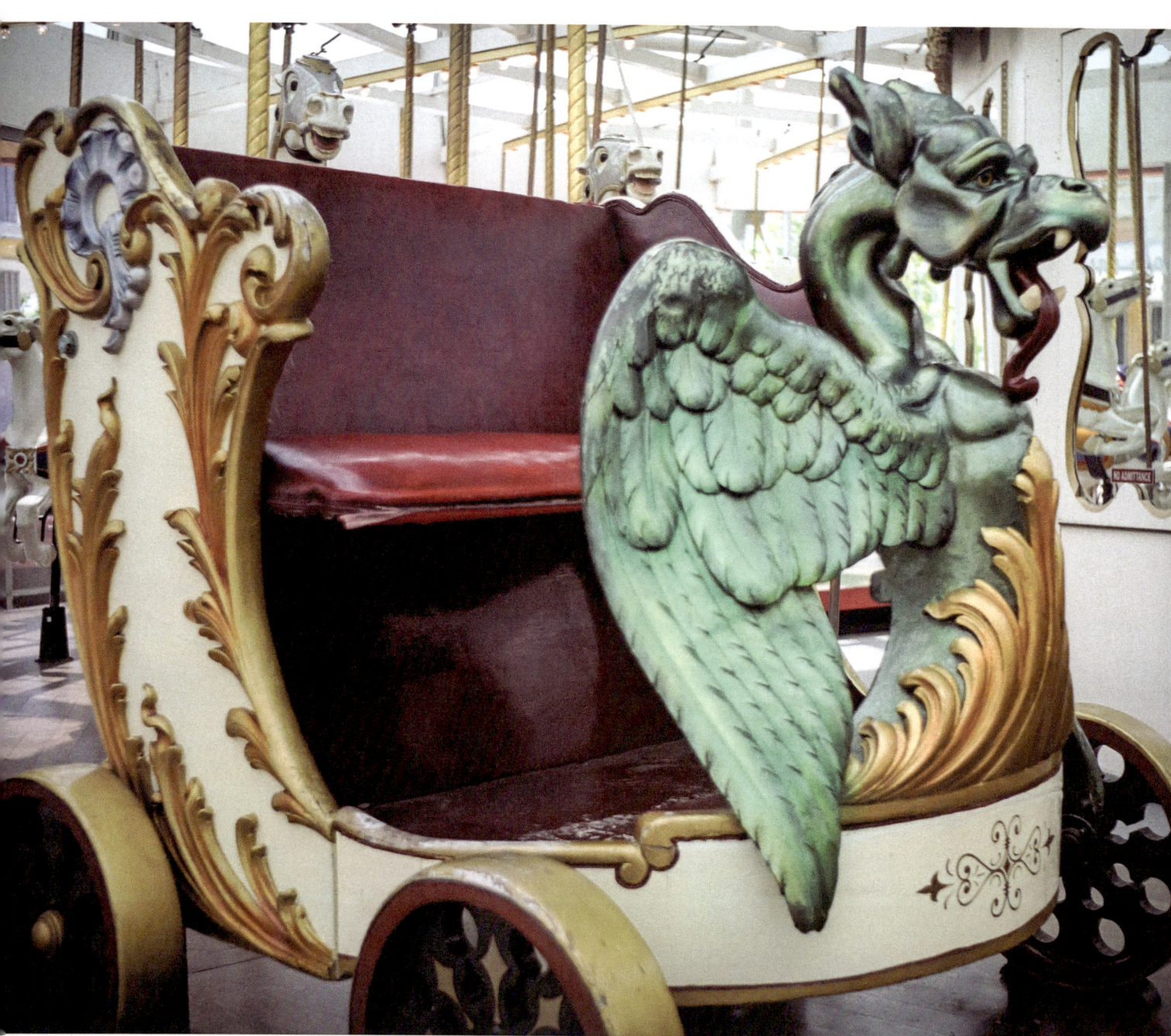

Chariot

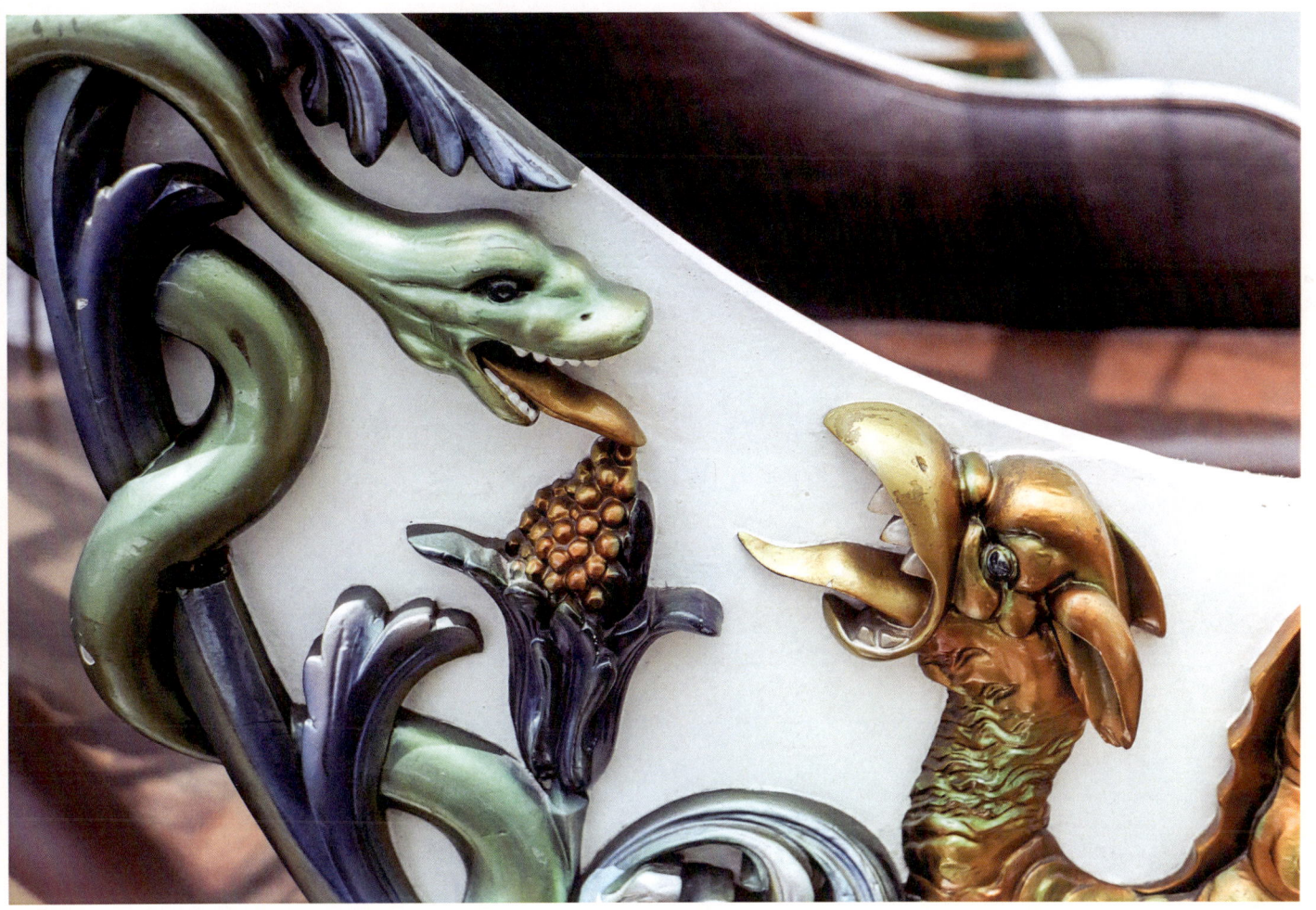

Chariot detail

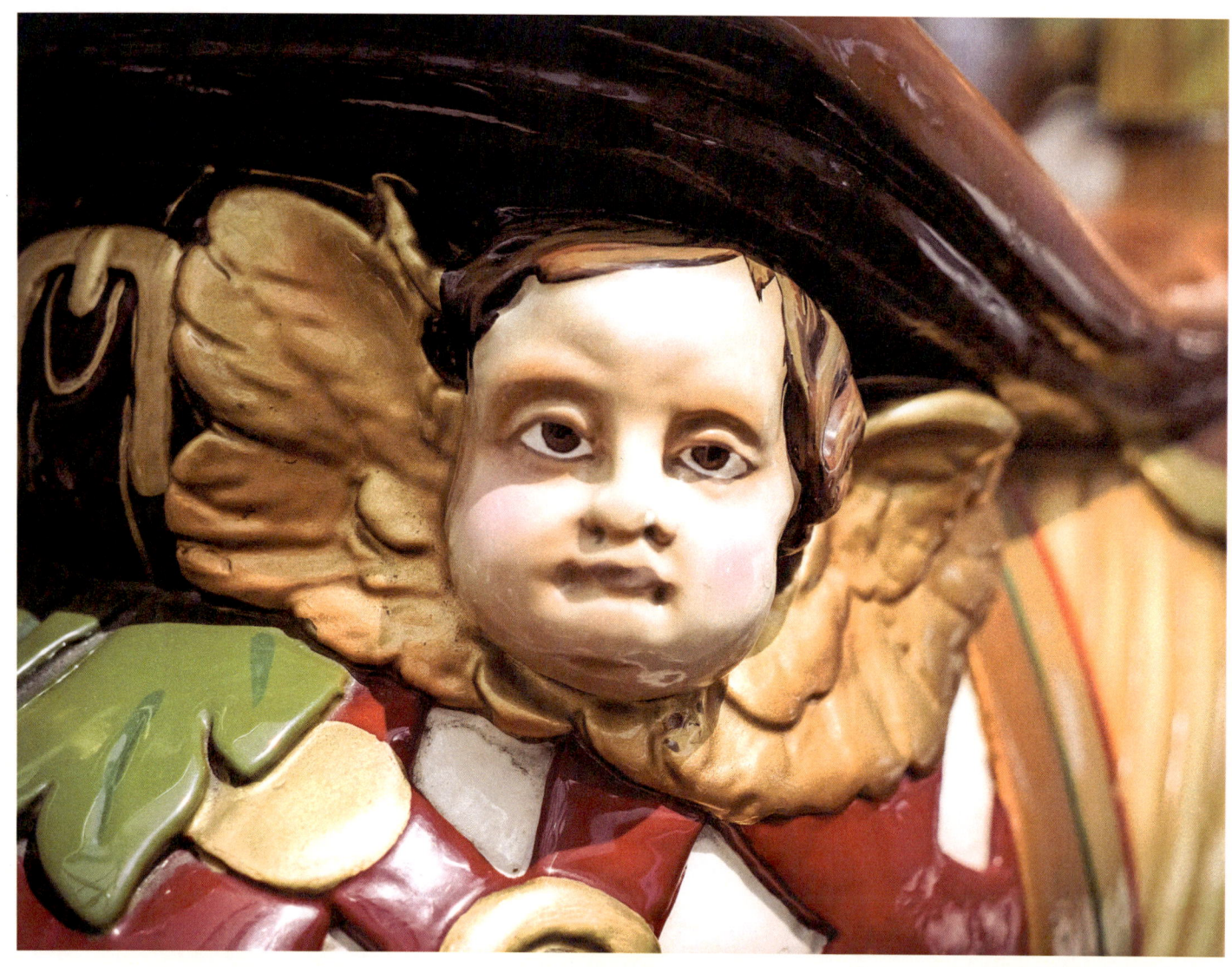

Saddle detail

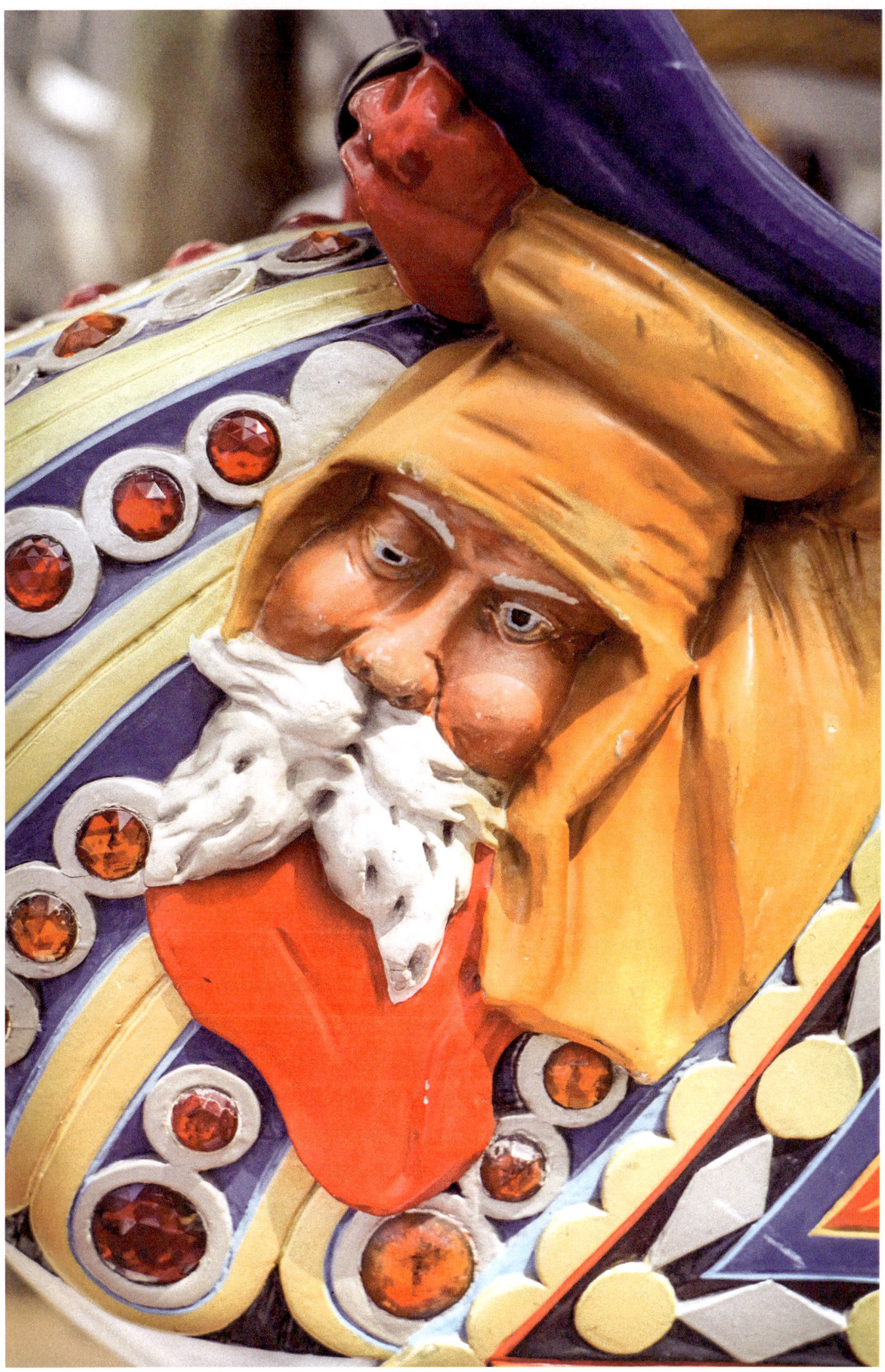

Saddle detail

Golden Gate Park Carousel

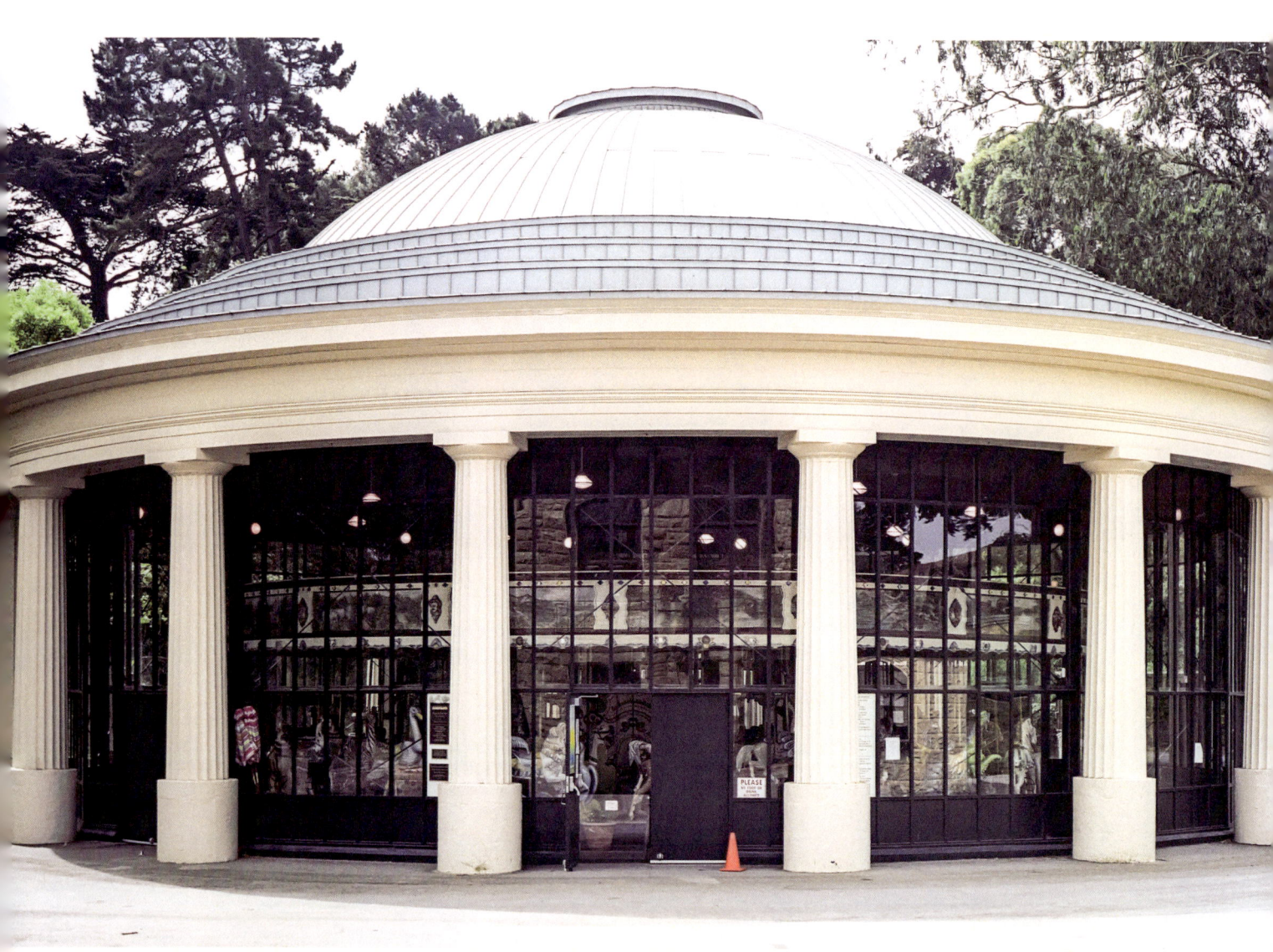

The Golden Gate Park Carousel was built in 1914 by the Herschell Spillman Company of North Tonawanda, New York, and is one of only two surviving four-row carousels by that company. (The other is at Tilden Park in Berkeley.) Before arriving at Golden Gate Park in 1940, the carousel operated at Lincoln Park in Los Angeles, 1914–1931; Lotus Isle in Portland, 1931–1933; and the Golden Gate International Exposition (World's Fair) on Treasure Island in San Francisco Bay, 1939–1940.

When the carousel broke down in 1977, the San Francisco Art Commission offered to help fund its complete restoration. The commission's choice for the job was Ruby Newman, a young muralist and theater set and costume designer. Heading a team that included a boat restorer from Seattle and a woodcarver born in Austria, Newman mostly completed the restoration by 1984.

Instead of trying to restore the carousel's original colors, Newman devised a color scheme of her own, but one that still aimed to accent the details of the carvings. The result was a stunning and unique carousel mingling the talents and conceptions of the carvers with the bold vision of a contemporary artist. Newman's coloring has been mostly maintained throughout a series of touch-up paintings—though not entirely. (At the time of these photos, another artist had recently been called in to make the lion's eyes less fierce!)

The carousel is the third to operate at this location, its earliest predecessor dating back to 1888, when it was powered by steam. The present pavilion was built in the early 1890s. A 1922 Gebrüder Bruder band organ was installed during Newman's restoration and is still operational. But music is normally supplied by recordings, because—as a carousel operator there put it—the organ is too loud!

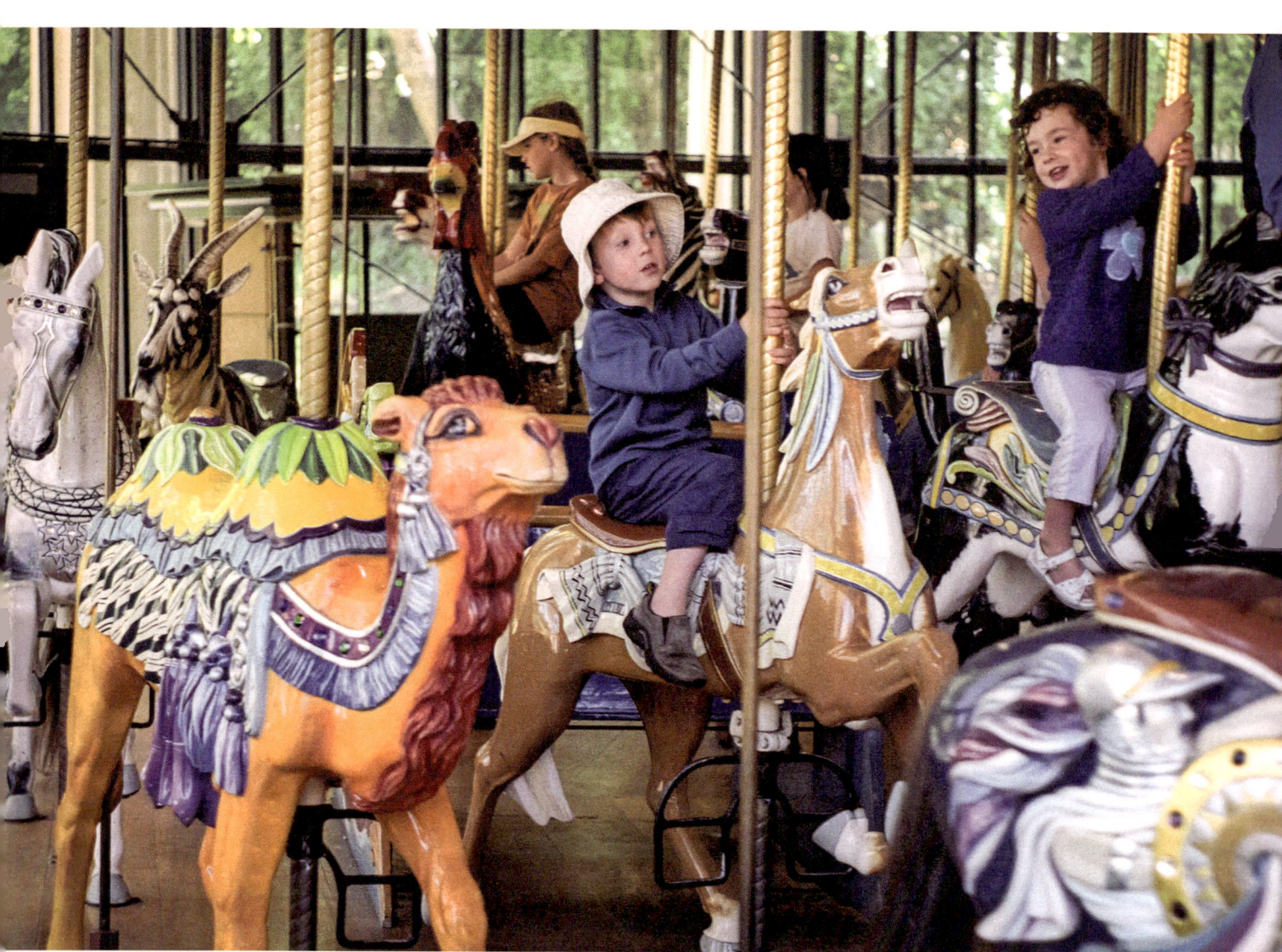

Carousel animals and riders

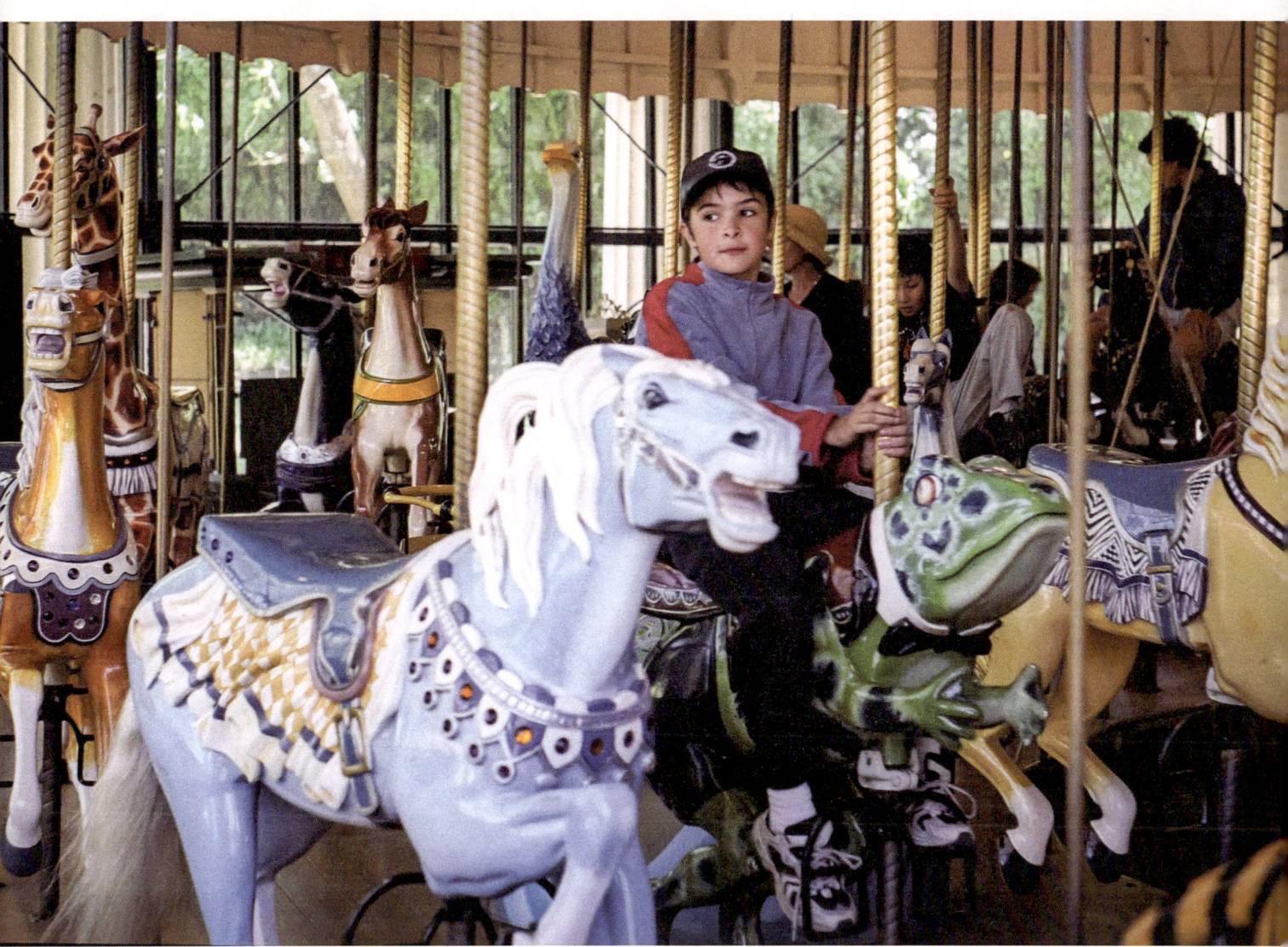

Carousel animals and riders

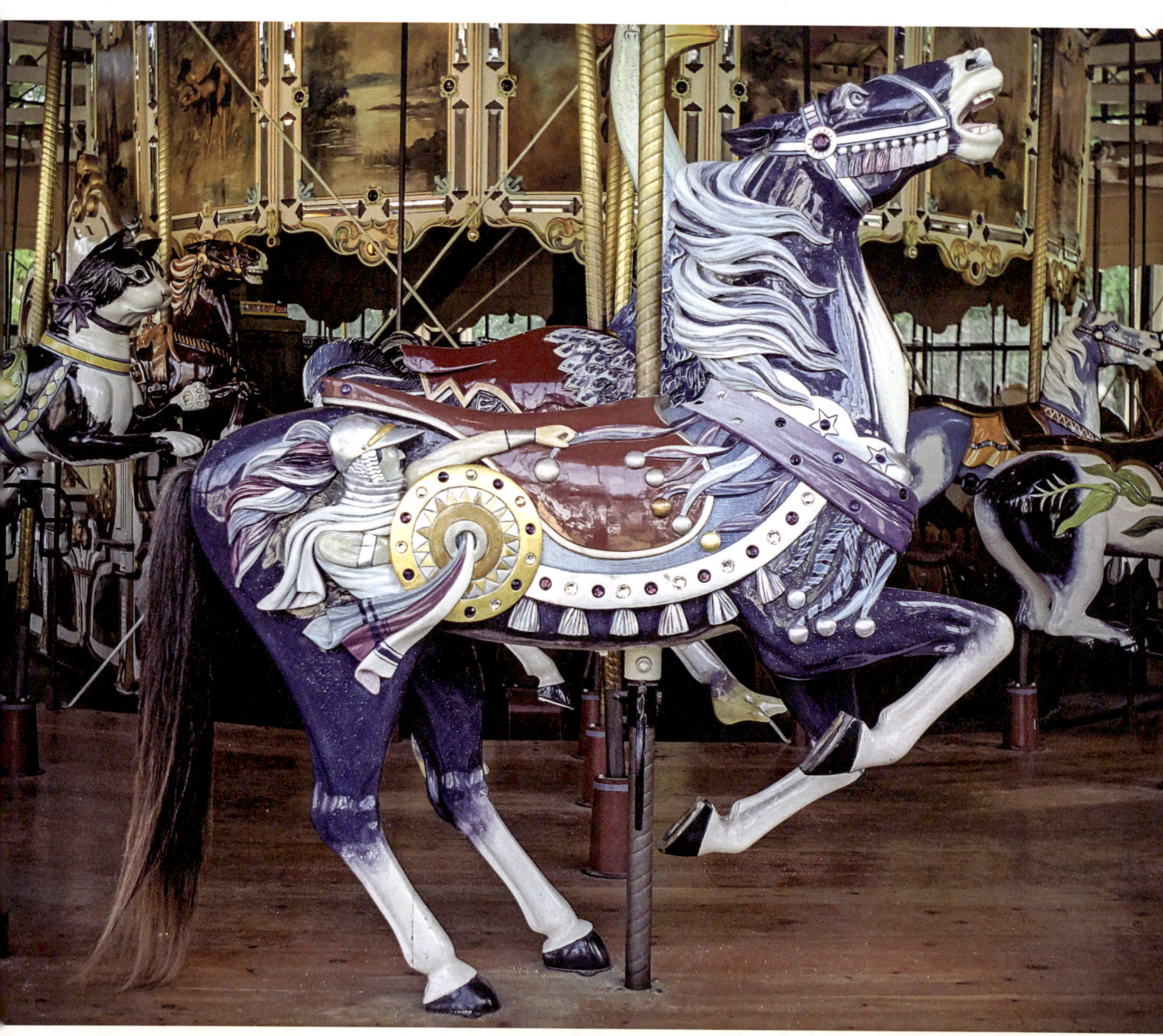

Prancer

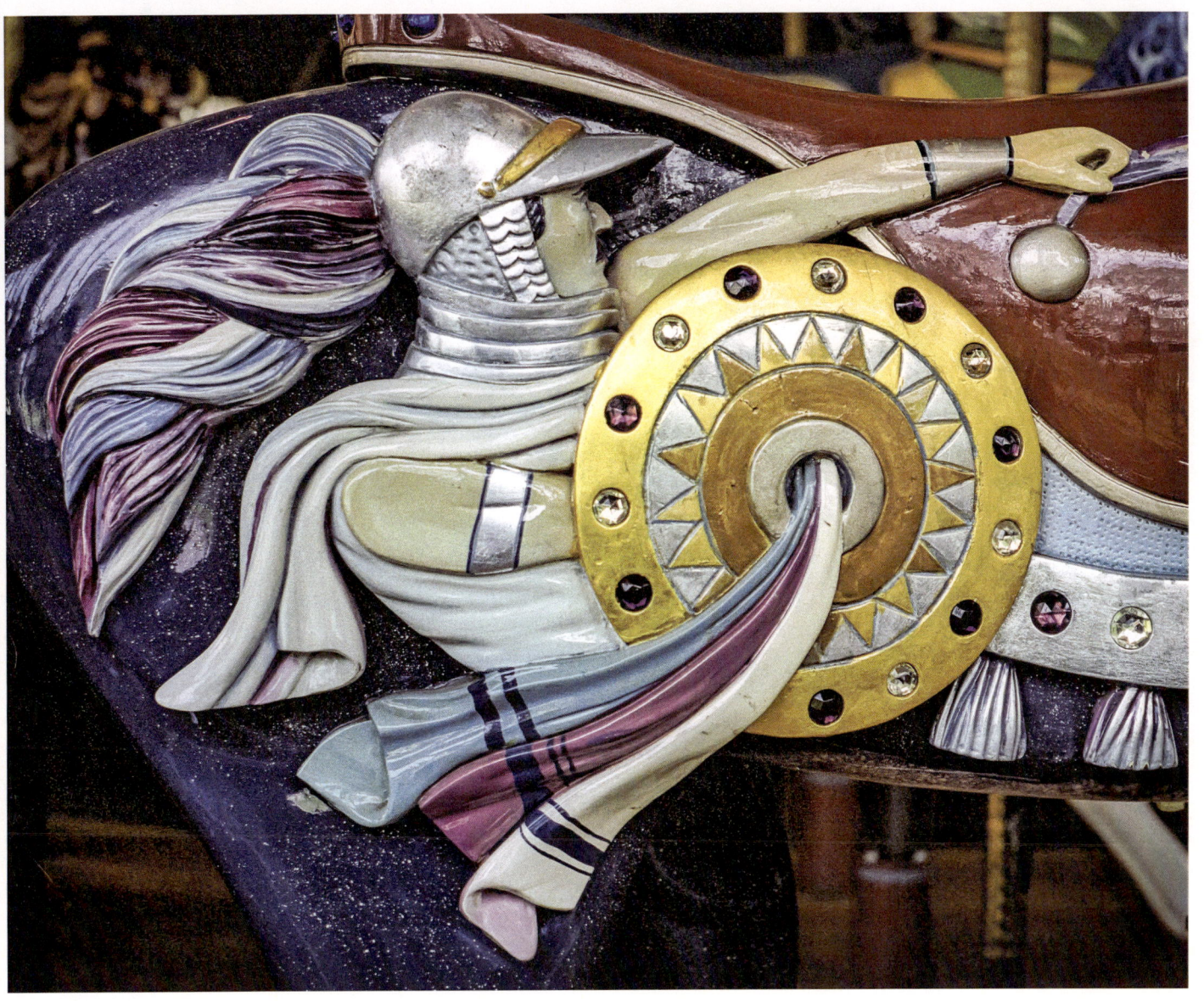

Prancer detail

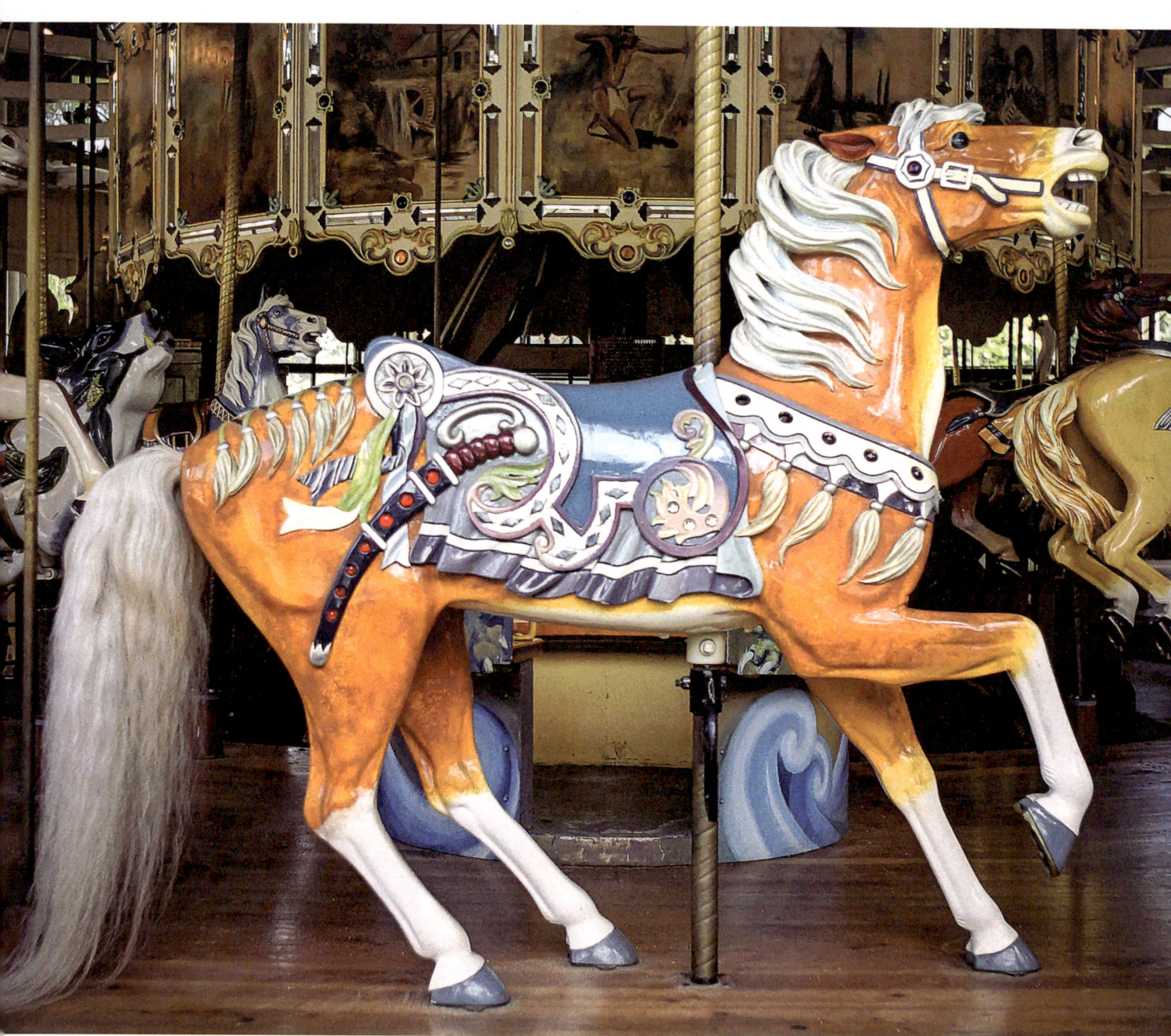

Stander

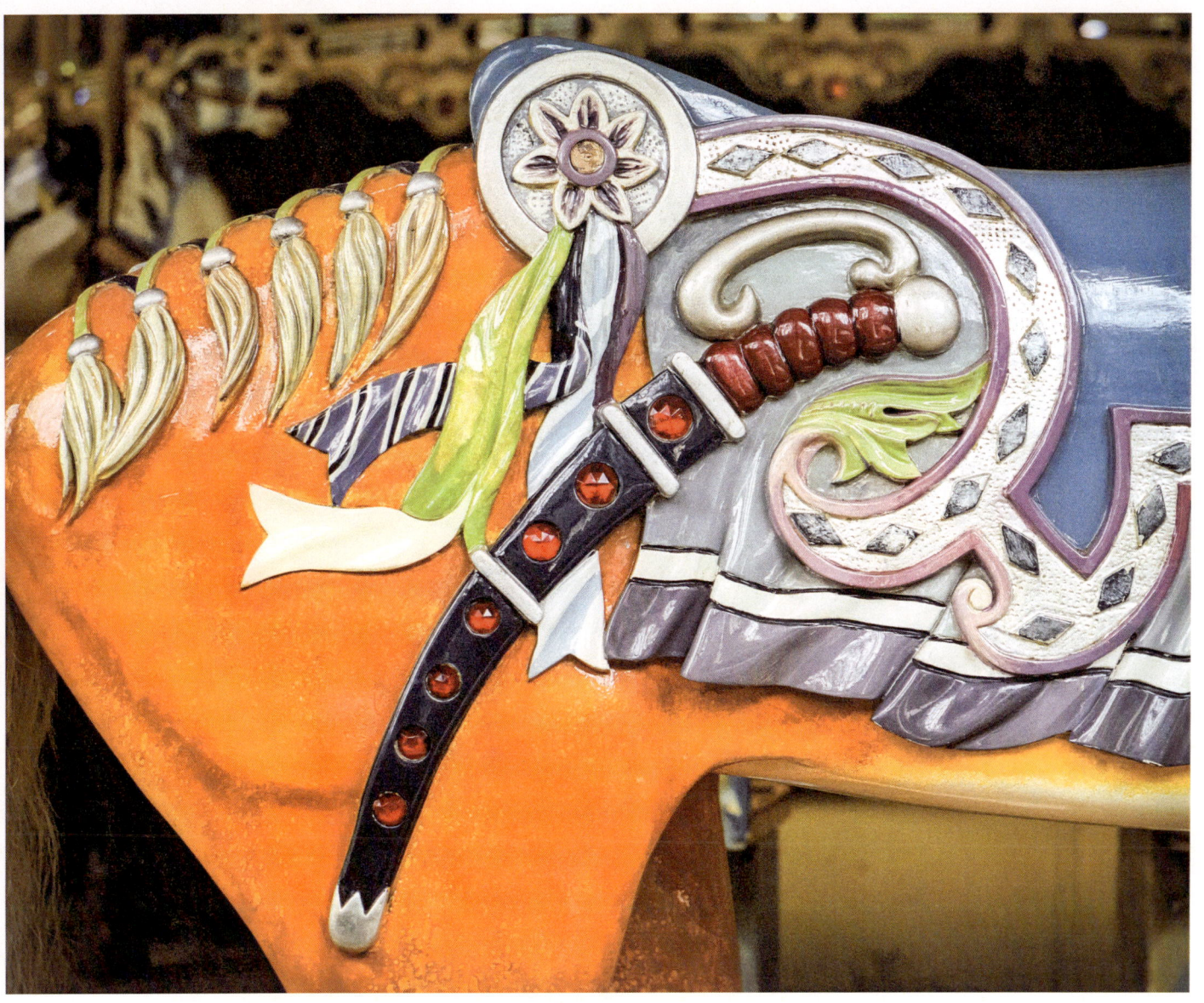

Stander saddle detail

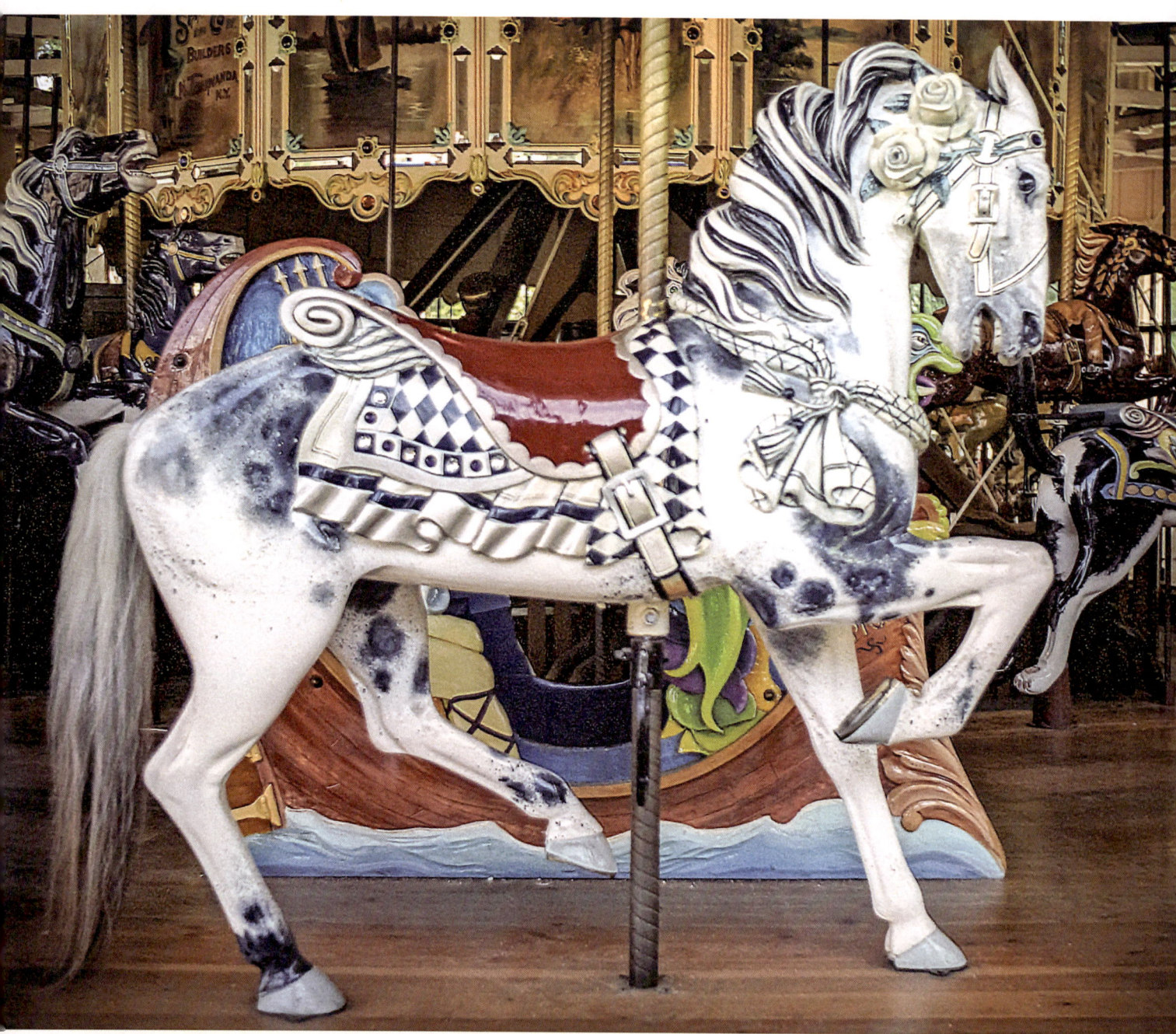

Stander

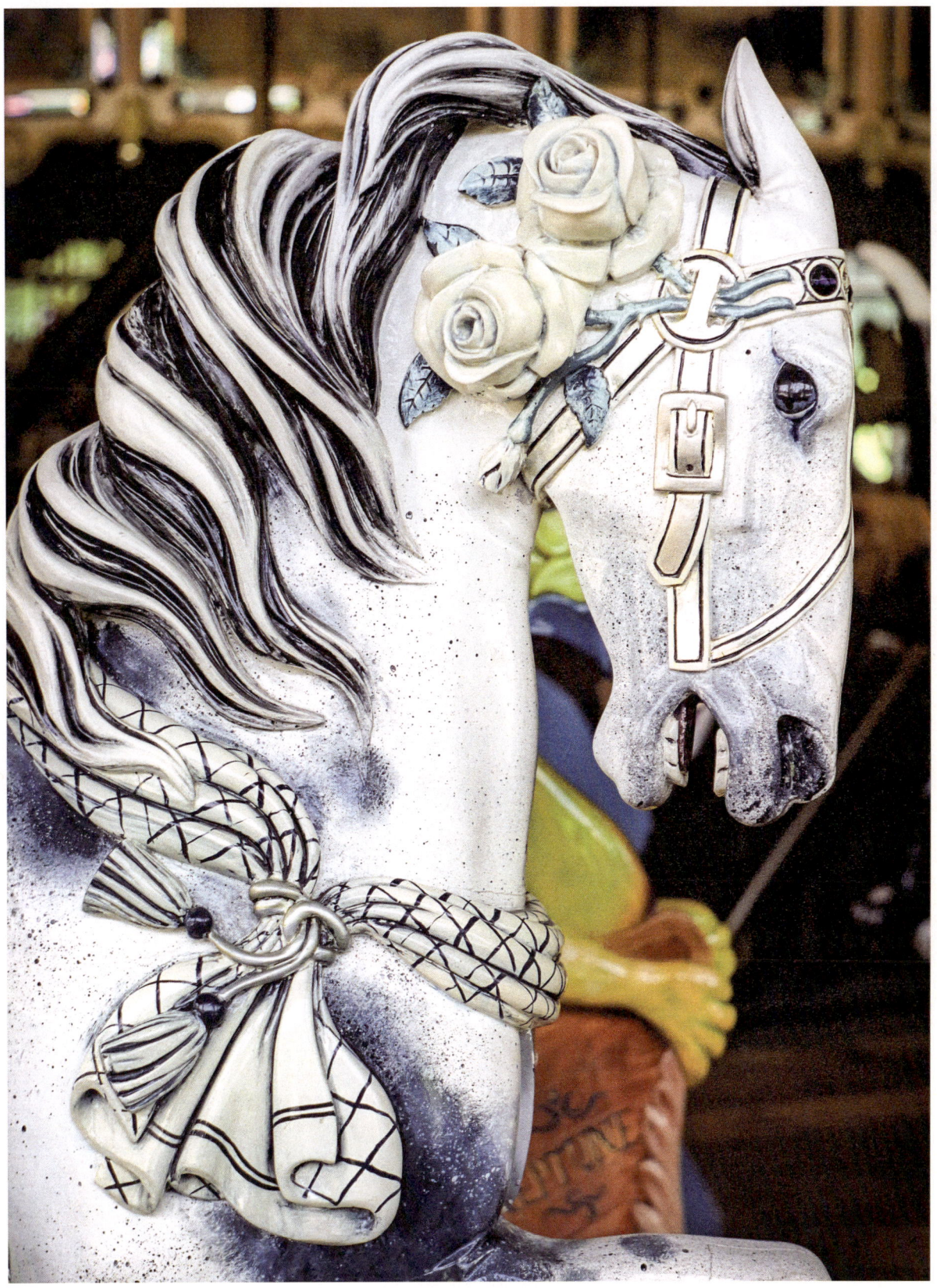

Stander head

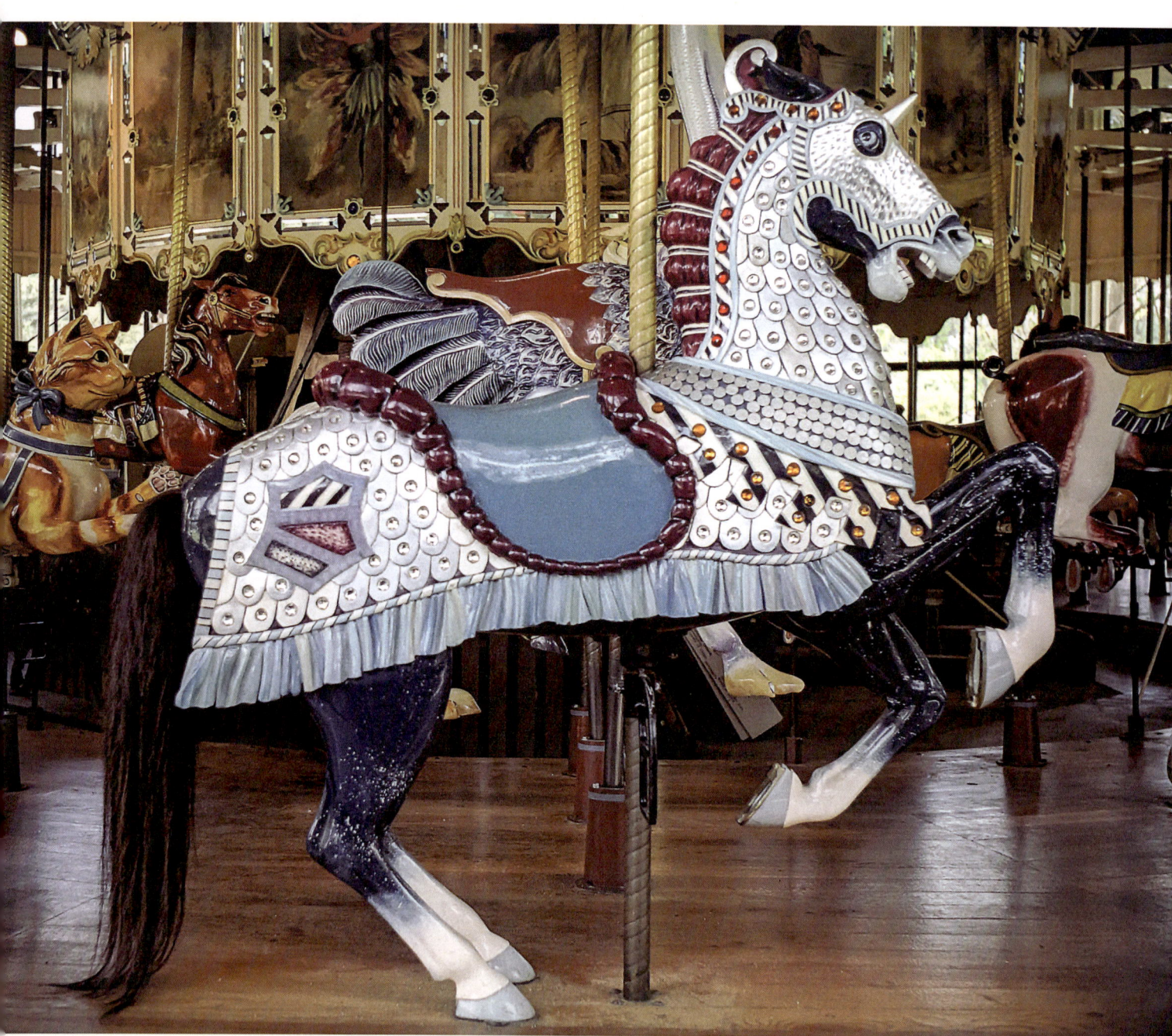

Prancer, "Armored" style

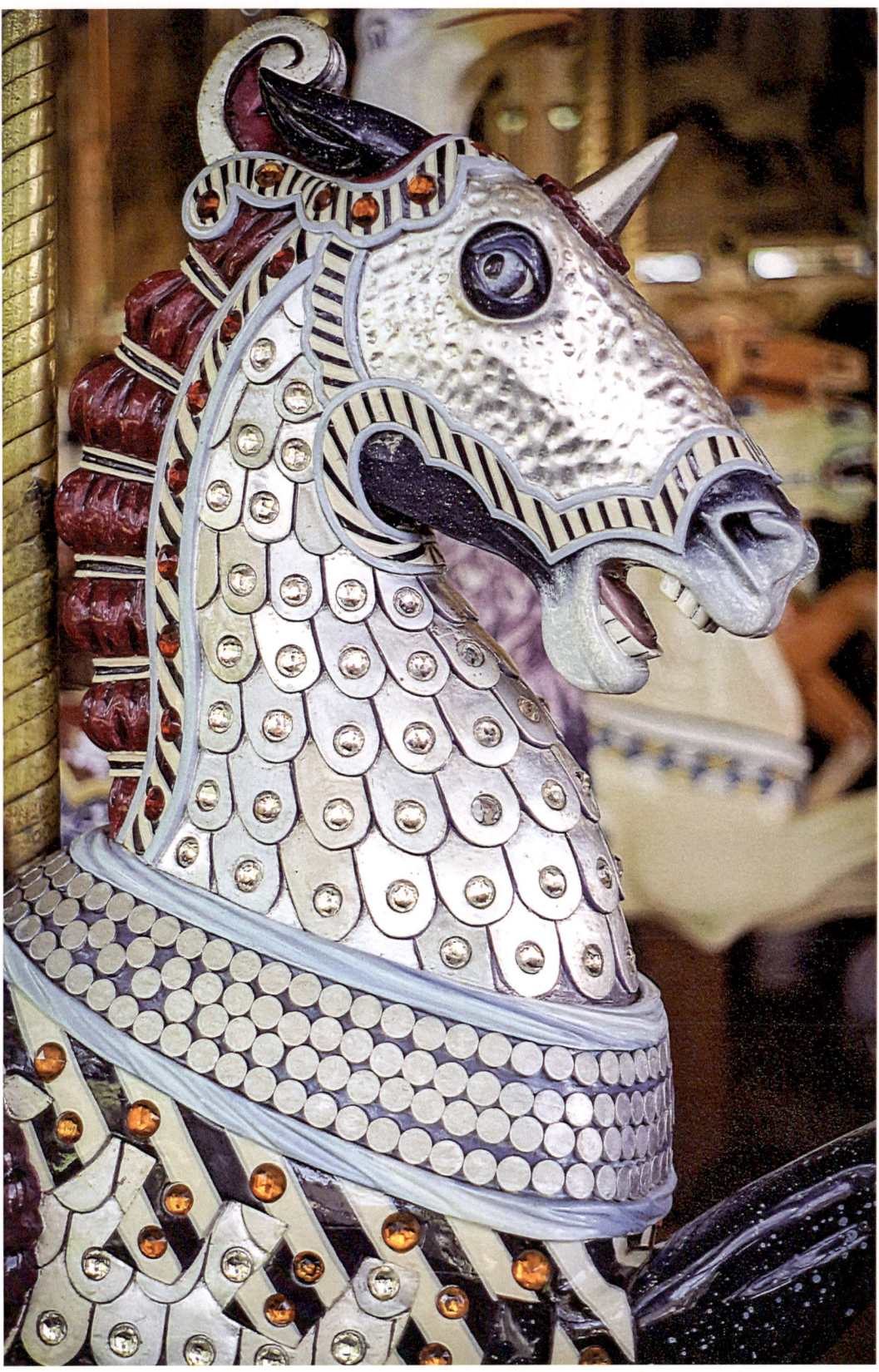

"Armored" prancer head

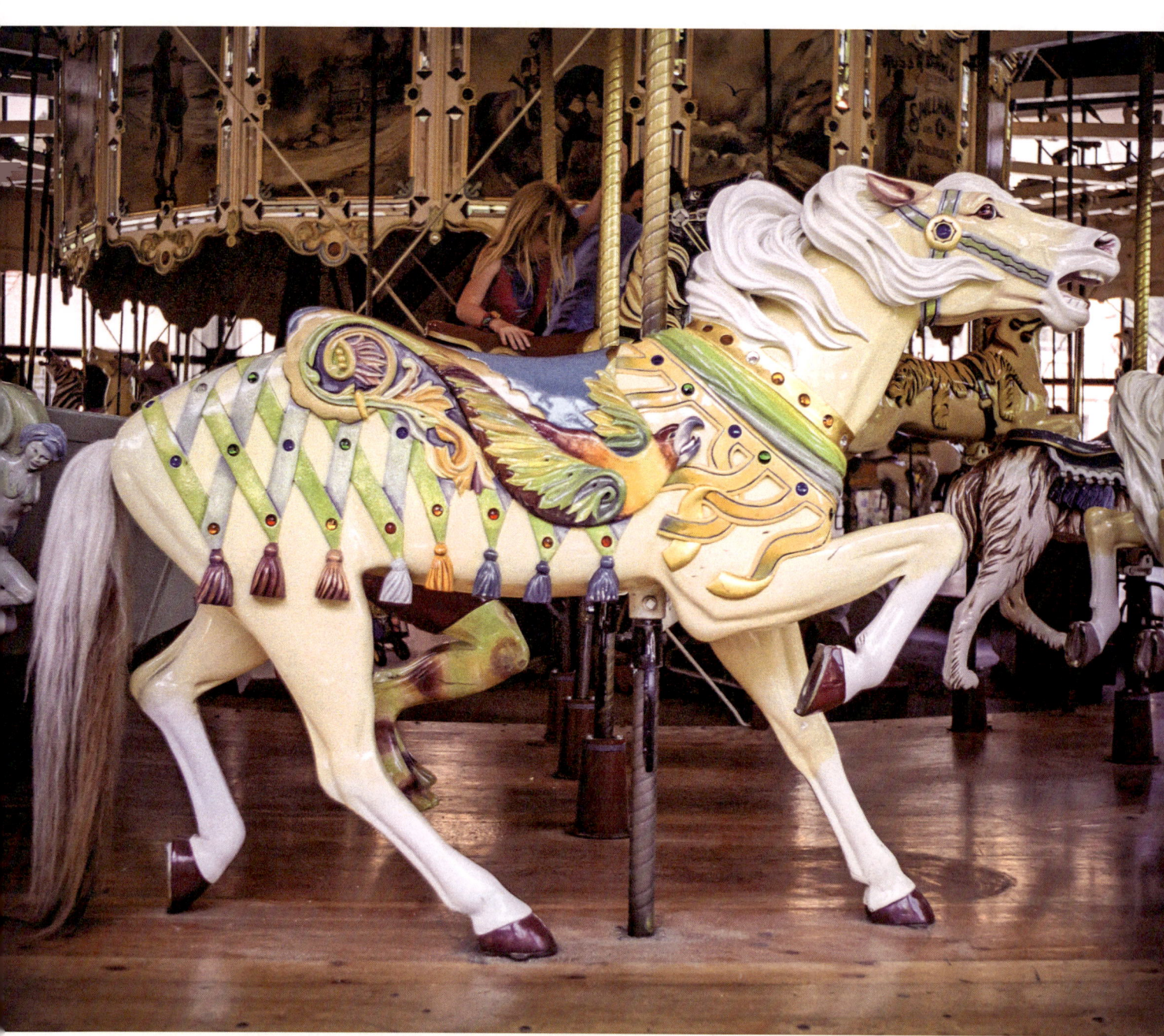

Stander

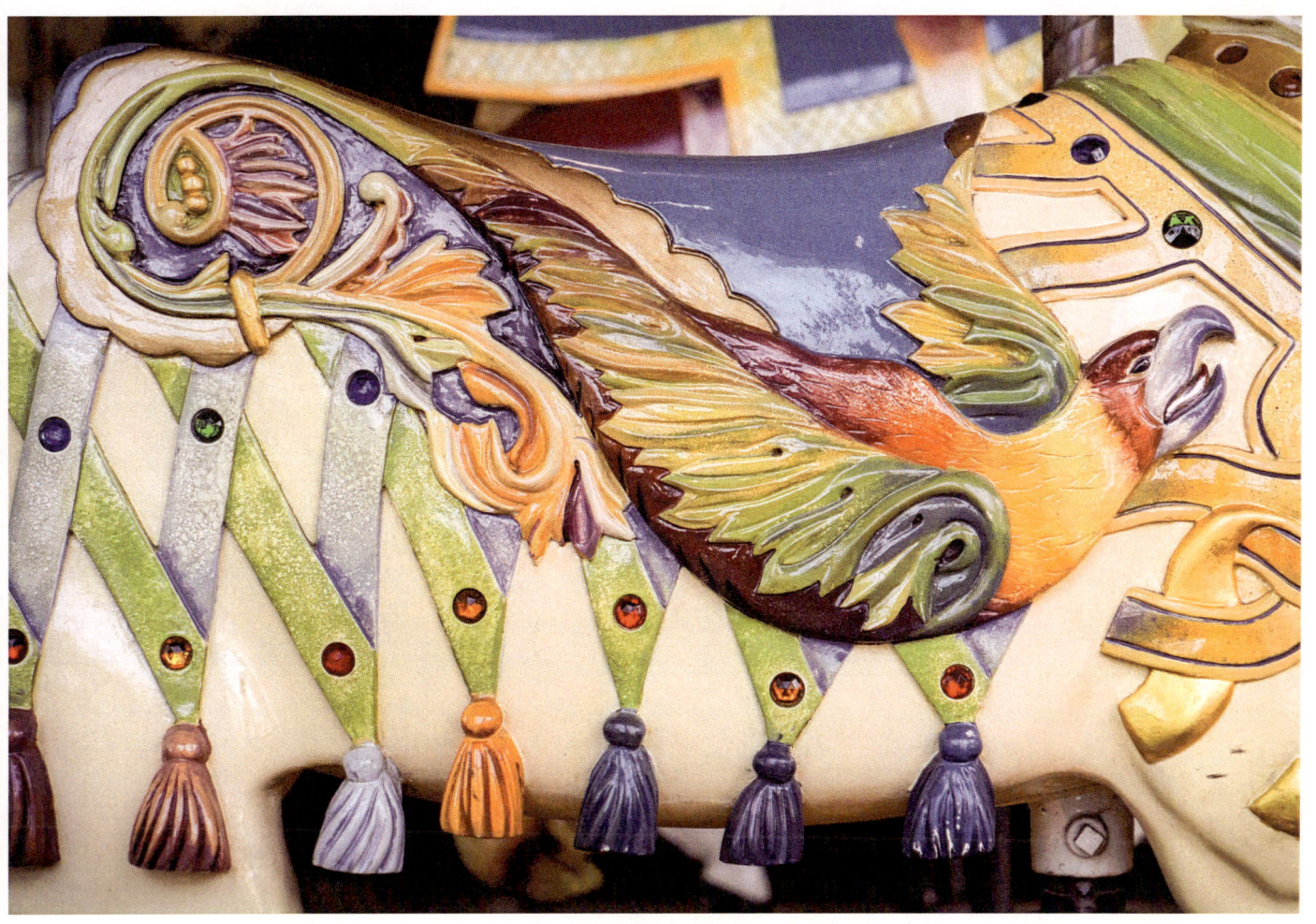

Stander saddle

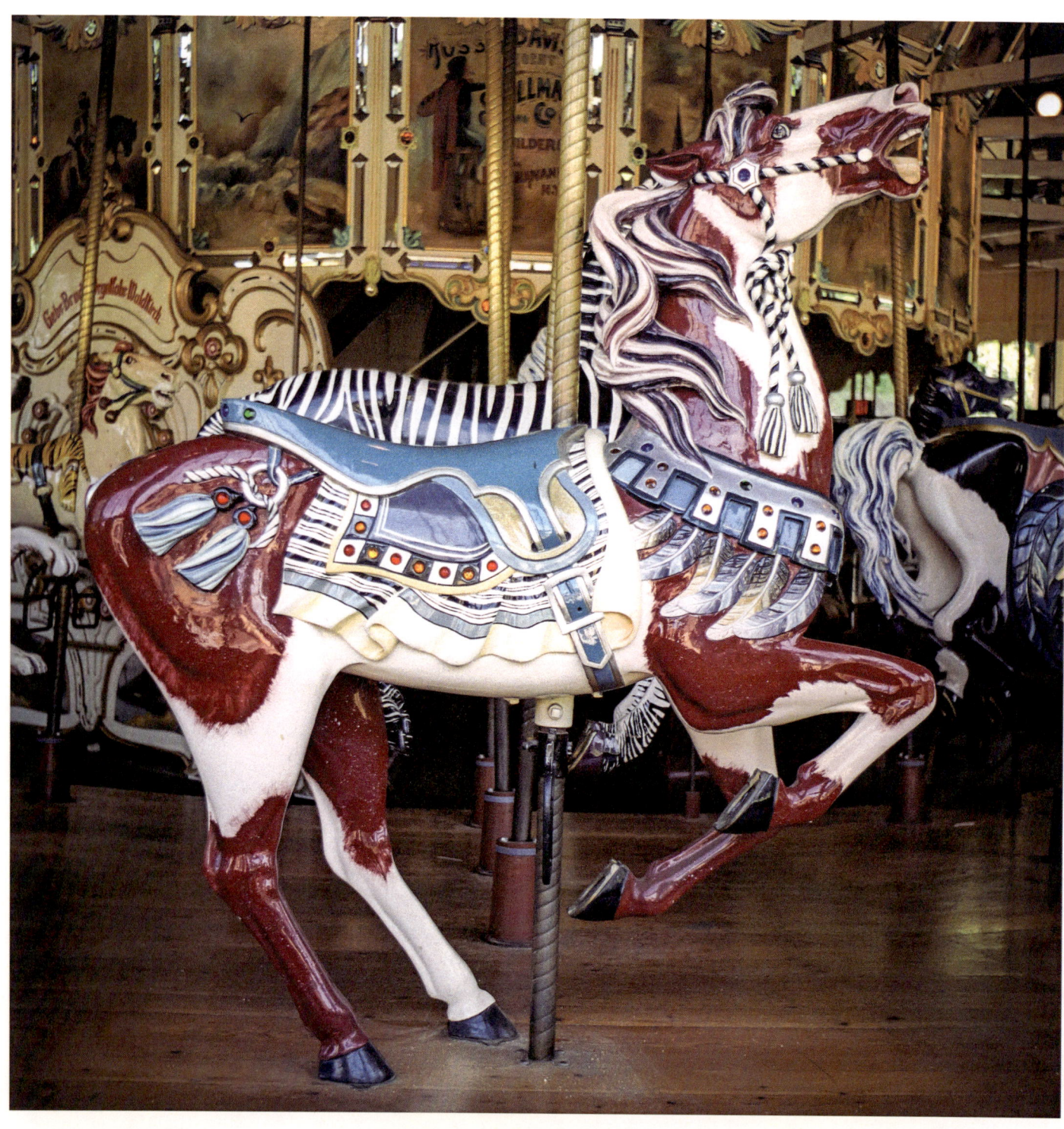

Prancer, "Lolling Tongue" style

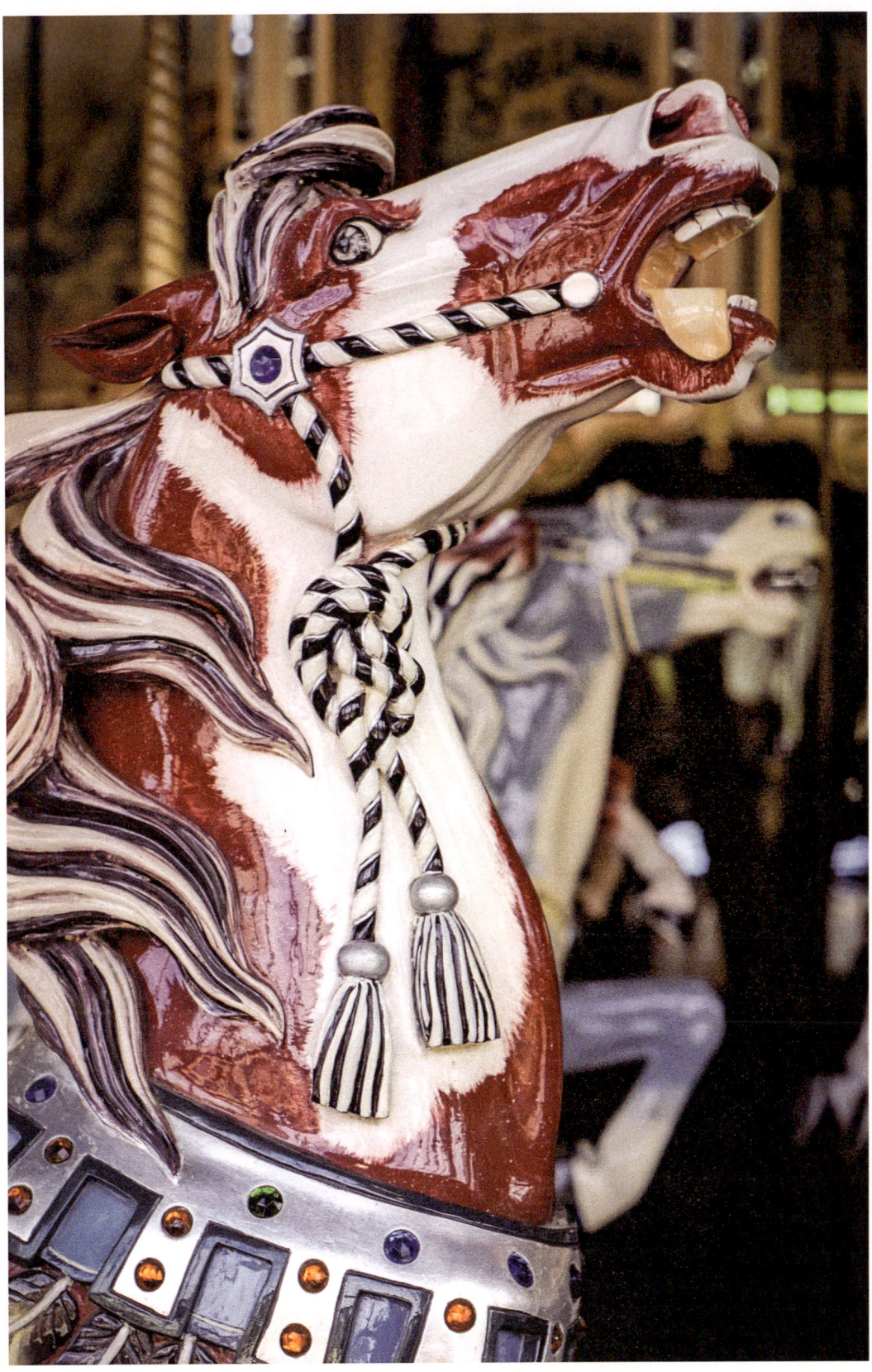

"Lolling Tongue" prancer head

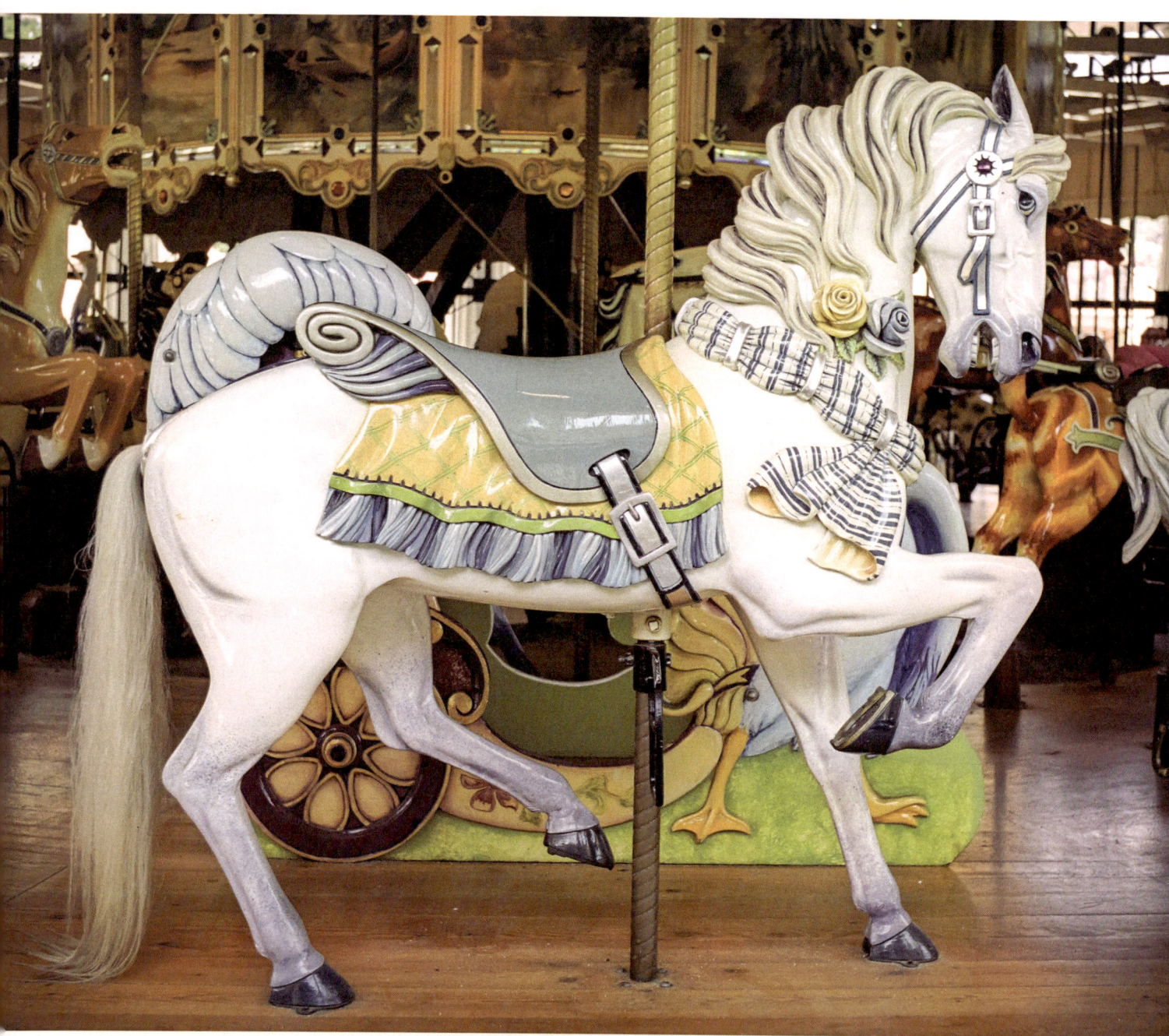

Stander

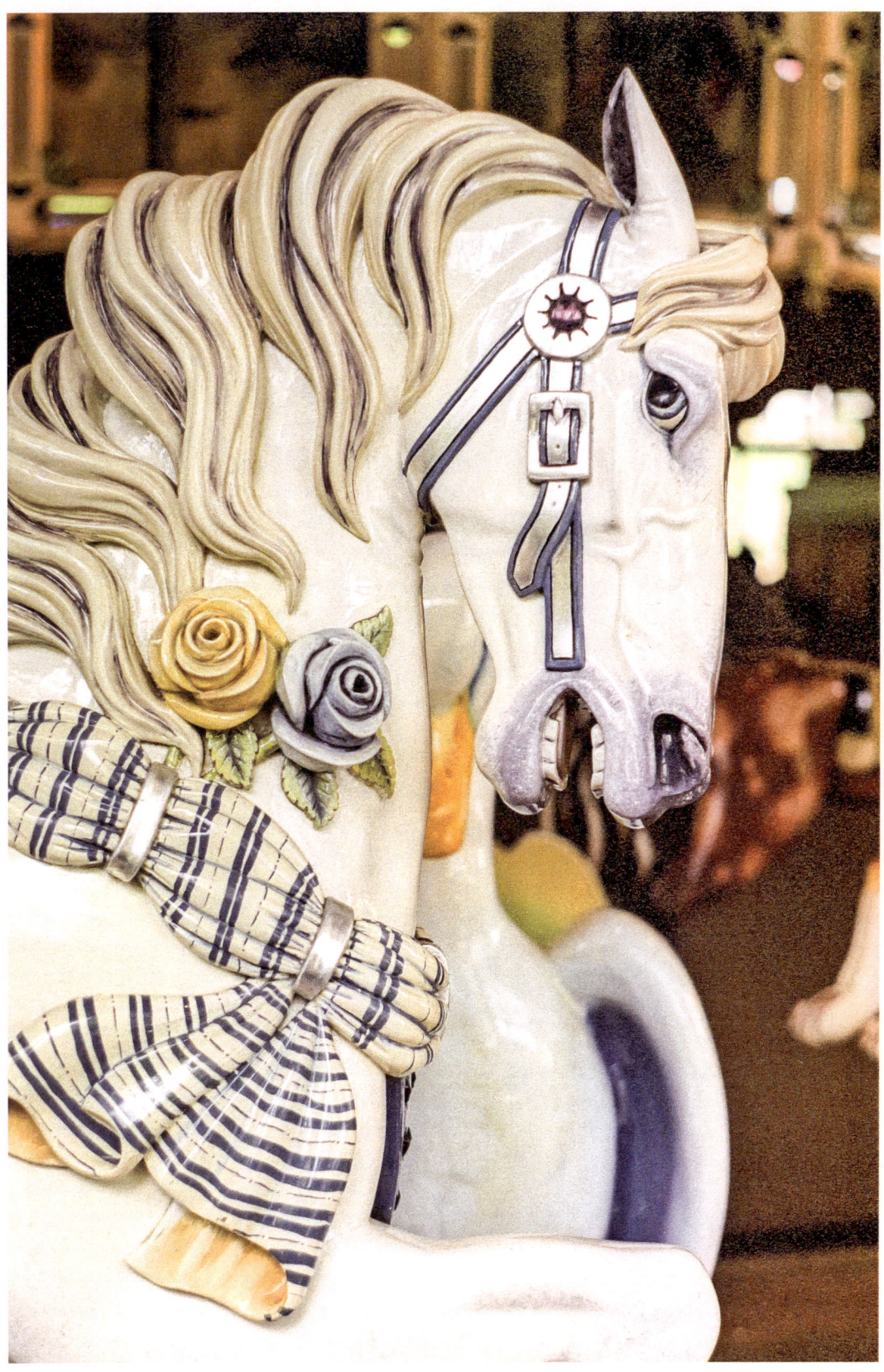

Stander head

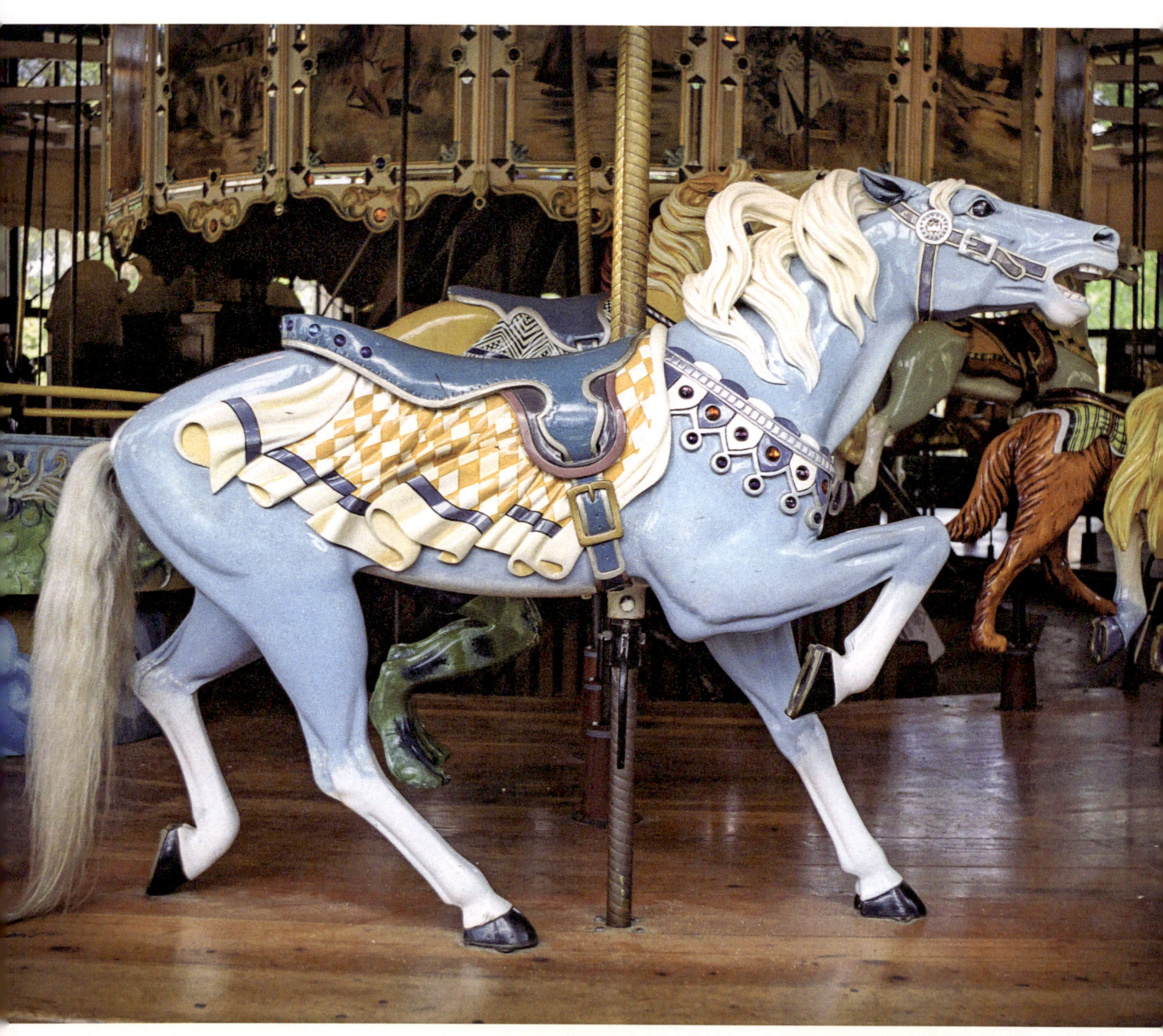

Stander

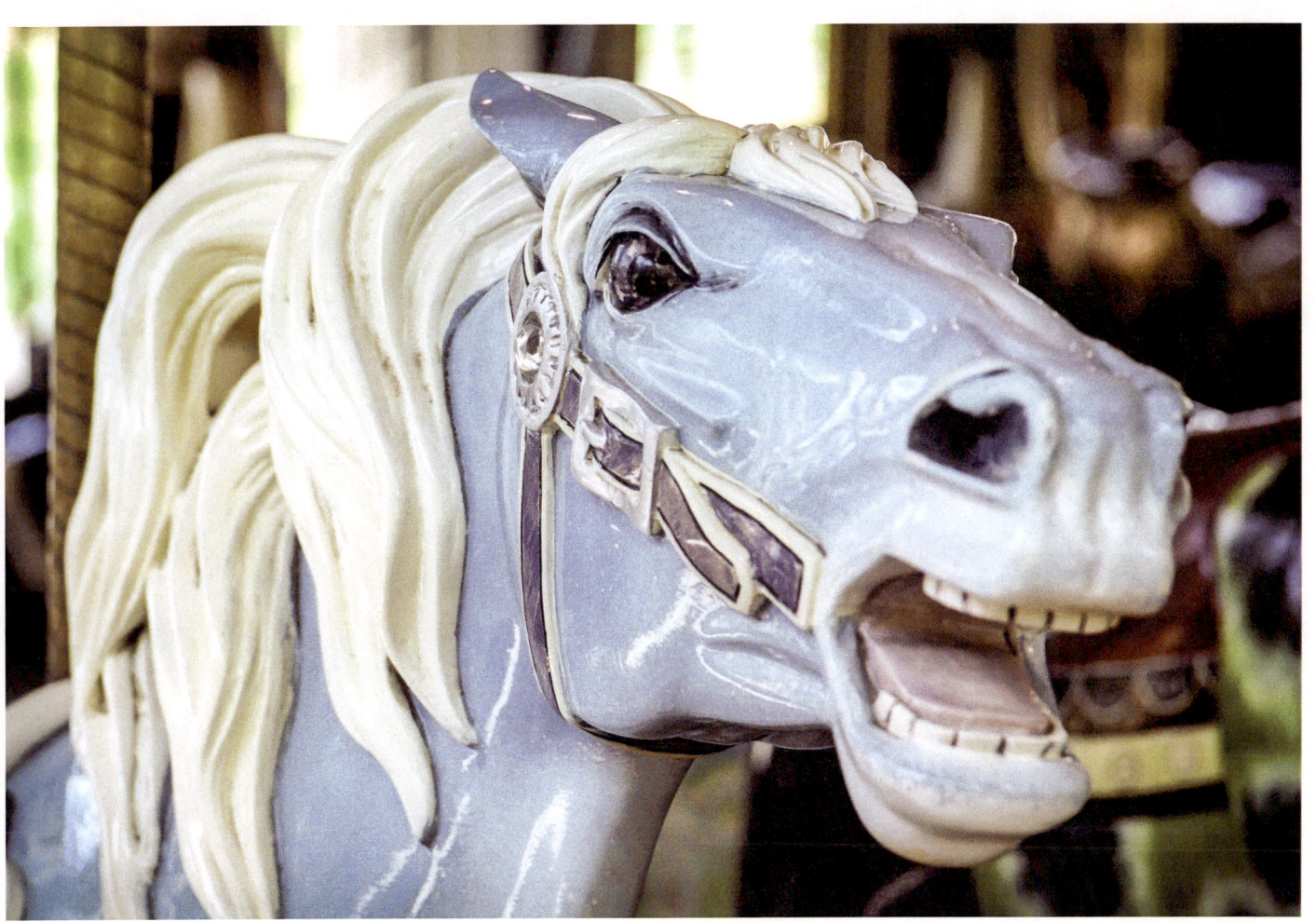

Stander head

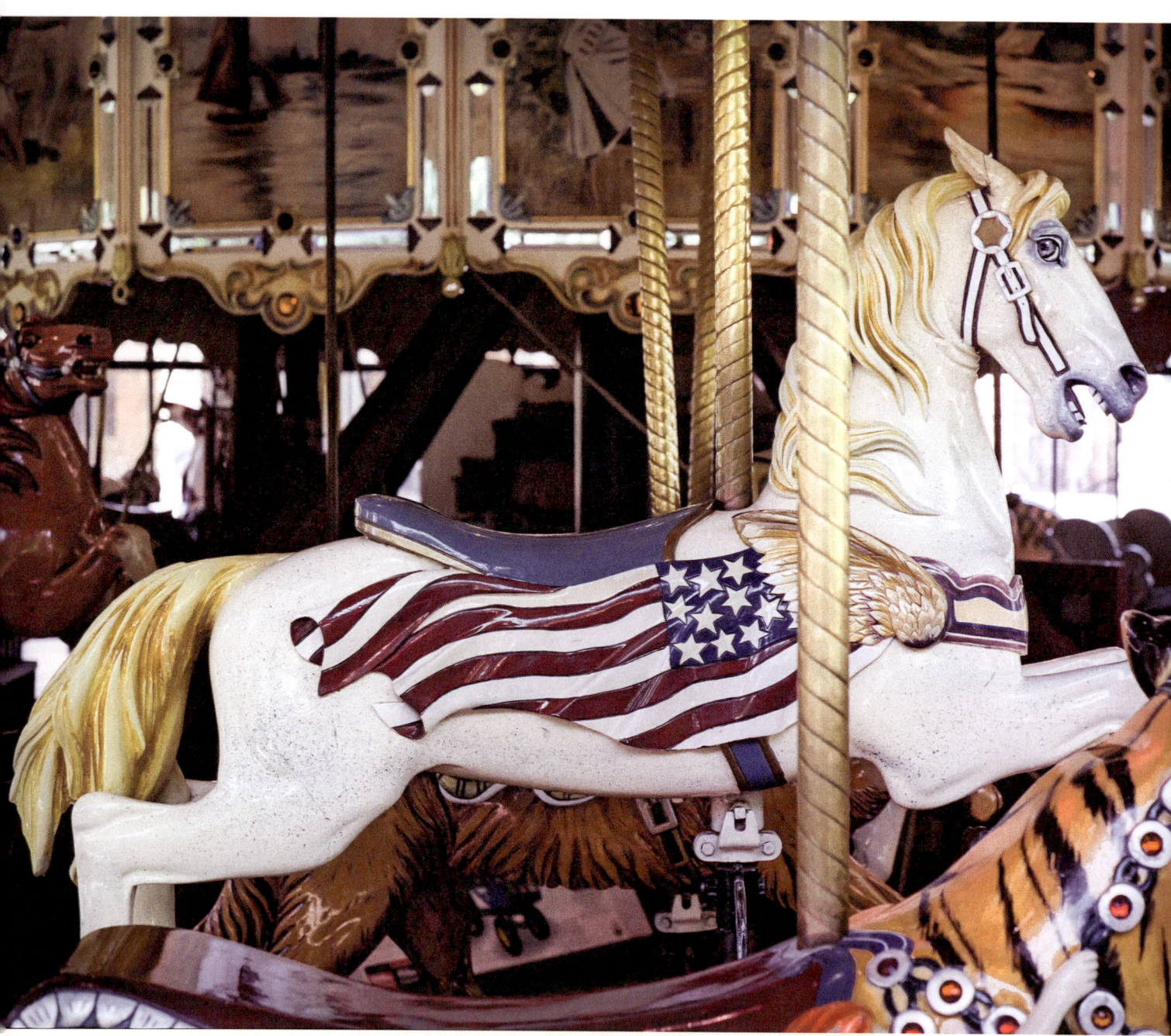

Jumper

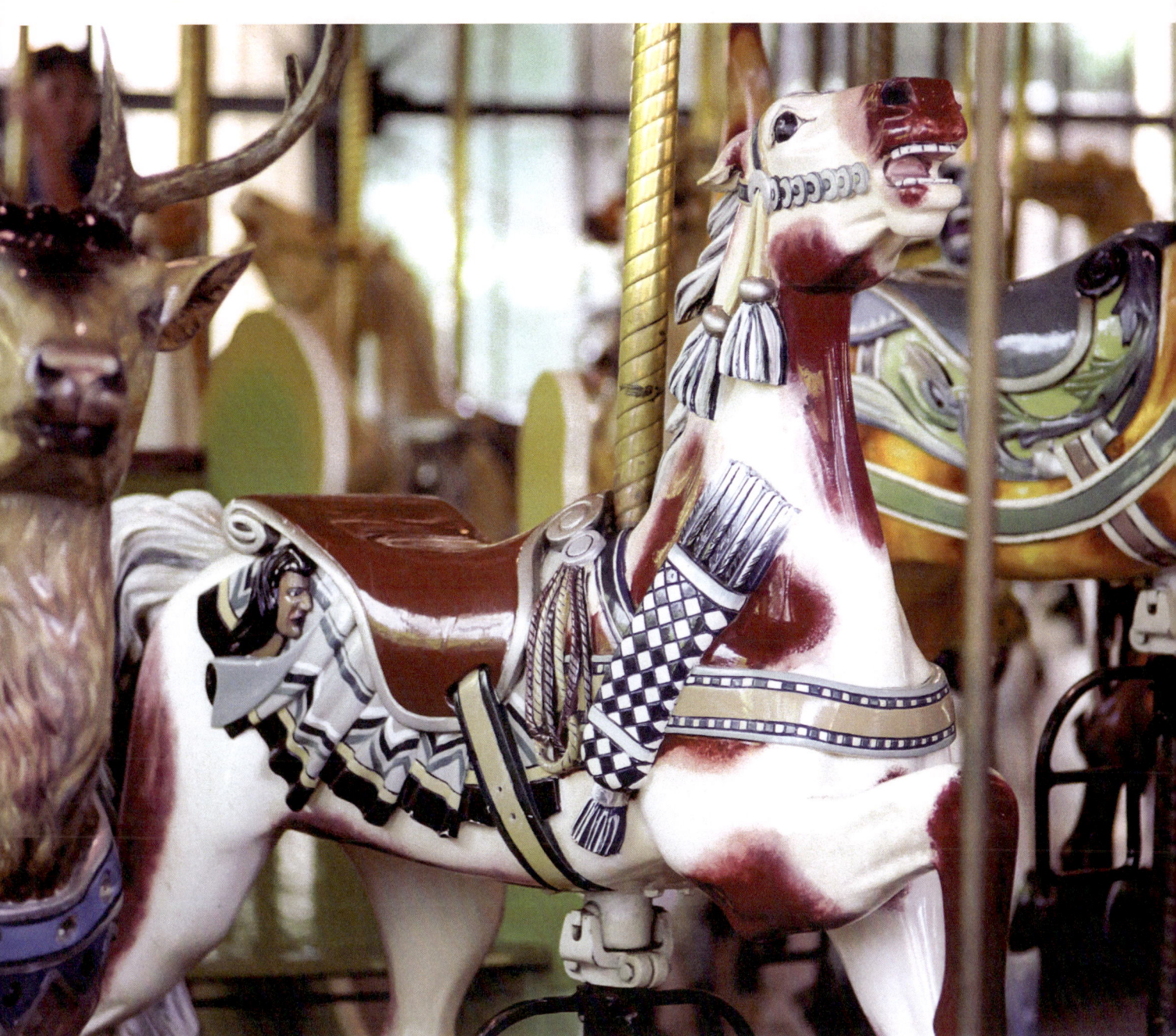

Stander

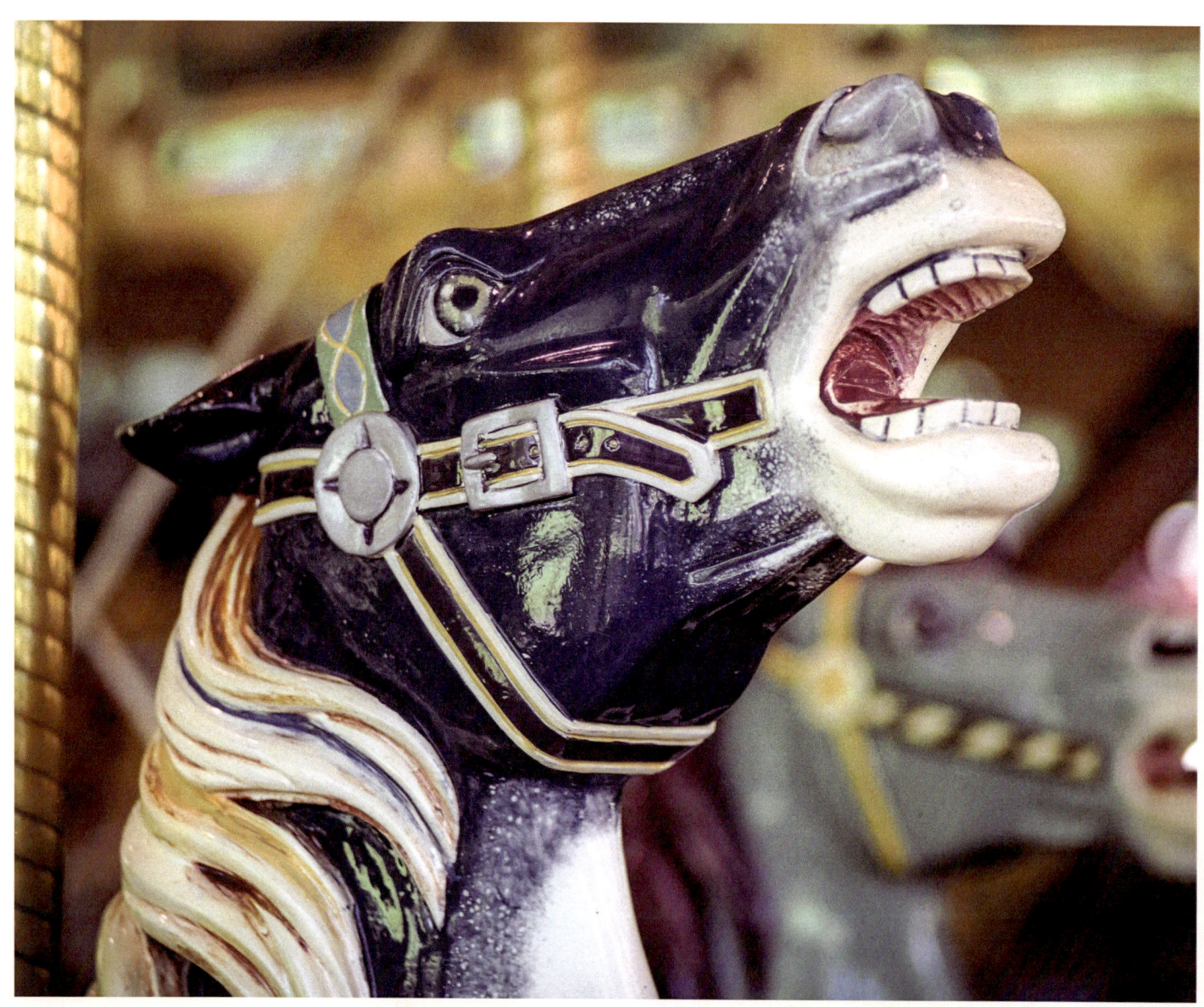

Jumper head

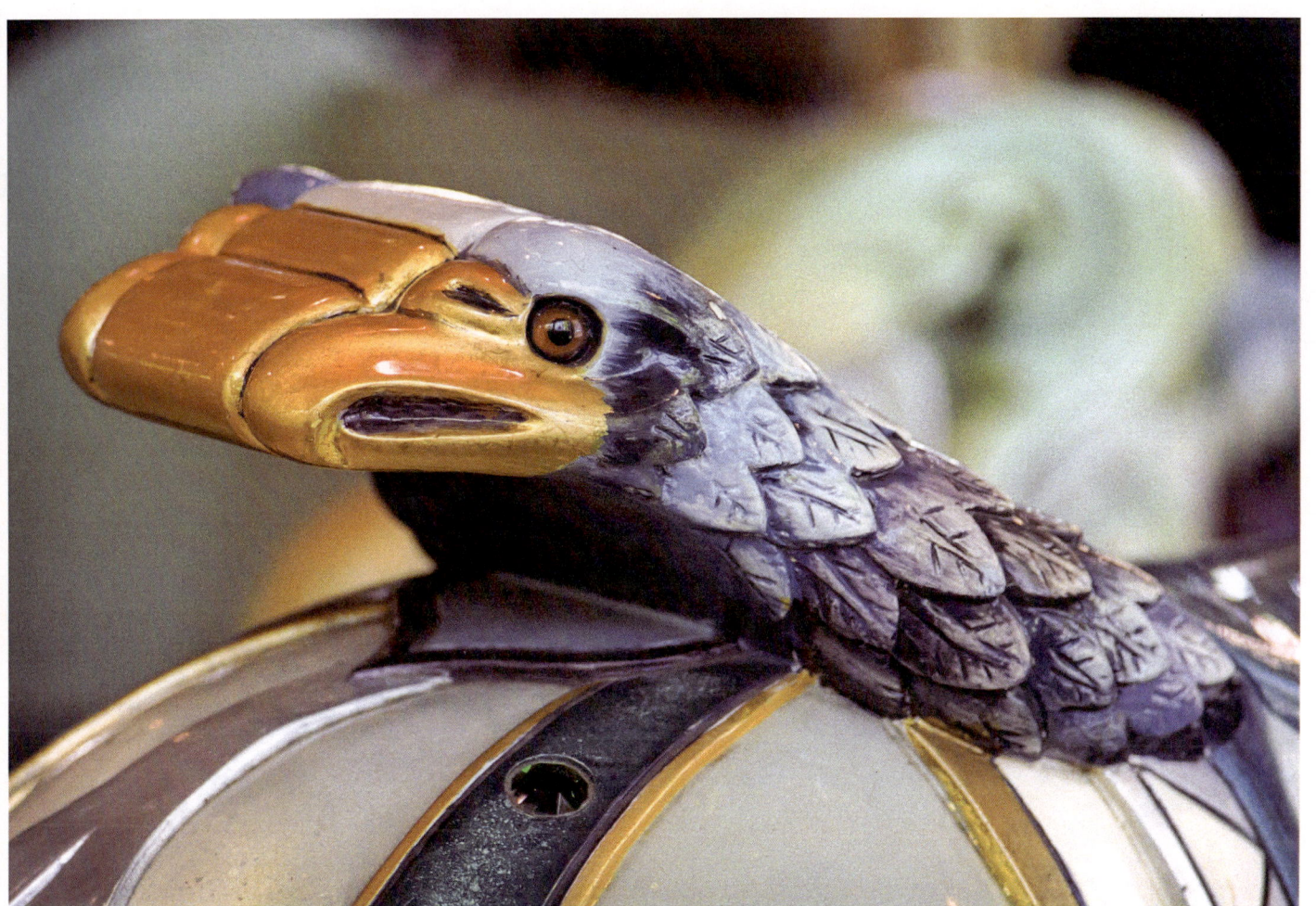

Saddle detail

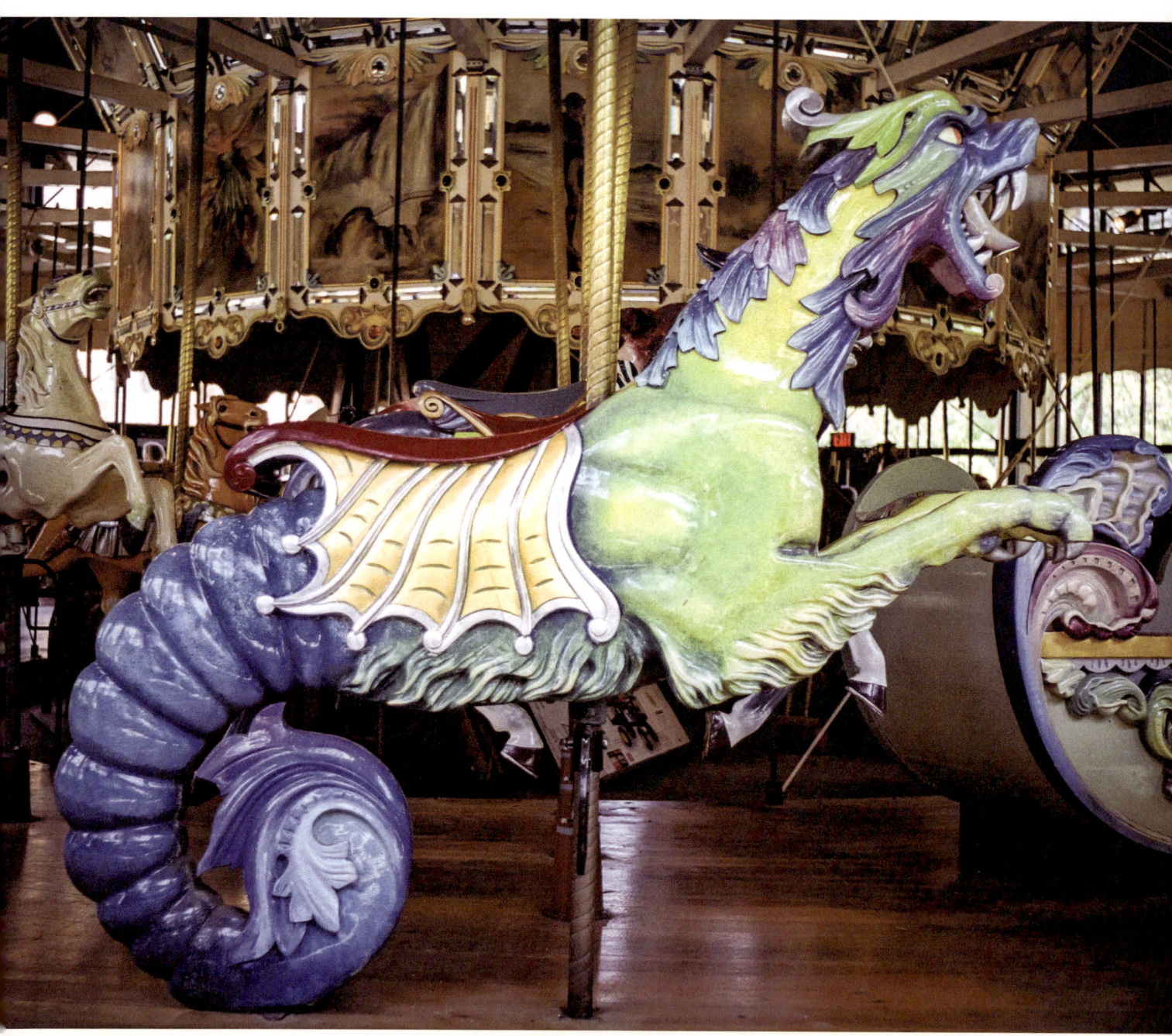

Prancing sea dragon

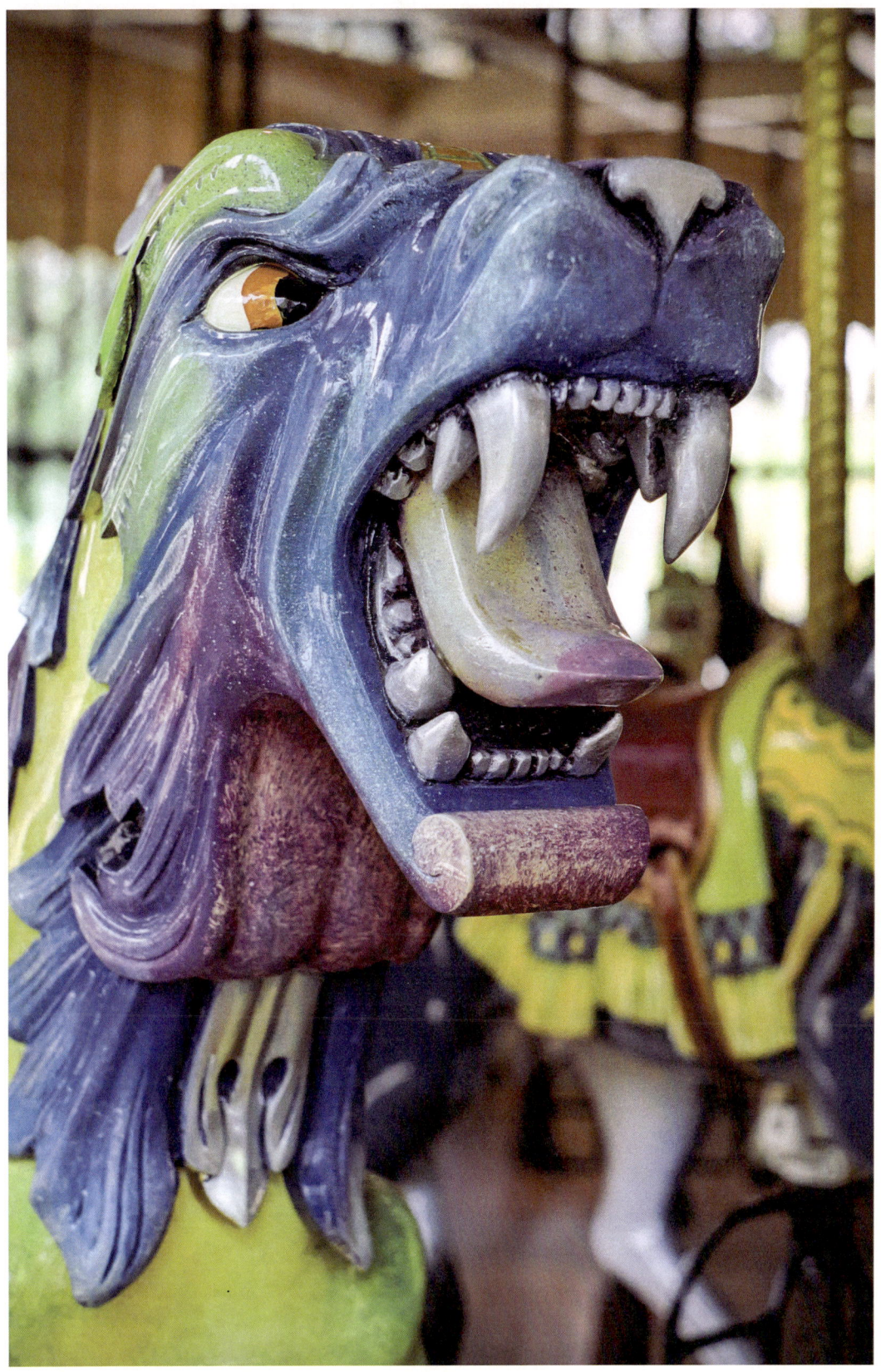

Sea dragon head

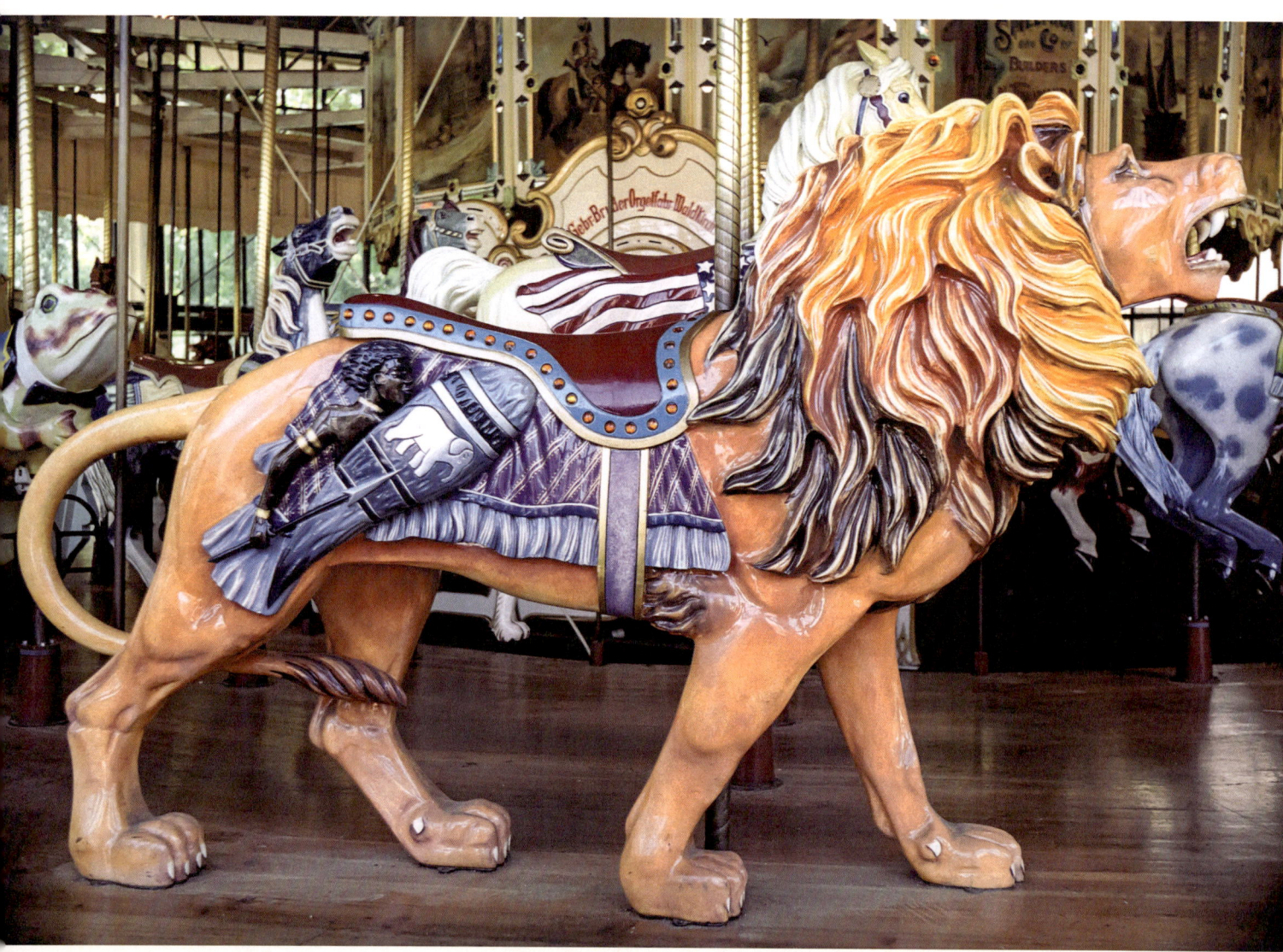

Standing lion

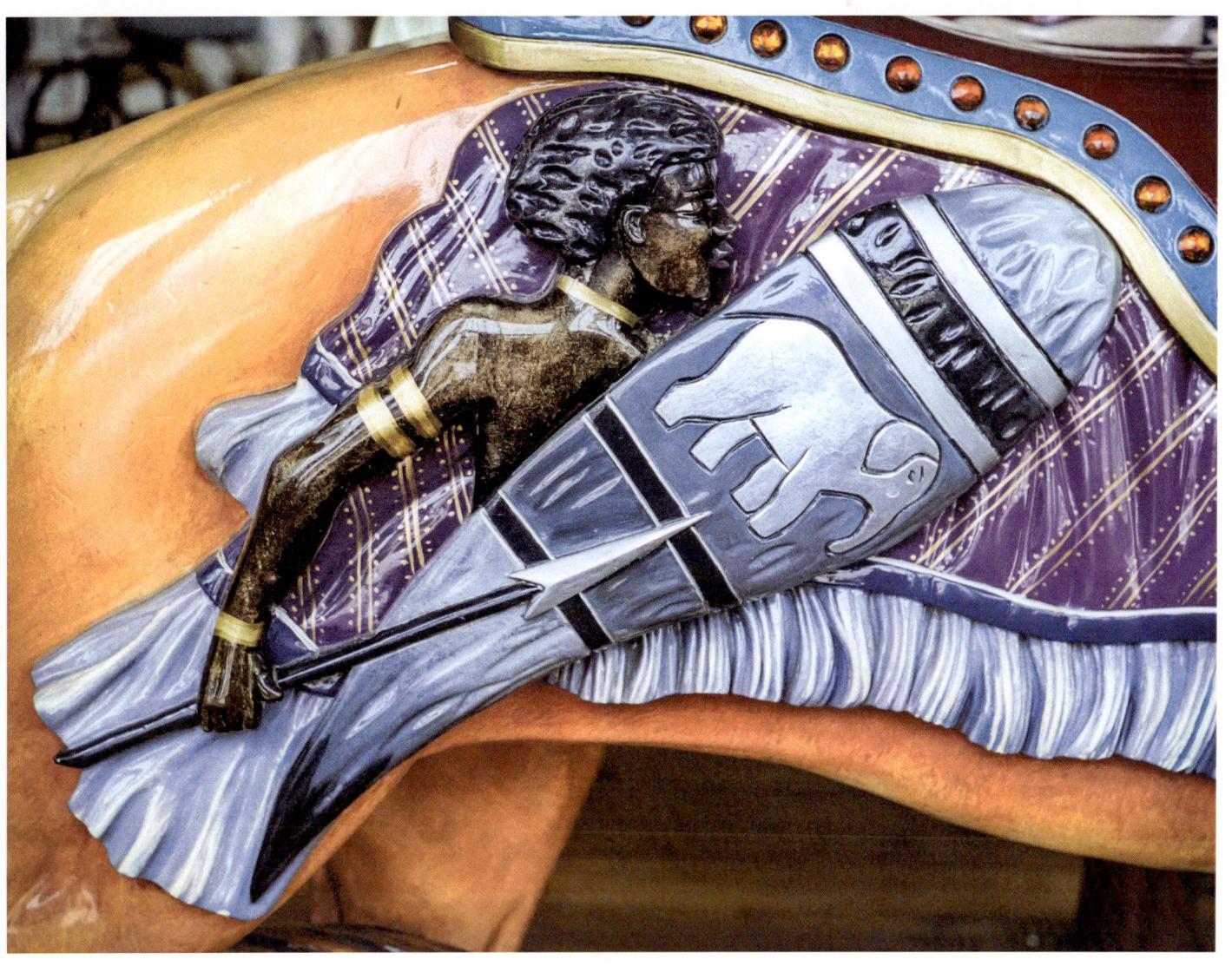

Lion saddle detail

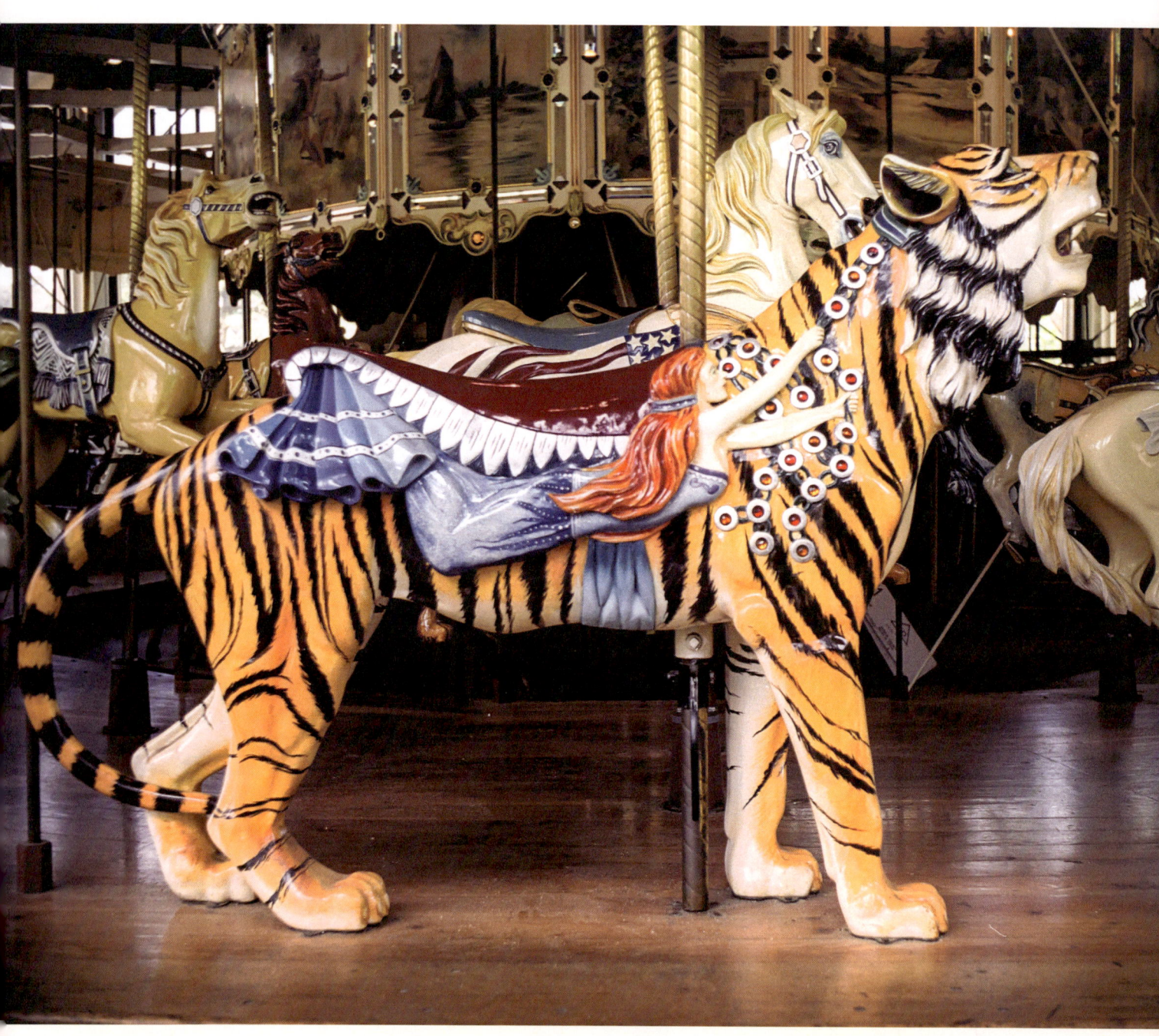

Standing tiger

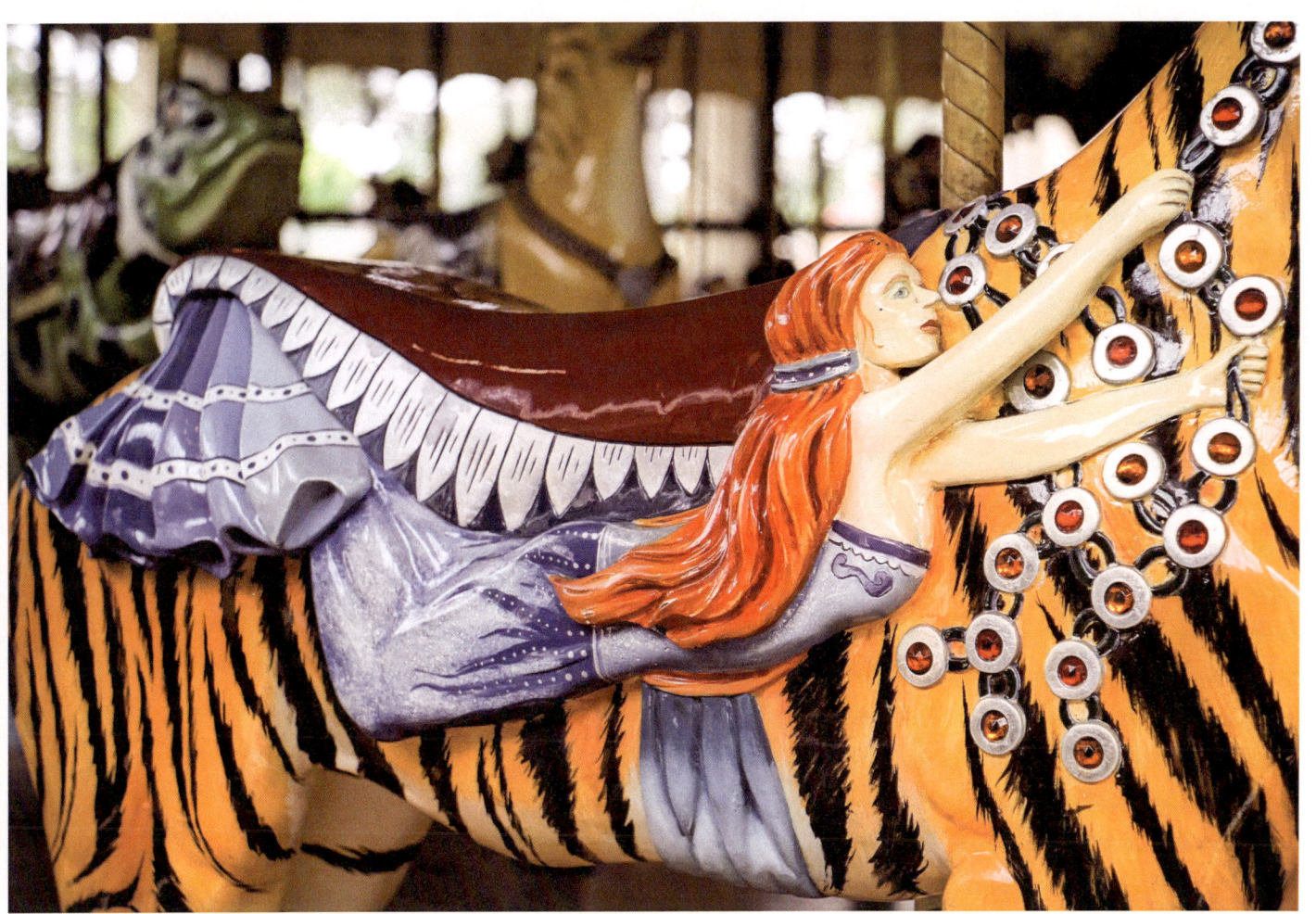

Tiger saddle

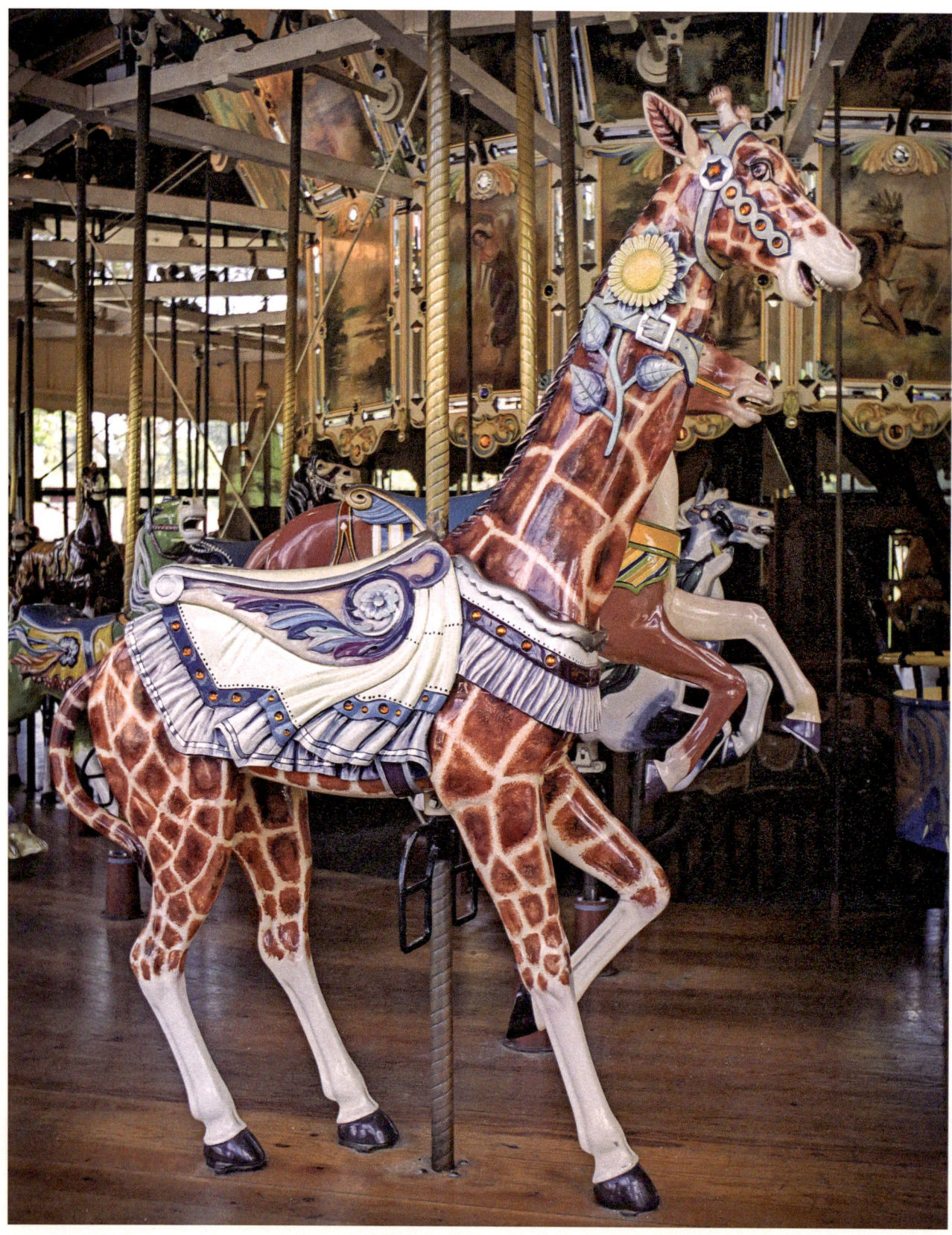

Standing giraffe

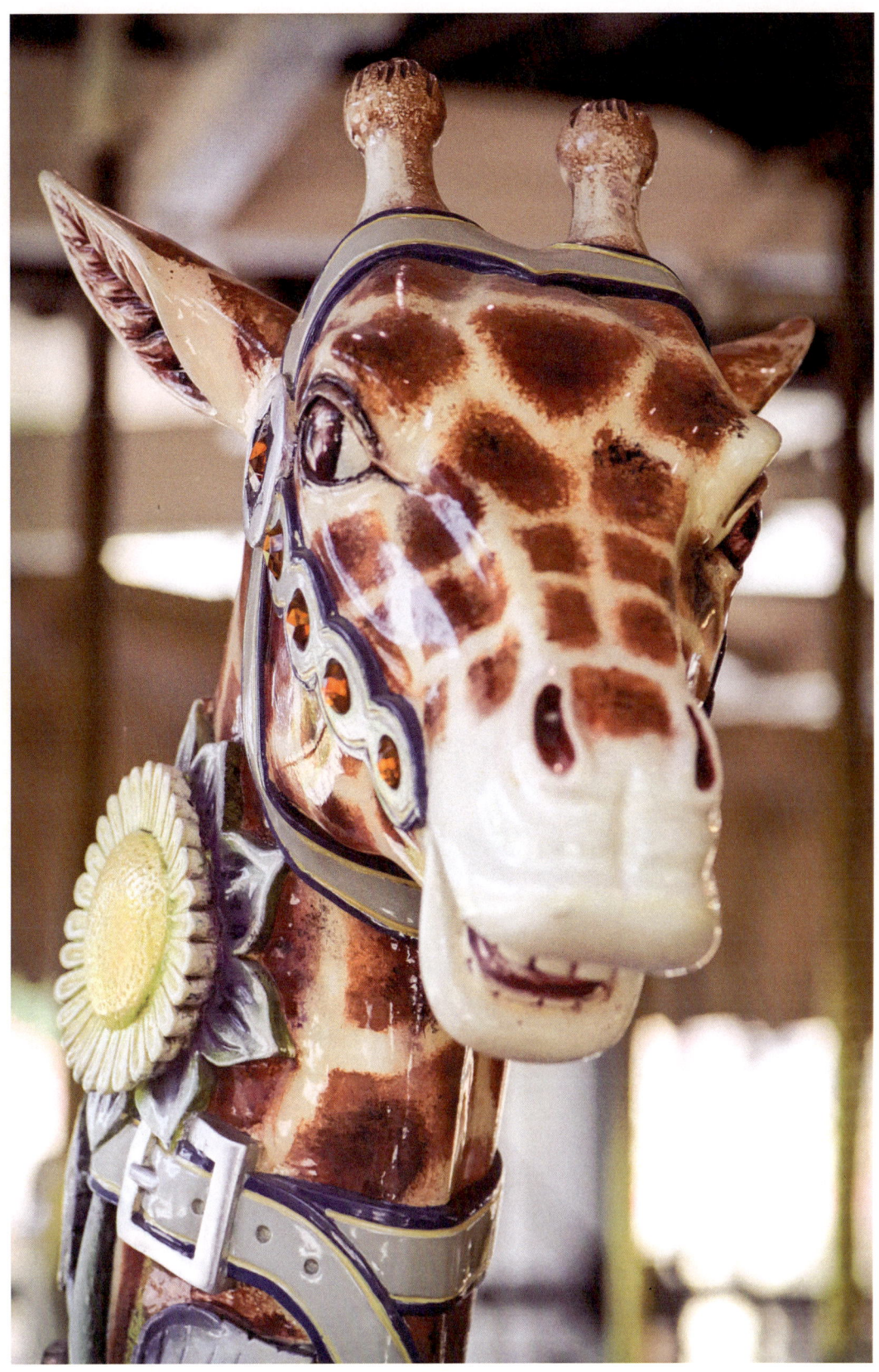

Giraffe head

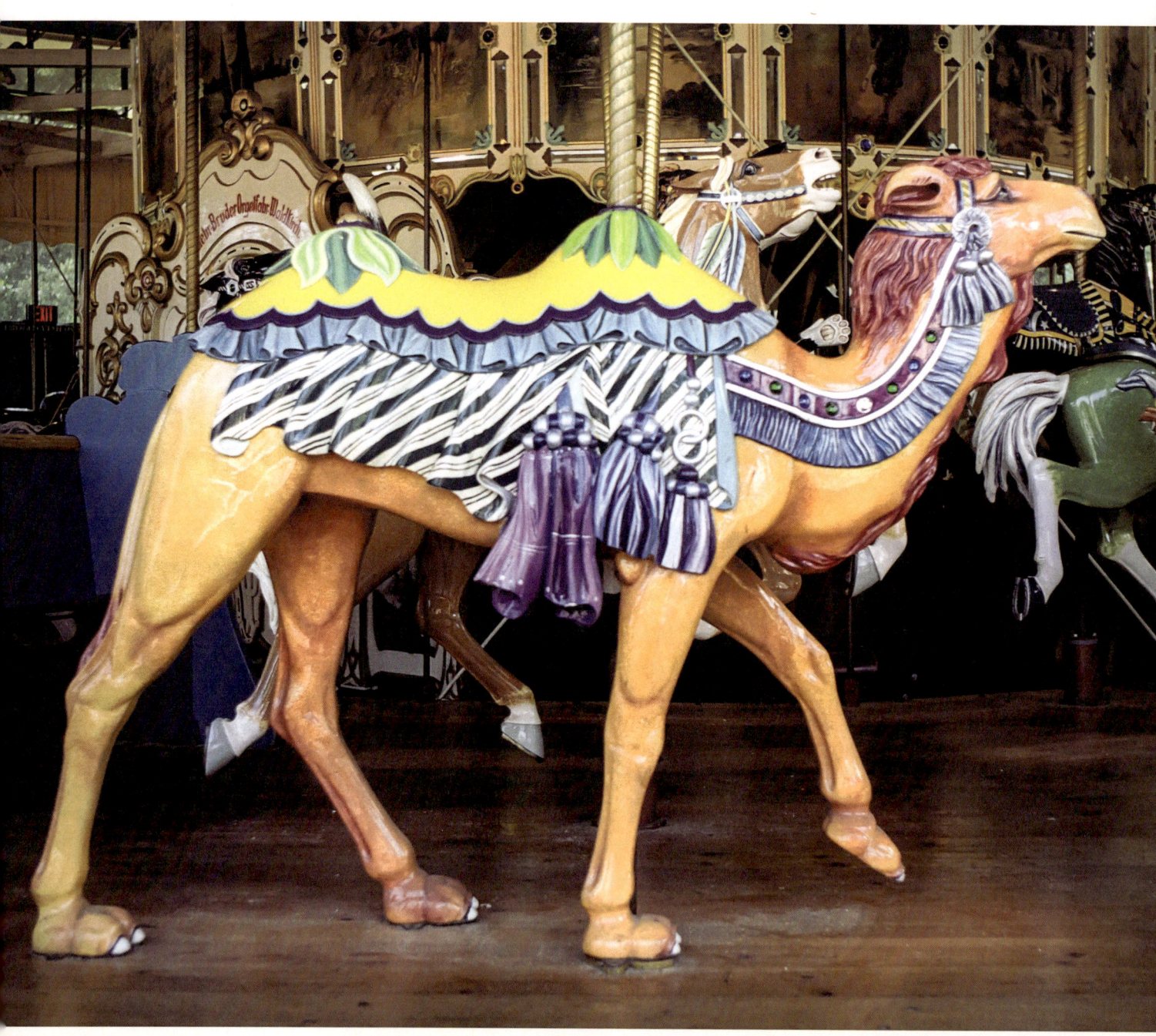

Standing camel

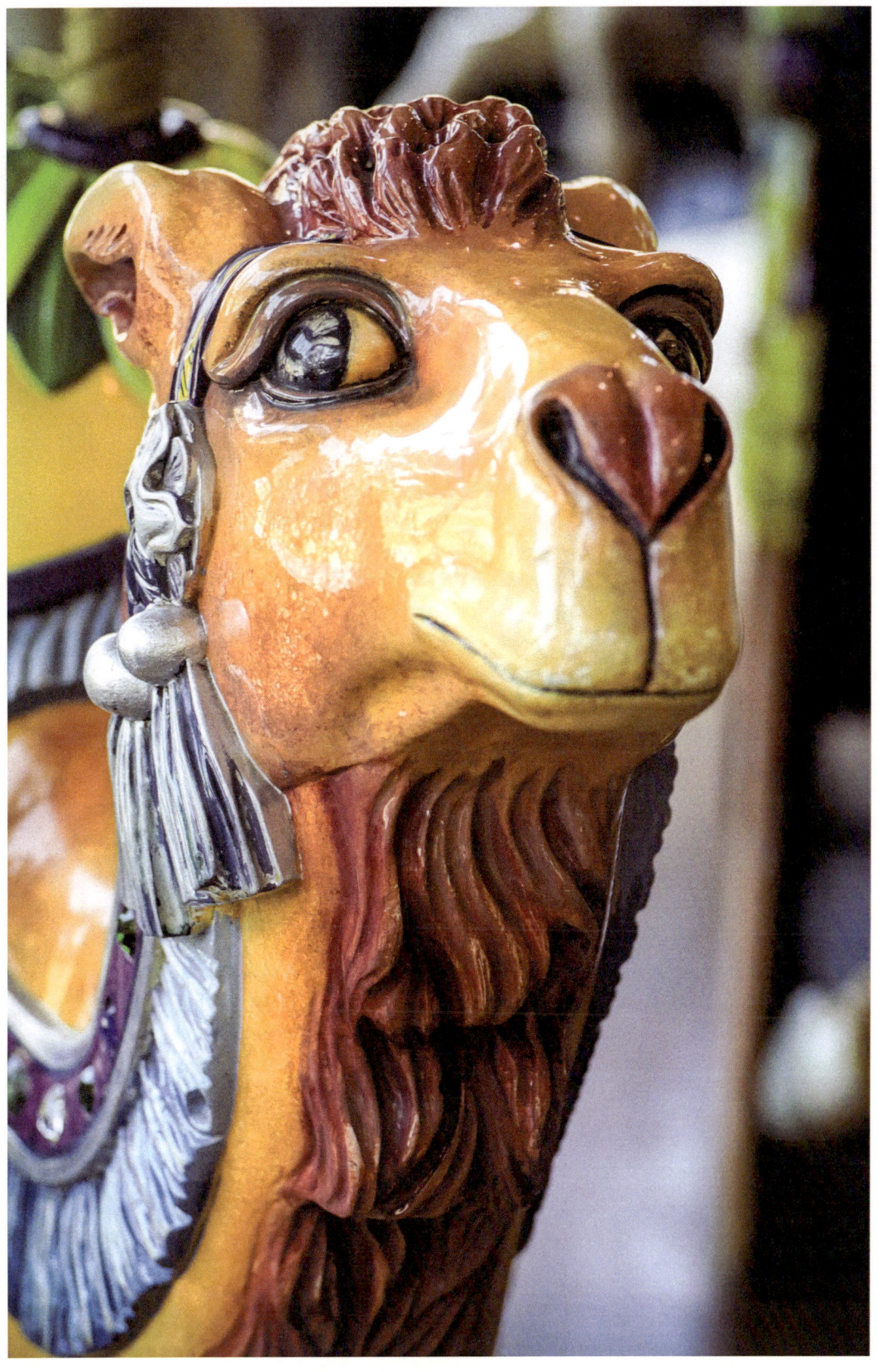

Camel head

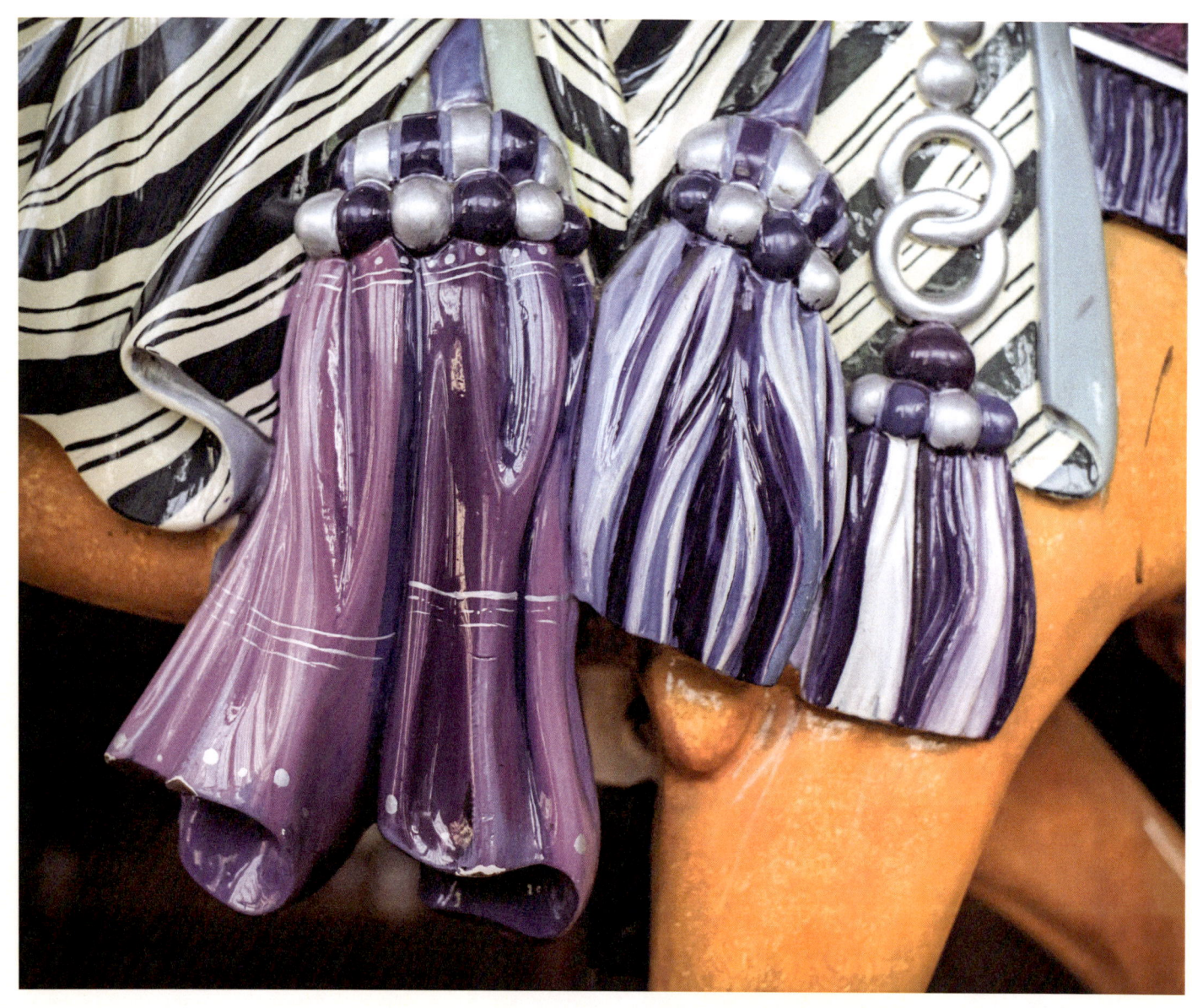

Camel saddle detail

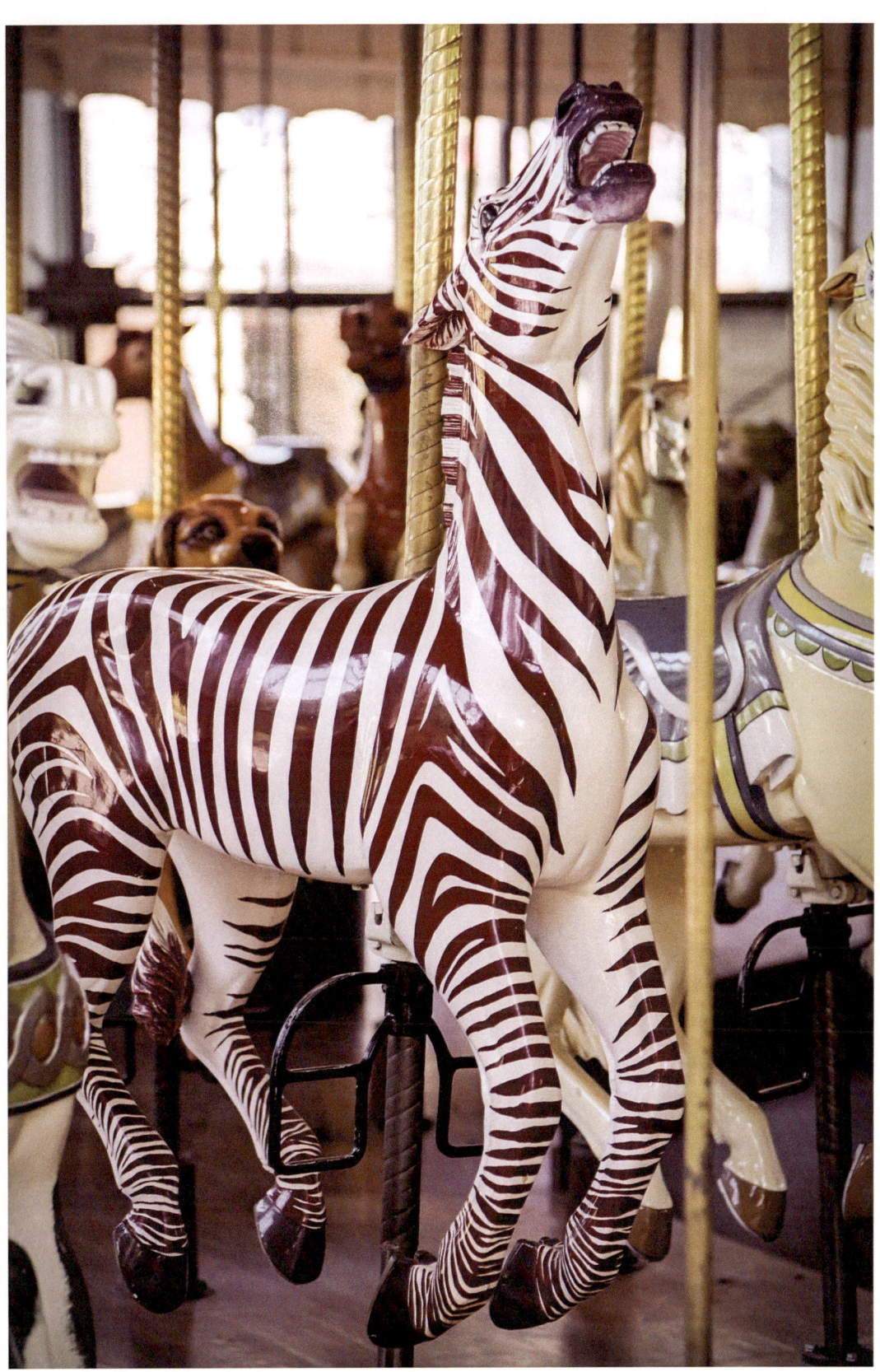

Jumping zebra

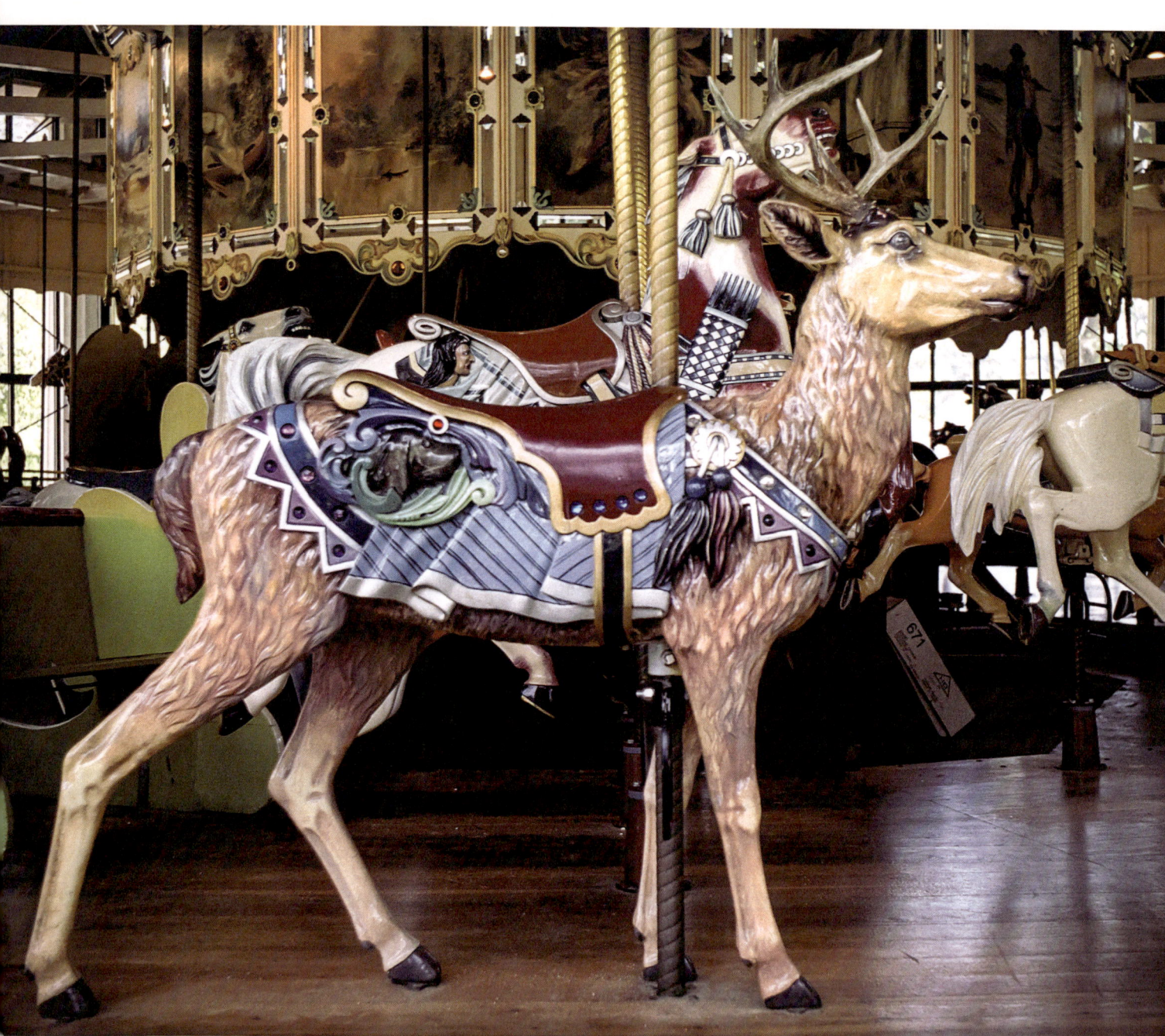

Standing stag

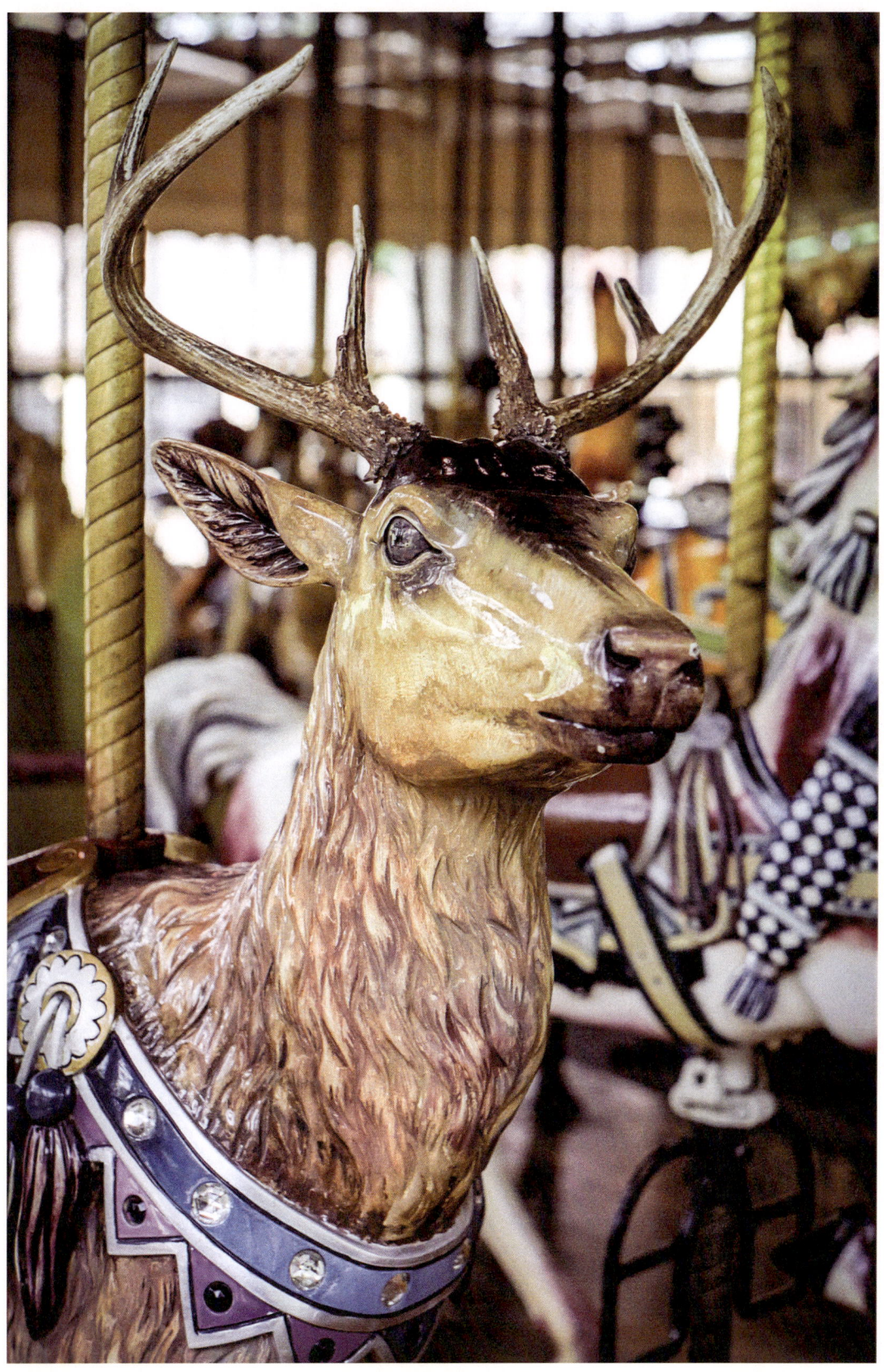

Stag head

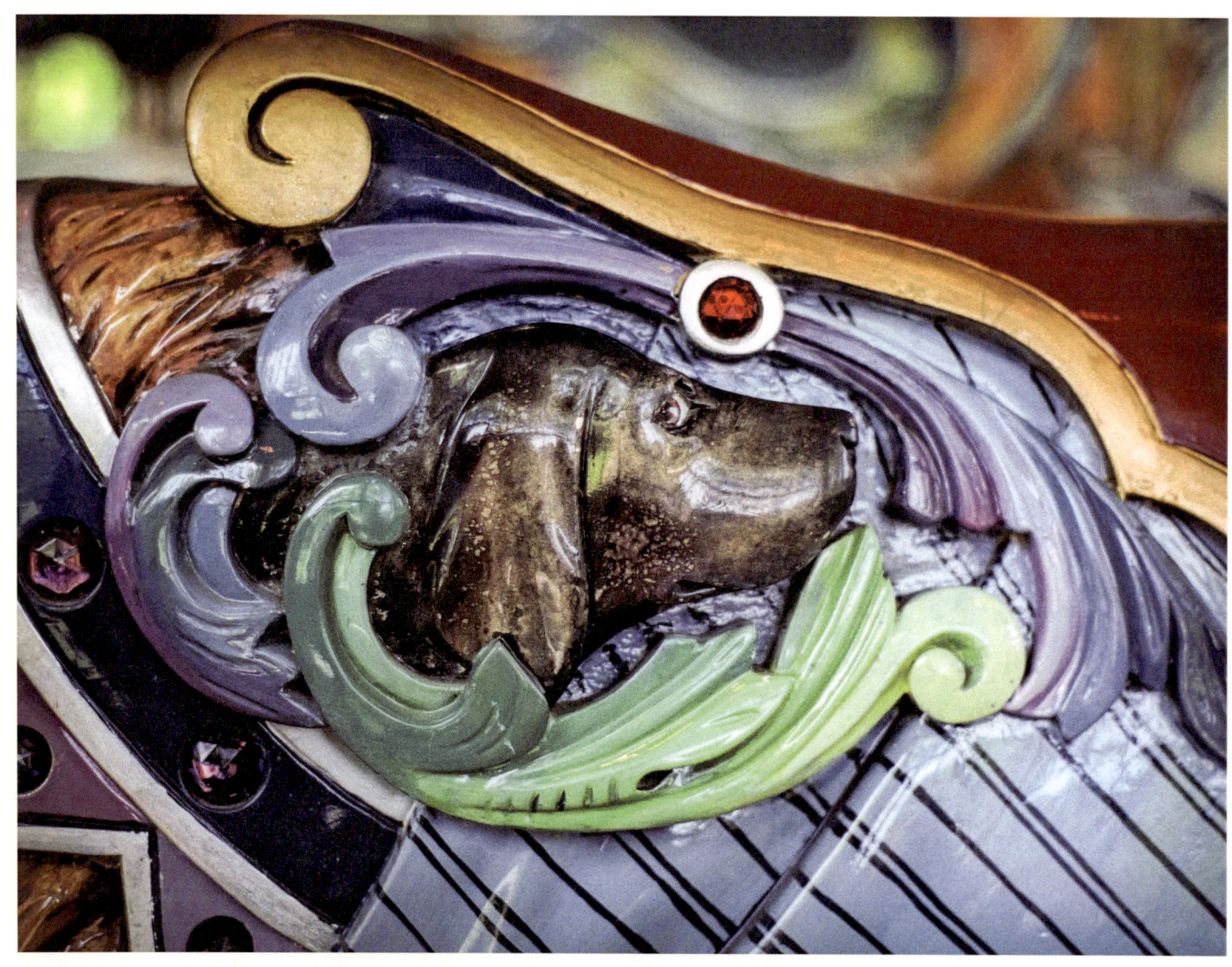

Stag saddle detail

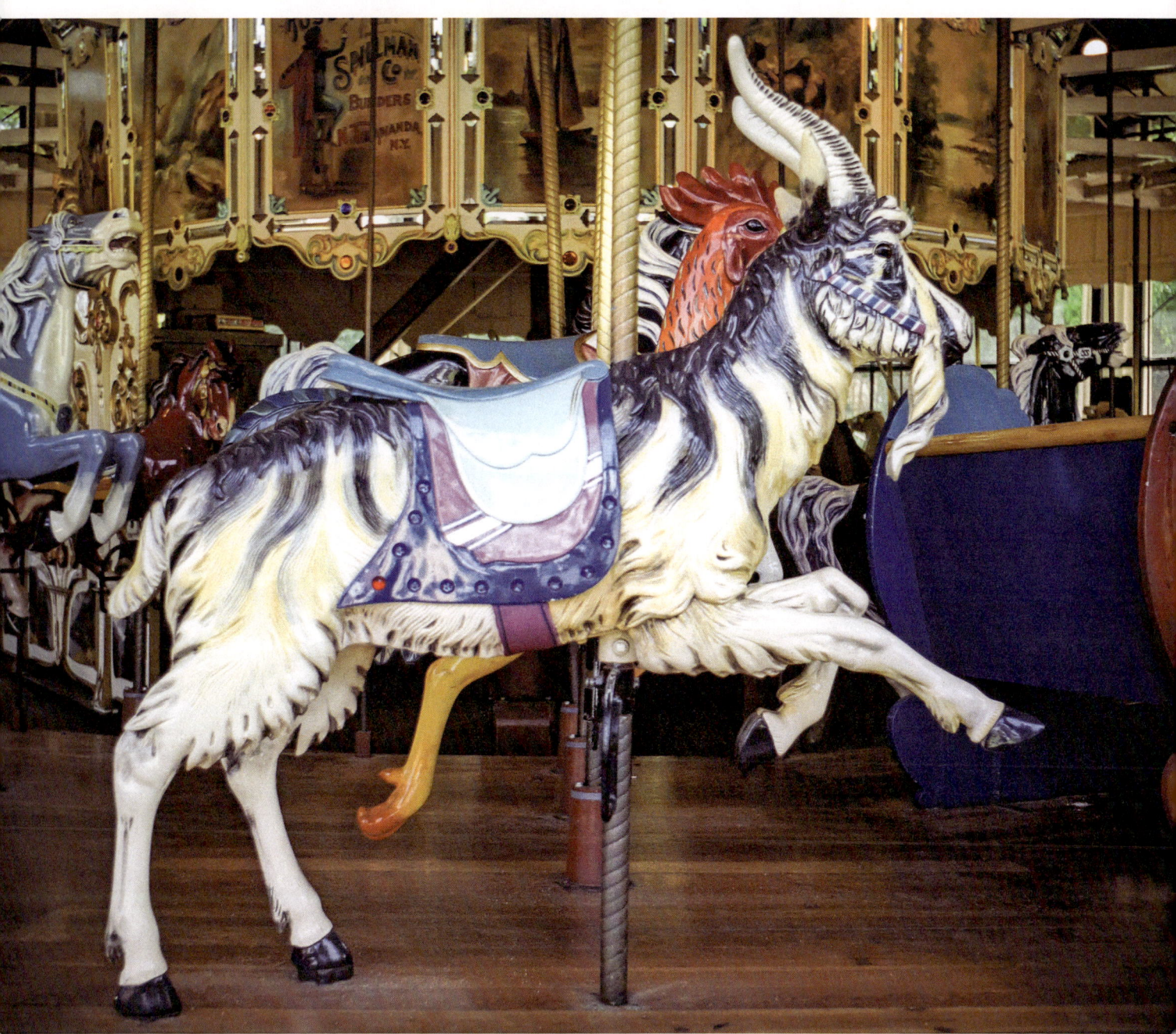

Prancing goat

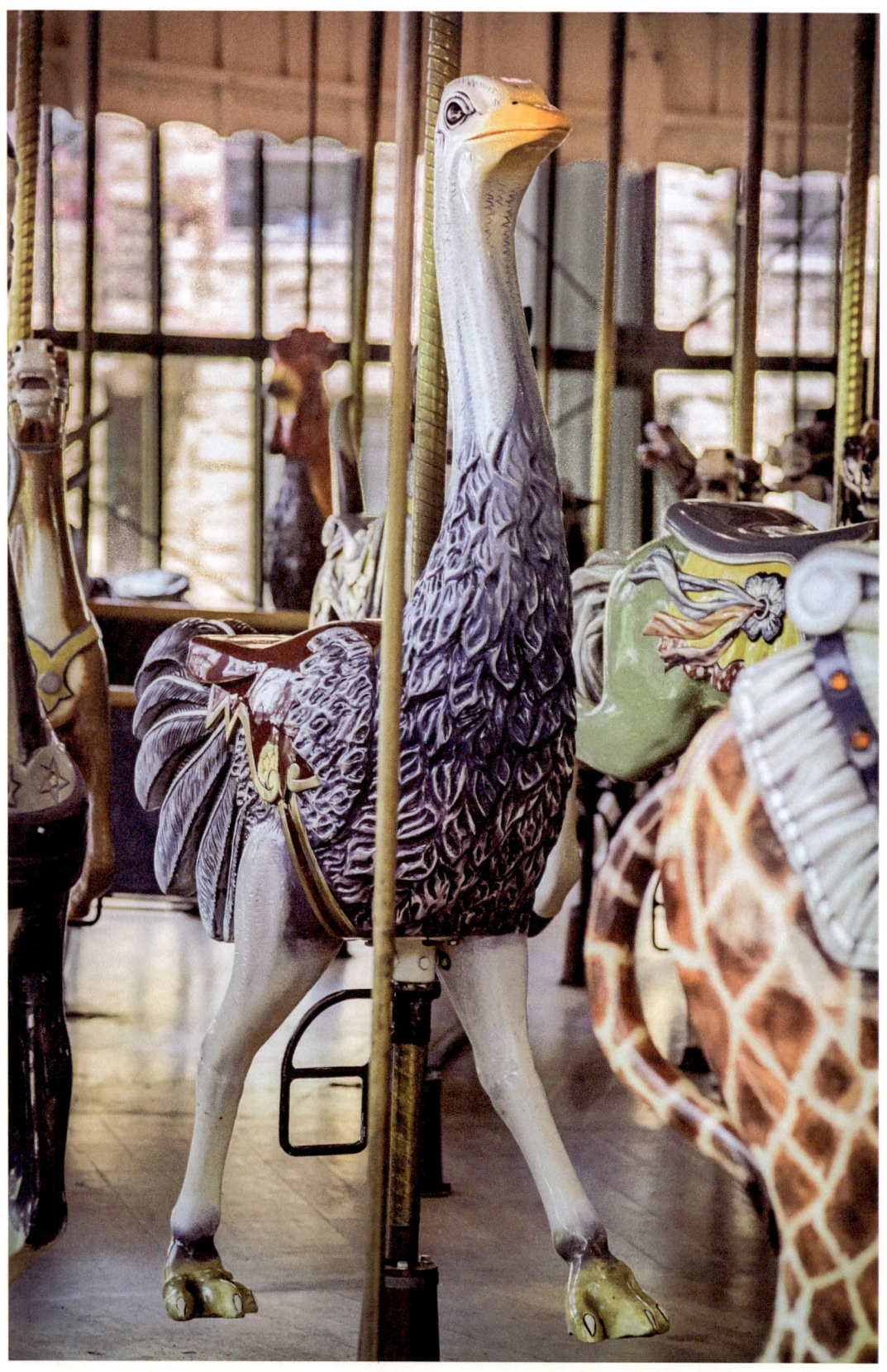

Jumping ostrich

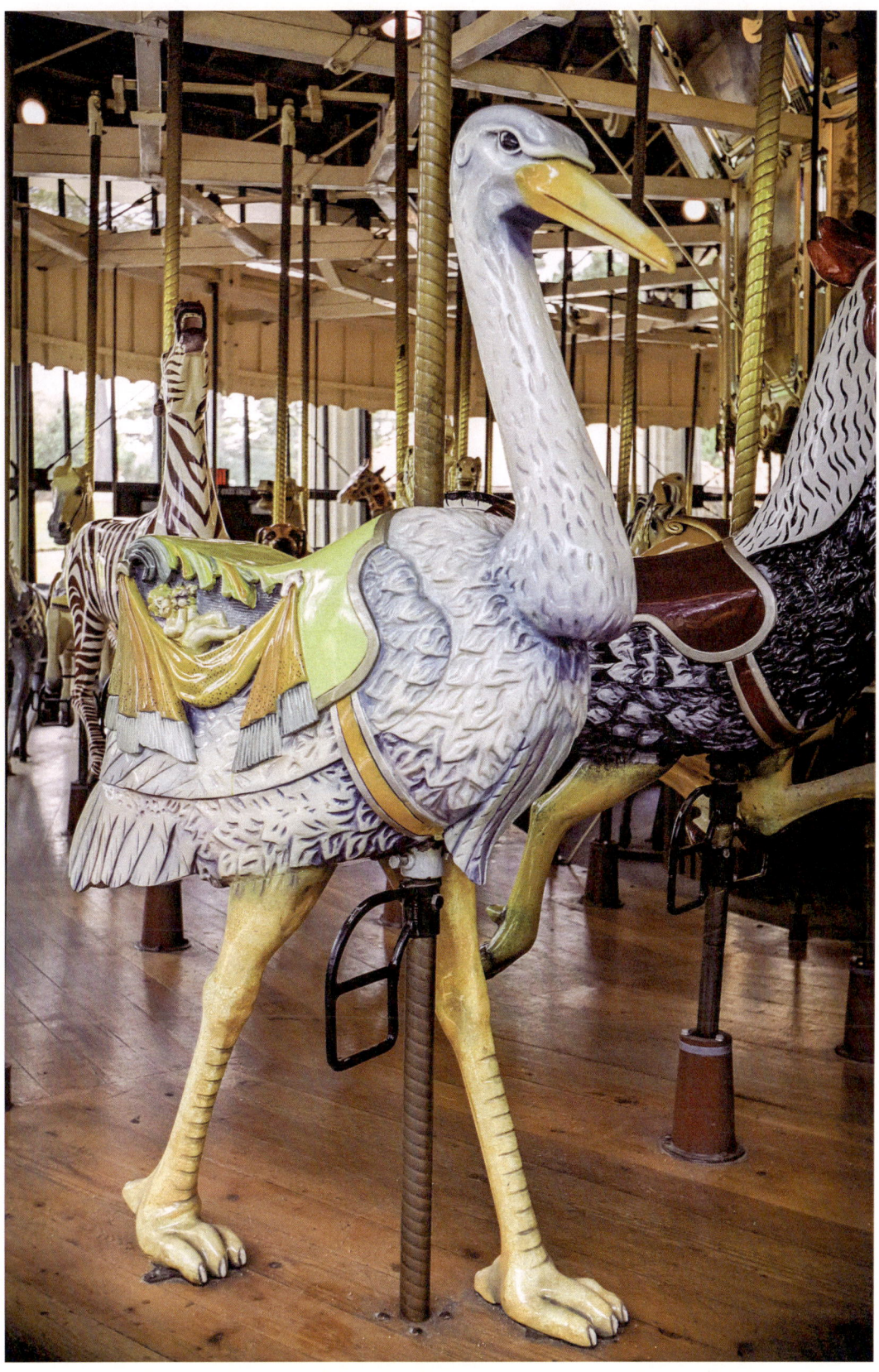

Standing stork

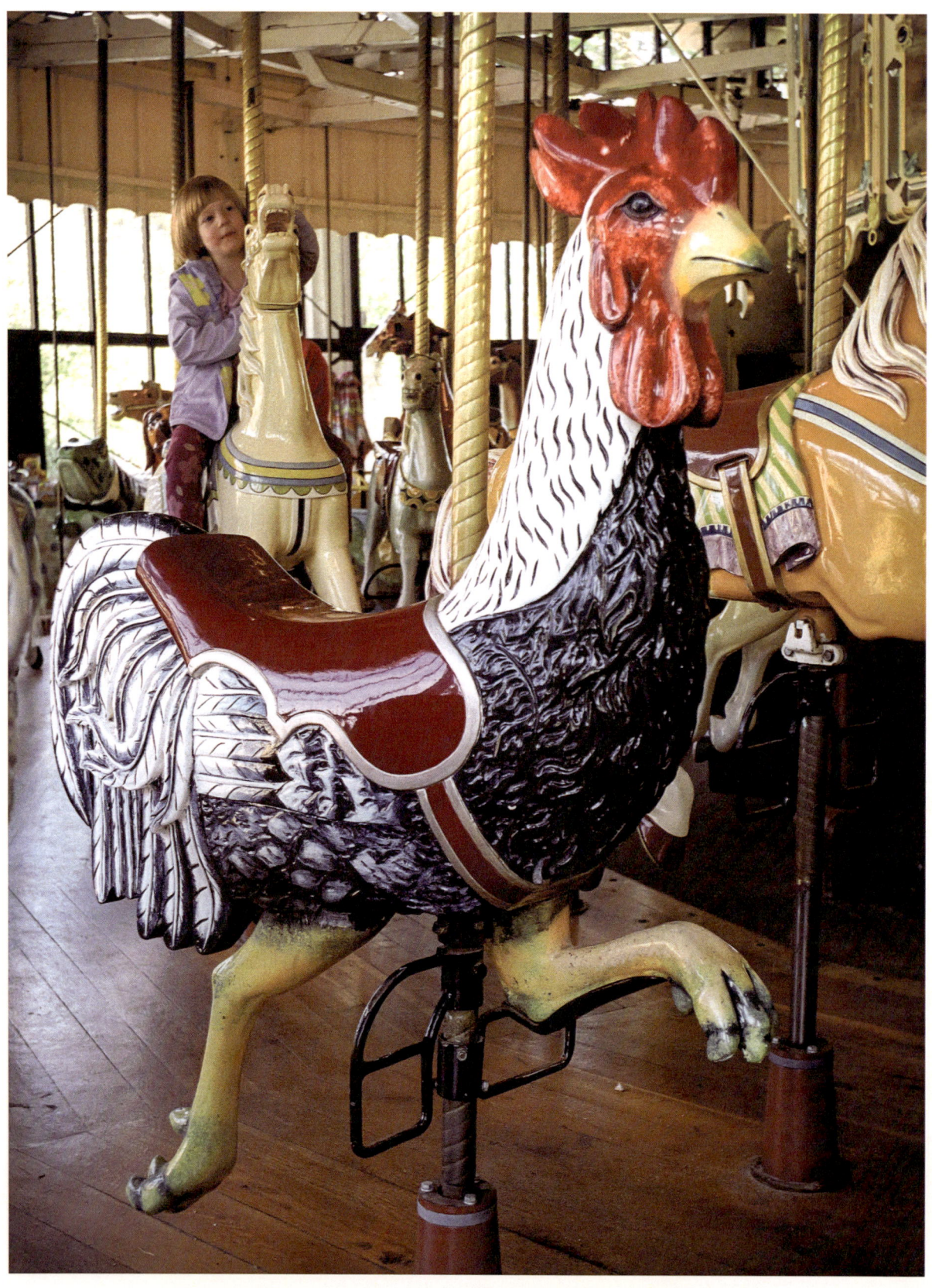

Jumping rooster

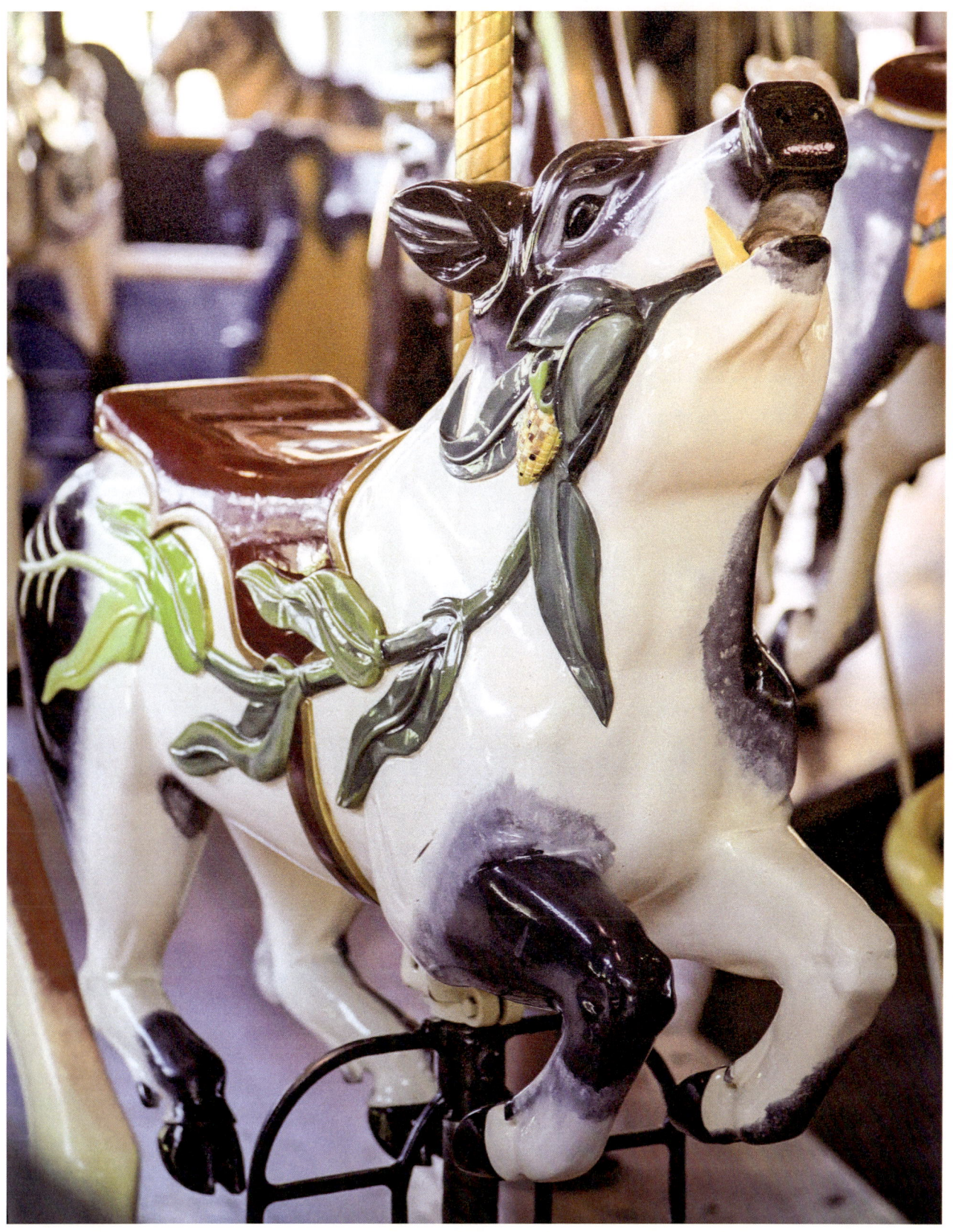

Jumping pig

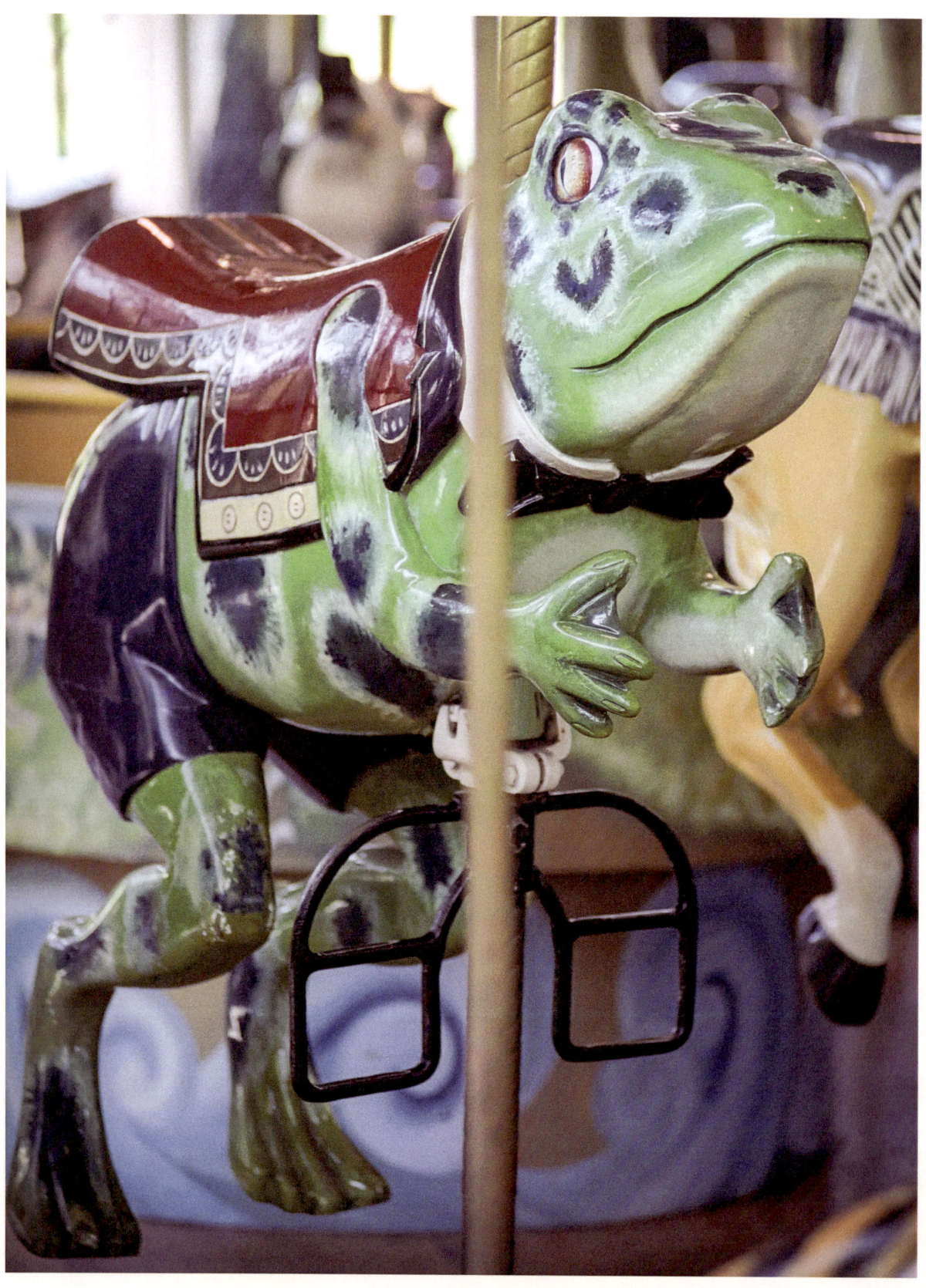

Jumping hop toad

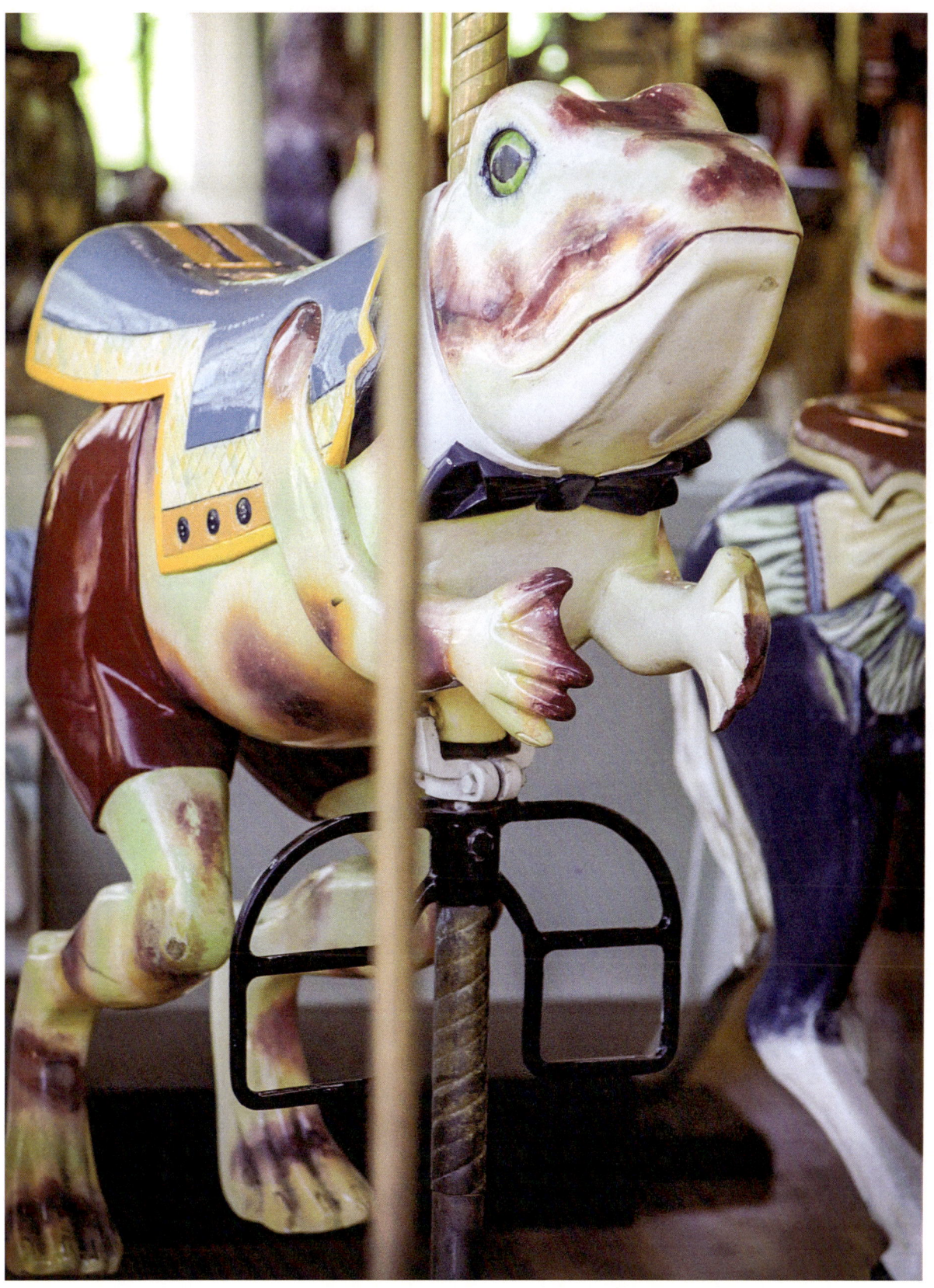

Jumping hop toad

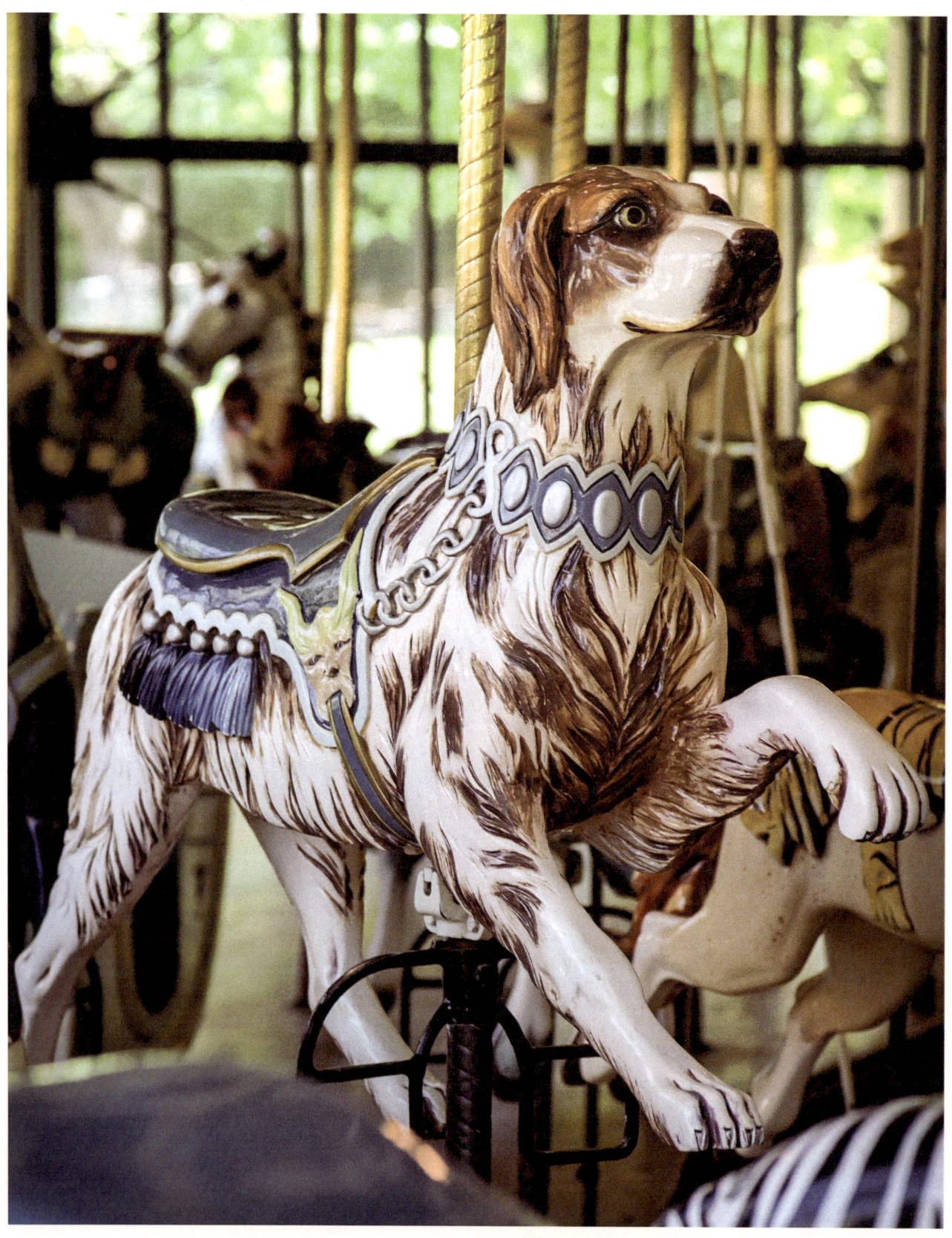

Jumping dog

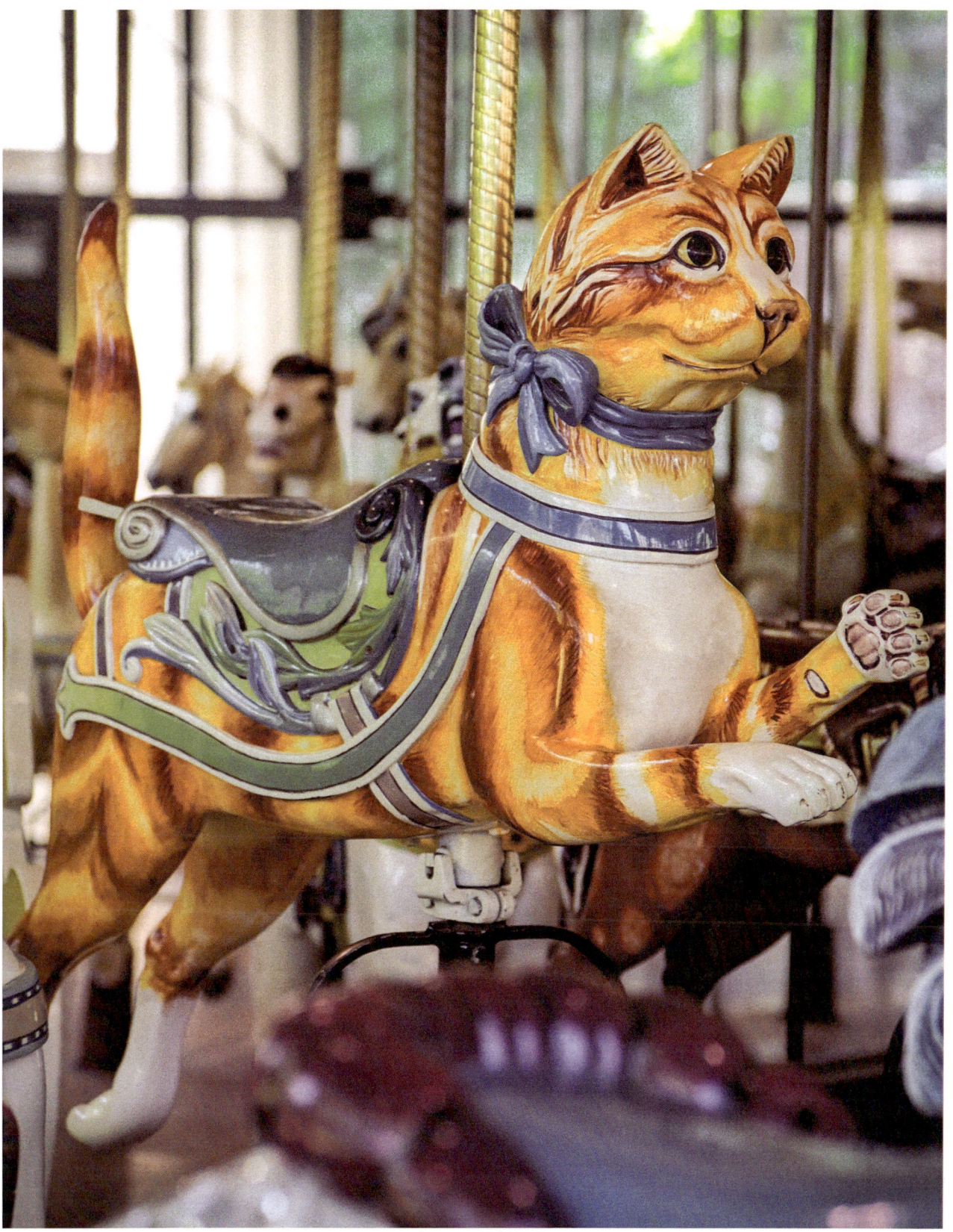

Jumping cat

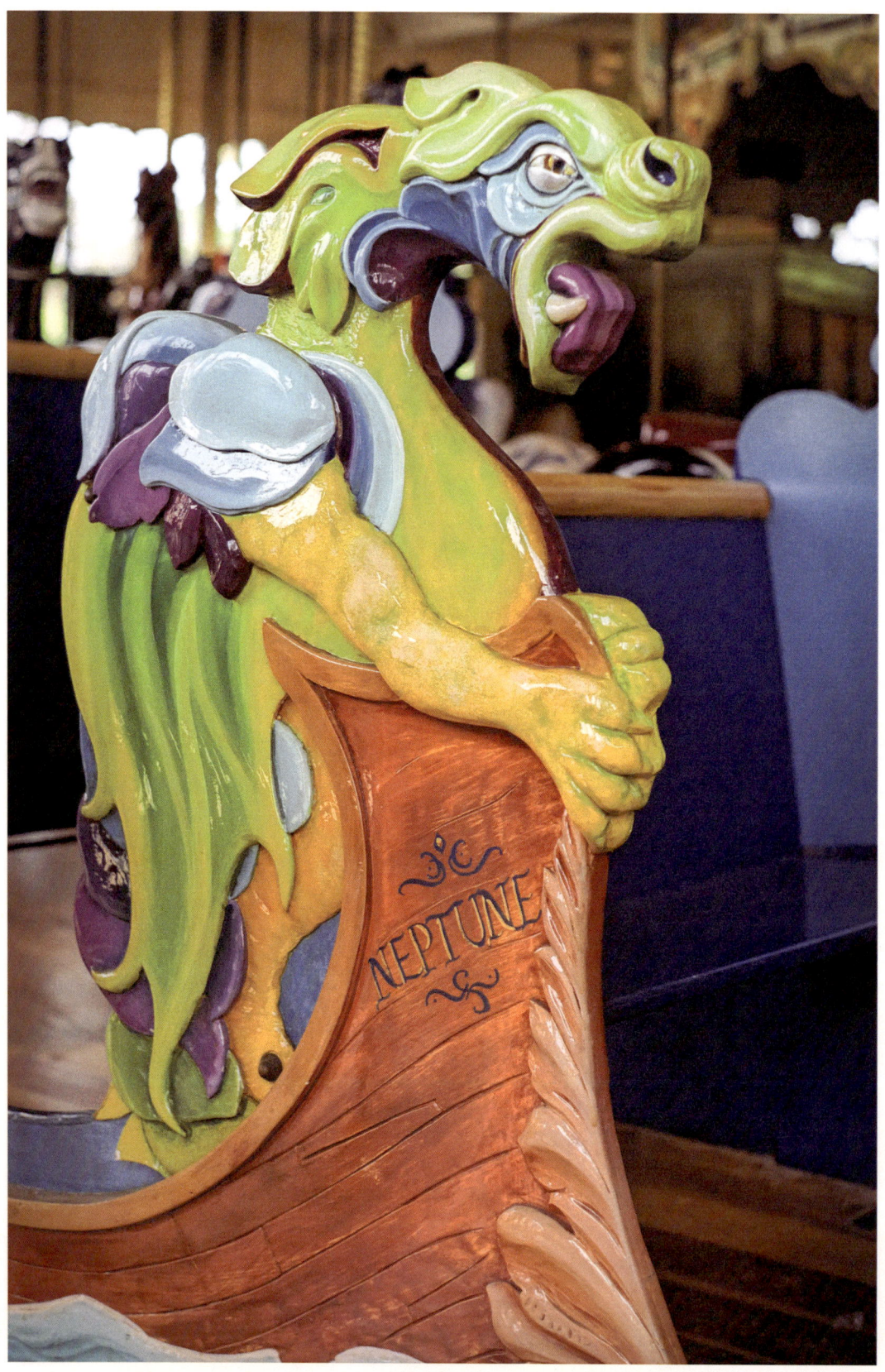

Chariot detail

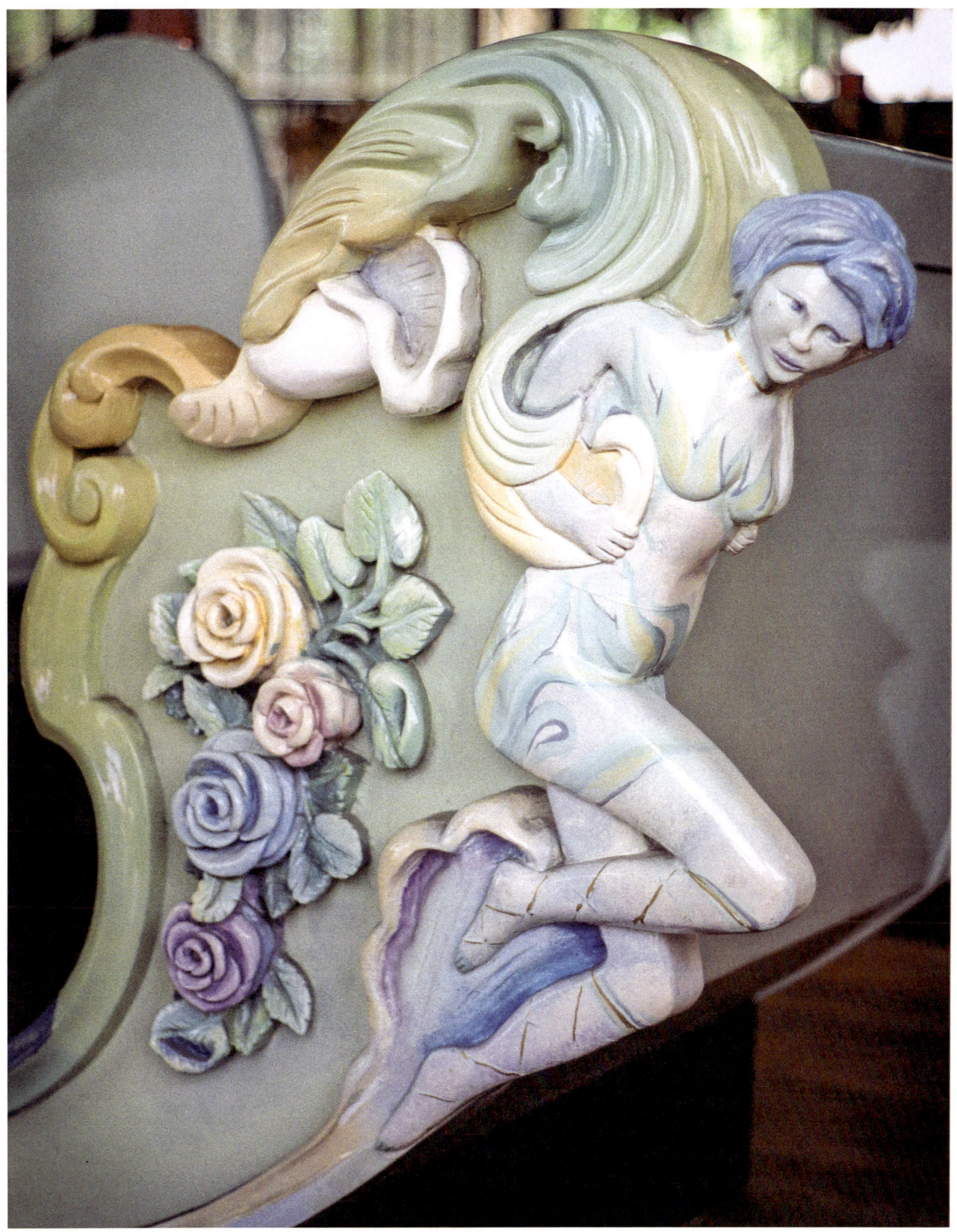

Chariot detail

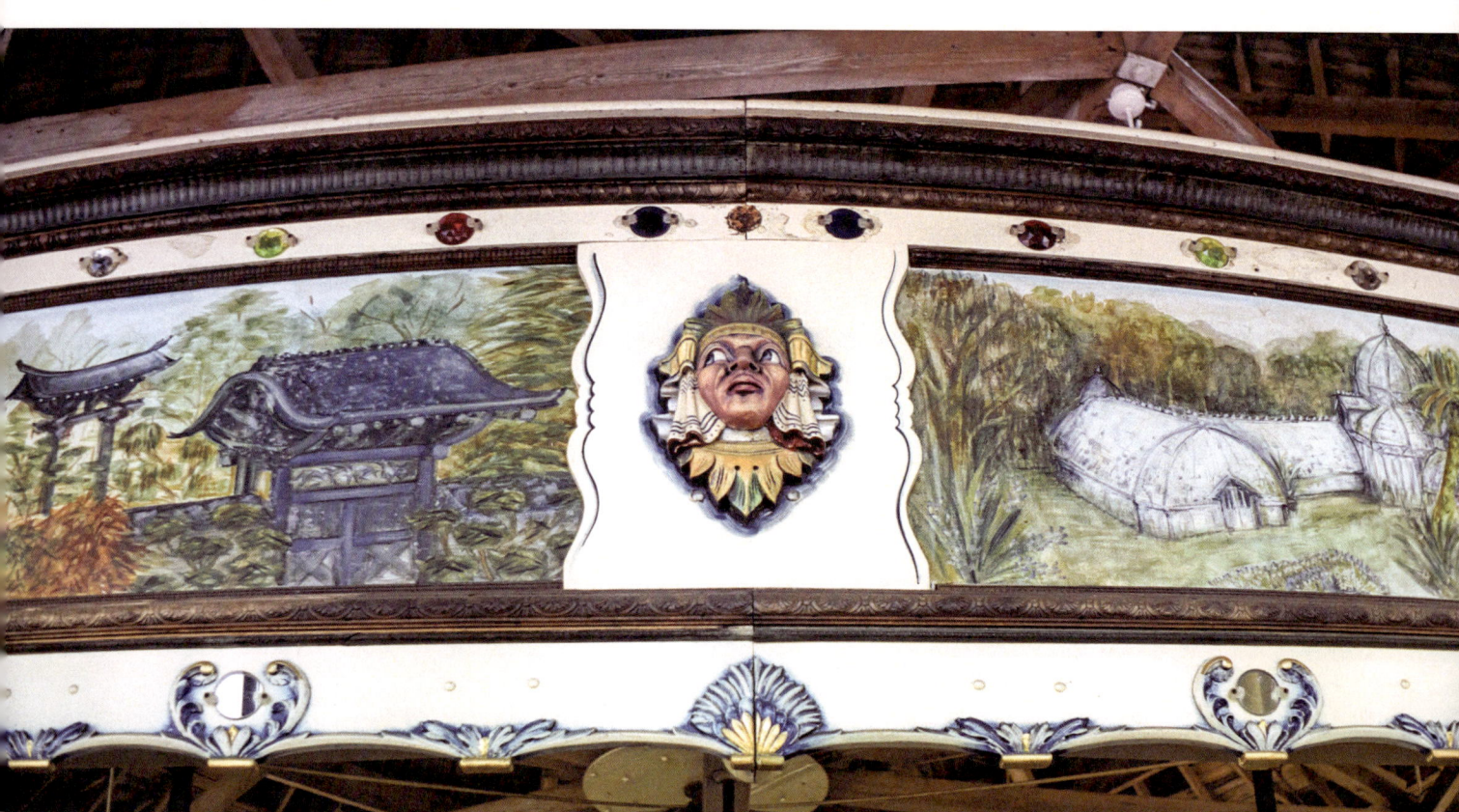

Rounding boards and shield

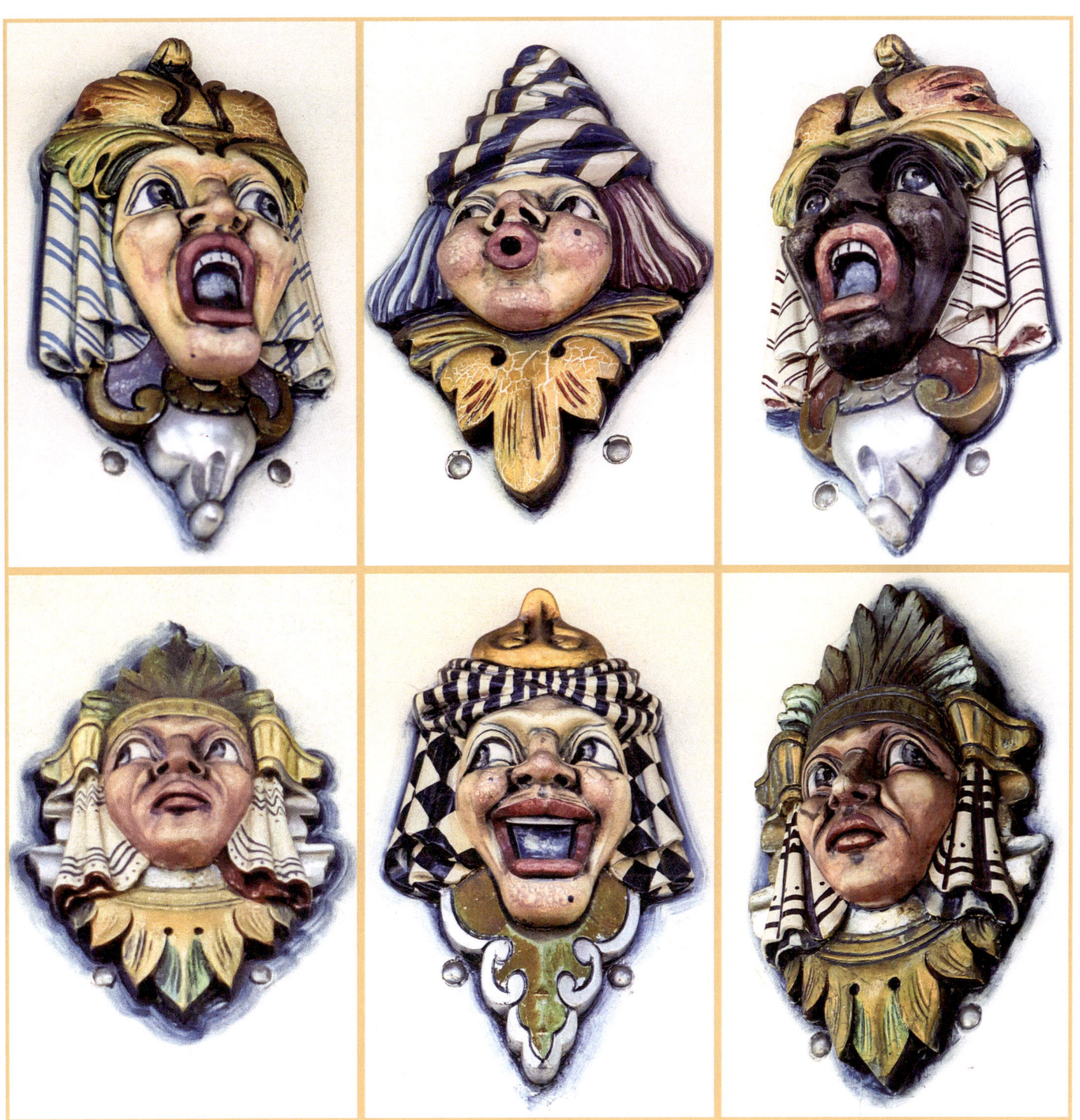

Shield details

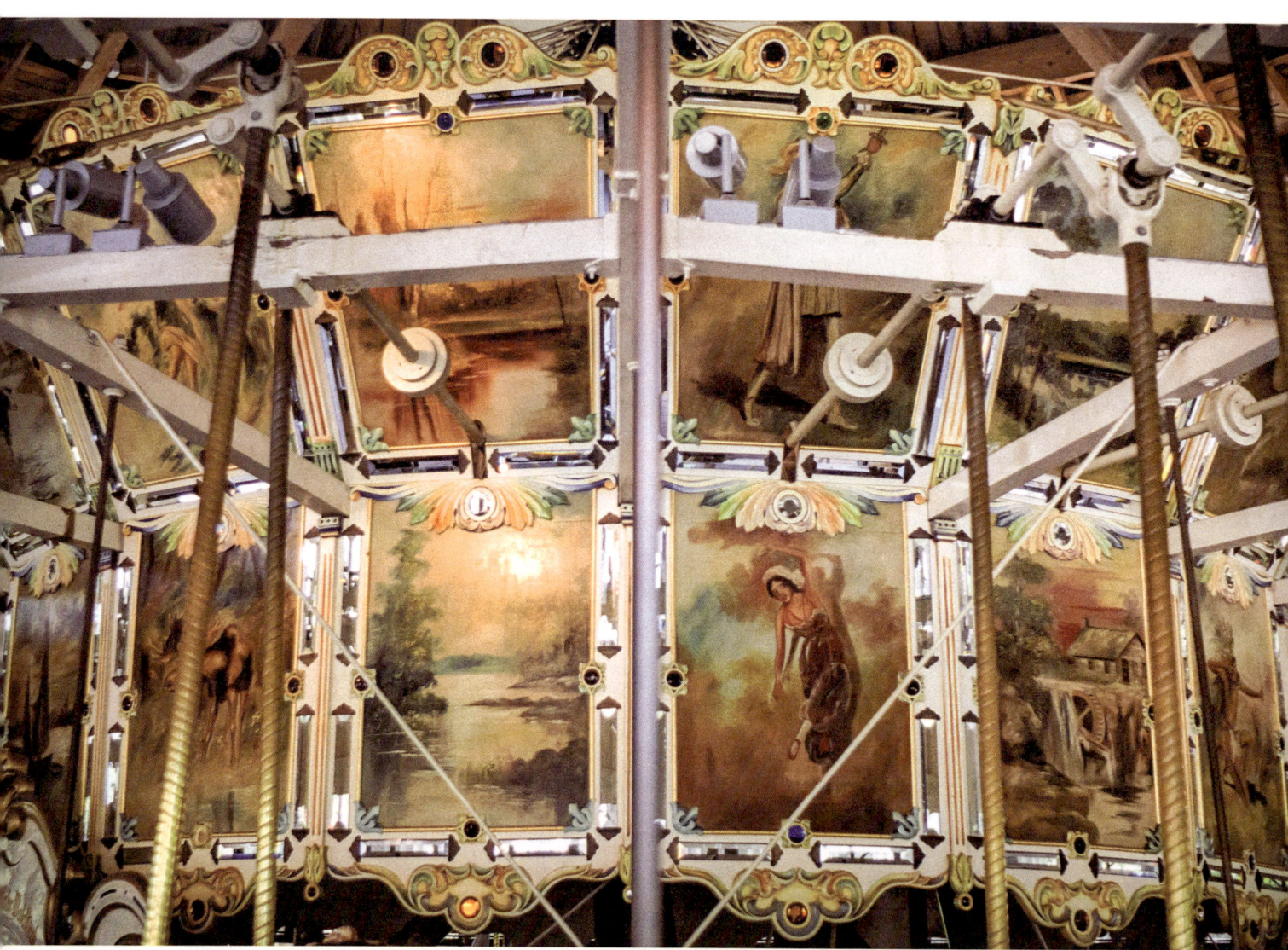

Scenery panels

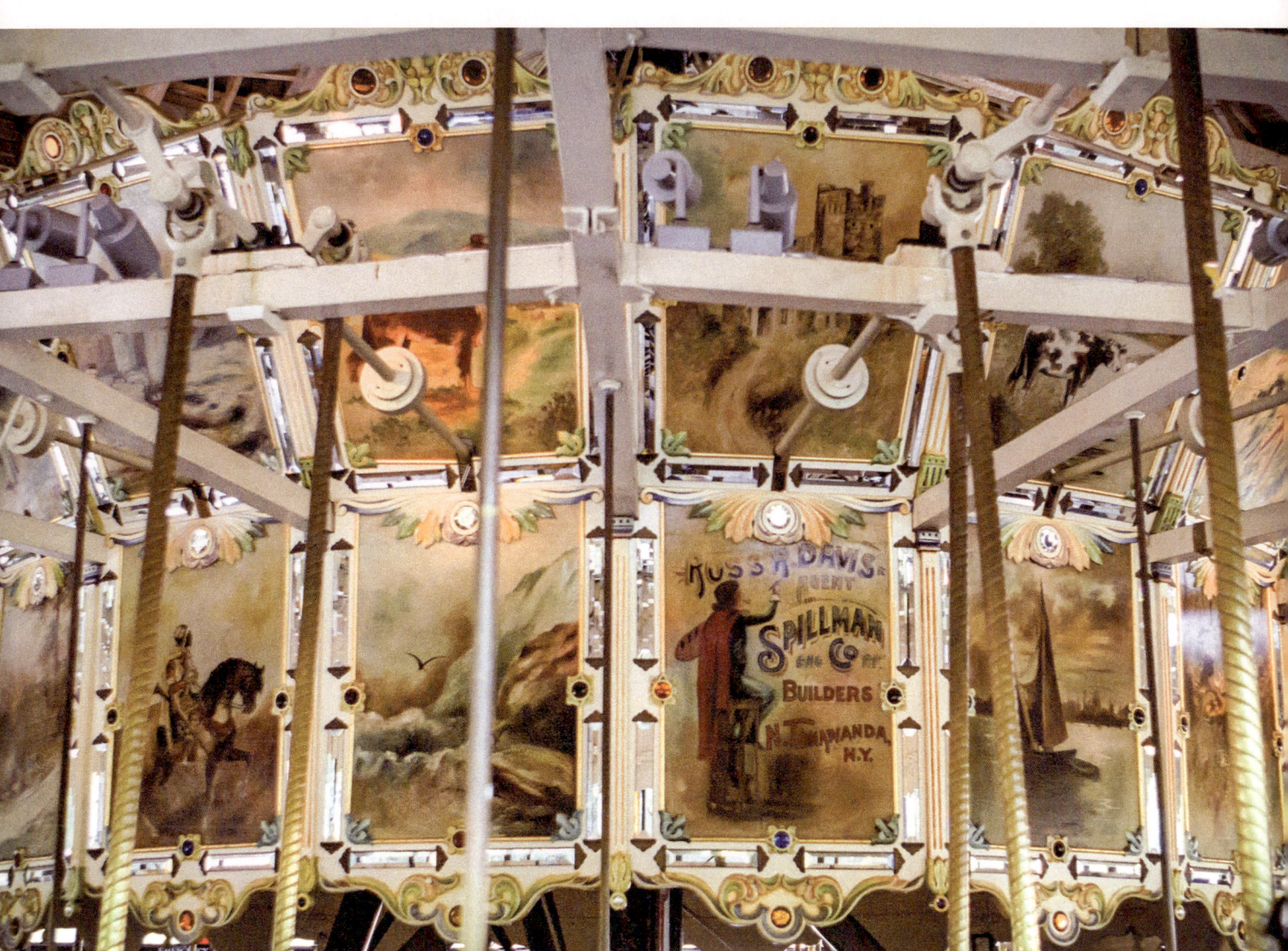

Scenery panels

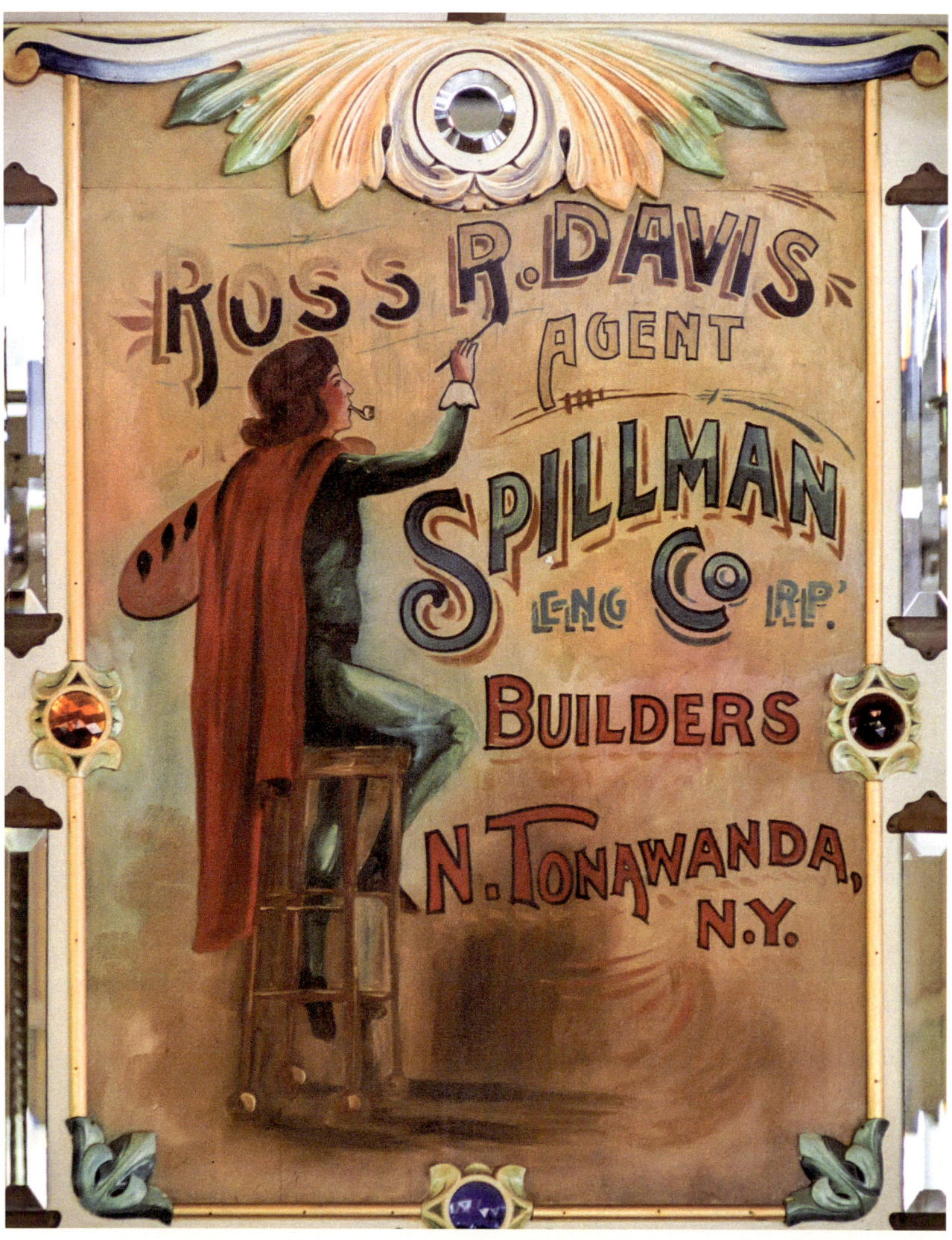

Scenery panel

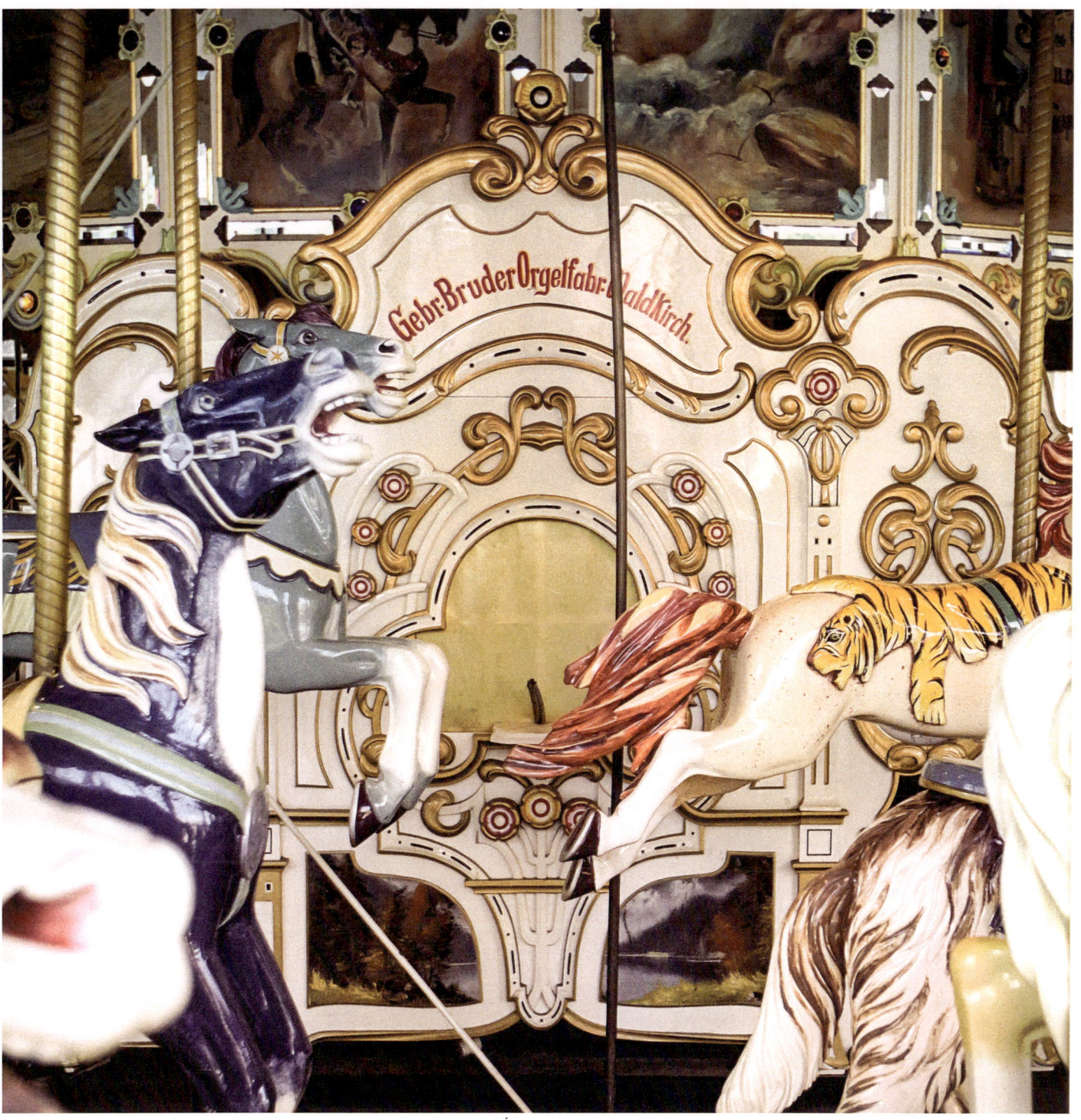

Band organ (Gebrüder Bruder)

Also for carousel lovers . . .

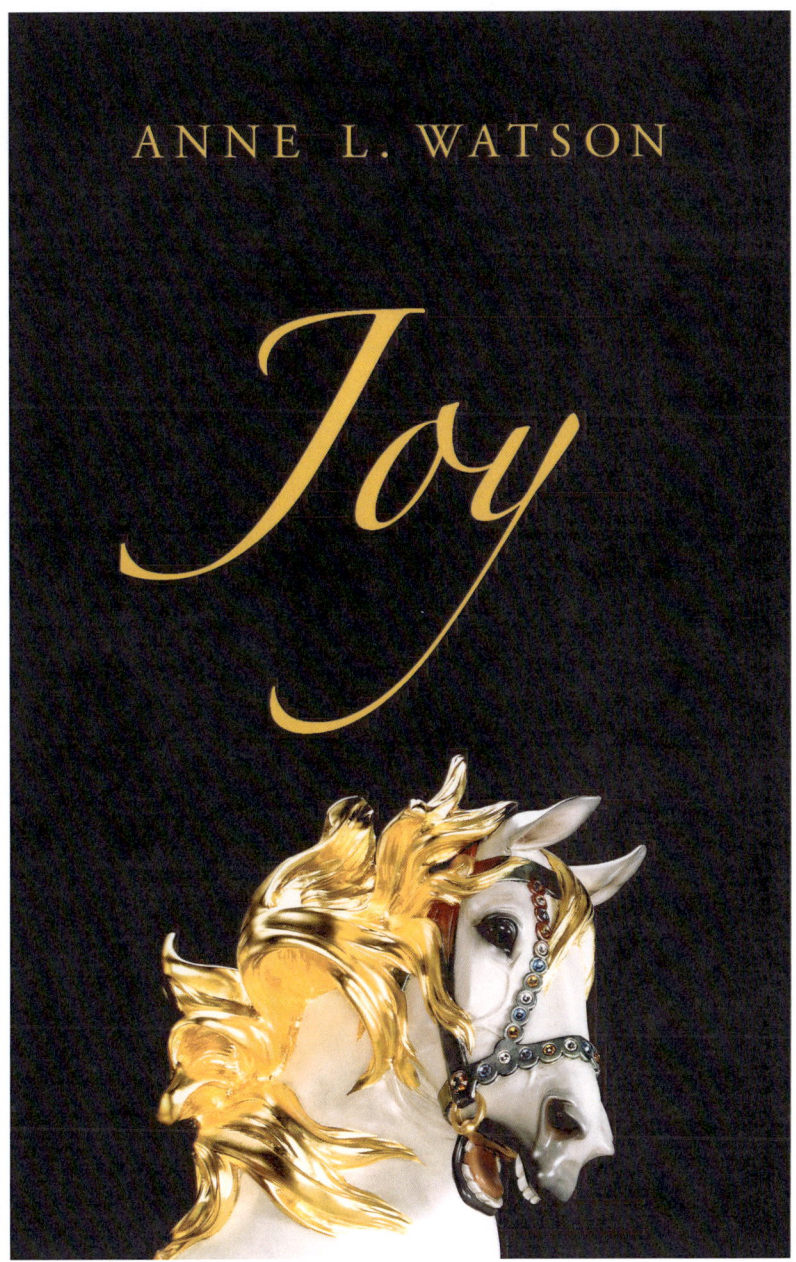

ANNE L. WATSON

Joy

In the Oakland, California, of 1989, Mirai San Julian is a young woman with a fascinating life and a rich past. She restores historic carousels—her dream career— working from her own studio in a former roller skating rink. Yes, Mirai has a lot going for her—but then why is everything in her life suddenly falling apart? And while she knows how to restore a carousel, will she know how to restore relationships with those she loves?

www.ingramcontent.com/pod-product-compliance
Lightning Source LLC
Chambersburg PA
CBRC092042170526
45172CB00008B/1252